Gender, Growth, and Trade

This book provides a comparative account of women's employment in Japan and Germany, situating the miracle economies of the postwar years within the context of other advanced economies.

Beginning with the formal independence of both countries in 1952 and following through to the period of high unemployment and low growth in the 1990s, *Gender, Growth, and Trade* examines the role of women as a flexible, contingent workforce. Using quantitative techniques with an emphasis on the importance of labor market institutions and other historical determinants of gender outcomes, the issues explored include:

- The role of labor market flexibility and the importance of broader macro-economic factors in accounting for the current differences in unemployment and employment growth among the OECD countries.
- The effects of reunification on men's and women's employment in the former East Germany, comparing the levels of child care provision and women's labor-force participation in East and West.
- The viability of the Japanese system of labor-management relations in the current recession in Japan.
- How labor dualism along gender lines plays a central role in keeping Japanese unemployment rates low and contributes to economic growth.
- The impact of trade expansion between developed and developing countries on women's employment.

David Kucera makes a significant contribution to gender mainstreaming and his findings will be of great interest to those studying and working within the fields of economics and gender studies.

David Kucera is Senior Research Officer at the International Institute for Labor Studies, Geneva, Switzerland.

Routledge frontiers of political economy

Gender, Growth, and Trade

The miracle economies of the postwar years

David Kucera

London and New York

First published 2001
by Routledge
11 New Fetter Lane, London EC4P 4EE

Simultaneously published in the USA and Canada
by Routledge
29 West 35th Street, New York, NY 10001

Routledge is an imprint of the Taylor & Francis Group

© 2001 David Kucera

Typeset in Times New Roman by
Curran Publishing Services Ltd, Norwich
Printed and bound in Great Britain by
Biddles Ltd, Guildford and King's Lynn

British Library Cataloguing in Publication Data
A catalogue record for this book is available from the British
Library

Library of Congress Cataloging in Publication Data
Kucera, David, 1960–
Gender, growth, and trade: the miracle economies of the postwar
years / David Kucera.
    p. cm. – (Routledge frontiers of political economy; 30)
    Includes bibliographical references and index.
    1. Women–Employment–Japan. 2. Women–Employment–
Germany. 3. Labor market–Japan. 4. Labor market–Germany. 5.
Japan–Economic policy–1945–1989. 6. Japan–Economic
policy–1989– 7. Germany–Economic policy–1945–1990. 8.
Germany–Economic policy–1990– I. Title. II. Series.

HD6197.K83 2001
331.4`0943–dc21   00–042488

ISBN 0–415–19862–3

In memory of Yoko Kasai Kucera

Contents

Figures

Tables

Acknowledgments

I have benefited from comments on various parts of the manuscript (or its rougher beginnings) by Günseli Berik, Thorsten Block, Ed Chilcote, David Howell, Ellen Mutari, Ute Pieper, Sabine Stebler, Yumiko Yamamoto, and especially the late David Gordon, my original dissertation advisor, and Will Milberg, who took over after David's death. In addition, working as Günseli's research assistant and taking her courses on the economics of gender introduced me to many of the issues addressed here; Ute and Thorsten provided much of the German employment data as well as other collegial support; Ed gave me a number of insights into input–output analysis, and the main results of earlier versions of Chapter 4 built on his work; Will and I co-authored a paper on the effects of manufacturing trade expansion on men and women's employment in ten OECD countries, and some results from that paper appear here. Mike Hanagan and Karin Müller Kucera provided comments on the entire manuscript and its workings as a whole, and their comments and encouragement were particularly important.

By good fortune, I have had three successive bosses who were supportive of this project in a number of ways: John Eatwell and Lance Taylor at the Center for Economic Policy Analysis (CEPA) in New York City, and Jean-Michel Servais at the International Institute for Labour Studies in Geneva. Work on earlier versions of Chapters 1 and 4 was supported by a grant to CEPA from the John D. and Catherine T. MacArthur Foundation. For all their efforts, thanks to the staff and editors at Routledge, especially to Alison Kirk, past editor who played a key role in getting this book off the ground.

Finally, my thanks to the international cast of characters who provided research assistance over the past several years, Natalia Filippova, Hui Gao, Friedrich Huebler, Ei Nagakubo, Pallavi Rai, and Frank Schroeder. Working with them provided one of the greatest pleasures in writing this book.

The views expressed in this book reflect those of the author and not necessarily the organizations with which he is affiliated.

Preface

Until the 1990s, Germany and Japan were regarded as the miracle economies of the postwar years. The outlines of their postwar development were broadly similar, from the rebuilding of devastated economies to rapid output and productivity growth and eventual world economic leadership. Germany and Japan are commonly characterized as "high-road" economies, noted by relatively cooperative labor–management relations and high real wage and productivity growth. At the firm level, this cooperativeness is manifested in works councils in Germany and enterprise unions and quality circles in Japan. These similarities motivate recent research comparing the industrial relations, economic policies, and macroeconomic performance of Germany and Japan. This book provides a comparative account of the evolving differences between men's and women's employment in Germany and Japan, beginning with the formal independence of both countries in 1952 and continuing into the deep recession experienced by both in the 1990s.

Central to this book are the issues of economic growth and the liberalization of international trade. Several different aspects of economic growth and macroeconomic performance are considered. Among these are the qualitatively different nature of German and Japanese women's integration into the workforce in the years of slower growth and higher unemployment since the early 1970s (in spite of the nearly identical increases in women's labor-force participation); the contrasting role of women as a buffer workforce in the face of business cycle up- and downswings; the way that Japanese women's disguised unemployment contributes to Japan's low unemployment rates; and the importance of Japanese women in facilitating Japan's "high-road" economic growth. Regarding trade liberalization, the key aspects considered are the different effects of trade expansion on men's and women's employment and earnings, particularly trade between richer and poorer countries.

Though the comparison of Germany and Japan makes up the heart of this book, both countries are situated throughout within the broader comparative context of the other developed countries. This holds for the book's main empirical analyses as well as the comparisons of labor market institutions and industrial relations that inform these empirical analyses. The main arguments of the book are summarized, chapter by chapter, as follows.

Chapter 1: Unemployment, labor market flexibility, and women as a buffer workforce

The opening chapter examines the relationship between unemployment and labor market flexibility. The latter is considered in the broadest sense, as it relates to labor markets at large (external flexibility) and to practices within firms (internal flexibility). The first part of the chapter addresses the argument that differences in unemployment and employment growth among the advanced economies result largely from differences in labor market flexibility. Empirical evidence is considered on nominal and real wage flexibility, wage-setting institutions, the trade-off between unemployment and inequality, social policy as a source of inflexibility, and Beveridge curves. With the exception of ambiguous evidence on the duration of unemployment insurance benefits, there is little solid evidence that high unemployment results from labor market rigidities.

Japan is the focus of the second part of this chapter. Japan merits special attention in these debates, for among the advanced economies it was the miracle economy without parallel, manifested in its dramatic growth, international competitiveness, and, even well into the 1990s recession, very low rates of unemployment. Moreover, Japan's low unemployment was commonly attributed to both highly flexible wages and high internal labor market flexibility. The argument that Japan's low rates of unemployment result from high internal labor market flexibility is suspect, or at least overstated, for several reasons. Japanese firms' reliance on internal flexibility is not an alternative to, but is rather complemented by, external flexibility. This external flexibility is provided disproportionately by women workers, who serve strongly as a buffer workforce. That is, the cyclic volatility of employment and labor-force participation is much greater for Japanese women than men. This holds not only for the labor market as a whole but also within firms, where temporary and part-time employees, who are mostly women, work alongside regular full-time employees, who are mostly men. The point is illustrated by the just-in-time production system as developed at Toyota Motors, for which the use of temporary employment plays a central role in accommodating fluctuations in demand.

Japanese women who lose their jobs tend to leave the labor force altogether and as such are not counted as unemployed. This is manifested in the remarkably high proportions of discouraged workers in Japan, particularly in the troughs of business cycles, with women making up the vast majority of these discouraged workers. Thus Japanese unemployment rates as well as unemployment volatility are deceptively low, much more so than for the other advanced economies. Most studies examining wage flexibility in relation to *unemployment* conclude that wage flexibility is comparatively high in Japan. In contrast, studies examining wage flexibility in relation to *output* conclude that Japan does not have comparatively high wage flexibility. The low volatility of Japanese unemployment rates suggests a resolution of these conflicting results and a sense of the particular role of Japanese women in the workings of the labor market and the economy at large.

Chapter 2: Women's integration into the workforce

The book's second chapter further investigates the role of women as a buffer workforce by undertaking empirical analyses of the buffer, job segregation, and substitution hypotheses. These hypotheses address the extent to which women serve as a buffer workforce over business cycle up- and downswings, how patterns of job segregation along gender lines relate to women serving as a buffer, and the substitution of women for men over both cycles and trends, particularly as a cost-cutting measure.

The most striking results from tests of the buffer hypothesis appear at the aggregate level, which considers in addition to Germany and Japan the other G7 and the Scandinavian countries. Among these countries, the evidence on the role of women as a buffer workforce is strongest for Japan, whereas there is little such evidence for Germany. Considering different periods indicates that Japanese women served particularly strongly as a buffer workforce after the mid-1950s, the period during which the predominately male lifetime employment system was consolidated. Among the countries considered, it is only in Japan that one observes the combination of women serving strongly as a buffer workforce and very high proportions of discouraged to unemployed women workers. Only in Japan, in other words, does the role of women as a buffer workforce provide a considerably altered view of macroeconomic performance. Counting discouraged workers as unemployed increases Japanese unemployment rates well over twofold for some recent years, bringing a substantial convergence with German unemployment rates.

For Germany, some evidence is found that foreign workers function as a buffer workforce. As there are sizeable numbers of foreign workers in Germany and the majority are men, the question arises whether this masks the extent to which German women function as a buffer workforce. To test this hypothesis, measures of women as a buffer workforce were derived both with and without the inclusion of foreign workers. This made no substantial difference in results, which consistently indicate that German women did not function strongly as a buffer workforce in the economy as a whole.

Measures of gender segregation – particularly the dissimilarity index – are considered using industry-level data for German and Japanese manufacturing. These measures are quite similar between Germany and Japan, evidence of similar patterns of gender segregation. More generally, patterns of women's employment among manufacturing industries are found to be remarkably similar among a sample of ten OECD countries. In both Germany and Japan, there were steady declines in dissimilarity indices over the postwar years, meaning steady declines in gender segregation. Movements of these measures can be broken down into two main effects: movements driven by changes in the relative size of industries (measured by employment) and movements driven by changes in women's share of employment within industries. In Germany, the decline in the measure of gender segregation was driven mostly by changes in the relative size of industries, whereas for Japan the decline was driven mostly by changes in women's share of employment within industries. Moreover, while the female percentage of manufacturing employment declined in Germany, it increased in Japan after the mid-1970s, suggesting a stronger trend substitution of women for men in Japanese than in German manufacturing.

Women's integration into the workforce in Japan was not associated with increased equality of men and women's employment conditions but rather the opposite, with a widening gender wage gap and women's declining representation in unions (for both manufacturing and non-agricultural employees). In Germany, on the other hand, the gender wage gap narrowed and women's representation in unions increased. Anecdotal evidence is presented for Japan suggesting that women were substituted for men since the mid-1970s as part of a long-term strategy by firms to cut costs and increase labor flexibility. These considerations were particularly pressing during these years in the face of slower economic growth, increased international competition, and an aging workforce in the context of Japan's system of seniority-based earnings.

Chapter 3: Industrial relations and labor market institutions

The previous chapter shows that women served strongly as a buffer workforce in Japan but not in Germany. Following up on this observation, Chapter 3 aims to account for this difference within the broader context of Germany's and Japan's systems of industrial relations and compares the nature of women's part-time and temporary employment, women's representation in unions, and policies supporting the employment of mothers.

It is argued that the patterns observed in Japan result from a highly dualistic employment system, with women under-represented in core employment and over-represented in peripheral employment. This dualism along gender lines describes both the labor market at large and practices within Japanese firms. Core employment in Japan is characterized by its so-called "three pillars": the lifetime employment system, seniority-based earnings, and membership in an enterprise union, all of which apply almost exclusively to full-time workers with regular employment status. On the periphery are those with temporary and part-time employment status. As to why Japanese women serve so strongly as a buffer workforce, the lifetime employment system is of central importance. For it is largely the province of men and imposes a rigidity in the face of economic fluctuations, a rigidity compensated for by the flexibility of Japanese women's employment and labor-force participation.

Japanese women's labor-force participation is volatile not only over business cycles but also over lifecycles. That is, Japanese women drop out of the labor force in large numbers in their mid-twenties and return in large numbers after their mid-thirties, typically as temporary or part-time workers. The two types of volatility are related, for it is in part through their employment as temporaries and part-timers that Japanese women so readily flow into and out of employment and the labor force. The very large gender earnings gap in Japan results in part from the volatility of women's employment and labor-force participation within the context of the Japanese system of seniority-based earnings.

The chapter argues that Japanese firms simultaneously pursue both high and low road strategies of labor–management relations, enabling them to reap the productivity advantages of a committed workforce and the cost and flexibility advantages of a dispensable workforce. The argument is related to that in Chapter 1 regarding Japan's simultaneous use of internal and external labor flexibility, both for the economy as a whole and within larger firms. These represent other aspects of Japan's labor market dualism, for which gender is a key marker of core and periphery.

Labor market dualism is much less marked in Germany than in Japan, suggested by the less marginal nature of temporary and part-time employment. In contrast with Japan, most temporary employees in Germany are men and they are generally young. Rather than providing a buffer workforce, temporary employment in Germany provides a means for employers to screen prospective employees, and temporaries generally move on to attain regular employment status. In this sense, temporary employment in Germany provides more of a stepping-stone than a buffer. As in Japan, the large majority of part-time employees in Germany are women. But a large number of part-timers in Germany enjoy similar pay, benefits, and job security to full-time employees. More generally, anecdotal evidence suggests that the rapid growth in part-time employment in both countries is driven more by the wishes of women and less by those of employers in Germany than Japan. The chapter also considers the role of women union activists in bettering German women's employment.

Chapter 4: Foreign trade, employment, and earnings

Chapter 4 shifts the focus of the book from domestic to global factors influencing men's and women's employment conditions. A good deal of research addresses the "skills bias" of labor demand – resulting from both skills-biased technical change and trade expansion with developing countries – and whether such a skills bias was an important cause of the increasing earnings inequality observed in a number of advanced economies in recent years. Less attention has been paid to the "gender bias" of labor demand, even though women's manufacturing employment in the ten OECD countries considered is strongly concentrated among industries identified by earlier studies as "trade losers." This chapter provides estimates of the effects of manufacturing trade expansion on men and women's employment, with breakdowns by world, OECD, and non-OECD trade. Evidence is found that foreign trade expansion had a more negative effect on women's than men's manufacturing employment in Japan and a roughly equal effect in Germany, with the difference driven by non-OECD trade – that is, trade with mostly developing countries. Results for the ten OECD countries reveal that, by and large, the determining factor in whether women's employment is more negatively affected than men's is a country's trade performance with respect to non-OECD countries for a small set of industries: textiles, apparel, leather and leather goods.

In contrast with labor demand shifts resulting specifically from trade expansion, overall labor demand shifted away from women's employment in Germany after the early 1970s, for both the manufacturing sector as a whole and manufacturing industries with high female percentages of employment. No such negative overall demand shifts occurred in Japan. The contrast between trade-induced and overall labor demand shifts suggests that trade was not the dominant determinant of men and women's relative employment in manufacturing, that other factors mattered more. Among the other factors considered are differences among industries in the pace of labor-displacing technical change and changes in the domestic composition of demand for goods.

In the face of the differences between Germany and Japan in overall demand shifts for men and women's manufacturing employment, male–female hourly wage differences narrowed in Germany and widened in Japan. On the labor supply side, increases in women's labor-force participation were remarkably similar in Germany and Japan after the early 1970s, and the rise in Japan of the female percentage of college graduates suggests that the skills of Japanese women increased. Taken together, neither labor demand nor labor supply sides provide a clear sense of why the gender earnings gap narrowed in Germany and, at least until the 1990s, widened in Japan.

For Japan, anecdotal evidence is provided suggesting that more purely institutional factors play a role in accounting for changes in the gender earnings gap. These factors are the closely parallel movement between the gender earnings gap and earnings inequality between large and small firms (for women in Japan are disproportionately concentrated in small firms) and changes in women's share of temporary and part-time employment and representation in unions. Union membership has a special significance in Japan. Along with lifetime employment and seniority-based earnings, union membership makes up one of the "three pillars" of the Japanese core employment system, with each pillar generally associated with the others. It is argued that the decline in women's union representation and the widening gender earnings gap since the mid-1970s reflect the fact that Japanese women's integration into the workforce was on the expanding periphery of a highly dualistic employment system, a system marked largely along gender lines.

Chapter 5: German reunification

The reunification of the former East and West Germany provides a historically unique circumstance for evaluating the rapid integration of two fundamentally different economies. Focusing on the regions of the former East Germany, the book's final chapter addresses the effects of reunification and the 1990s recession on men's and women's employment, and returns to the themes of the buffer and job segregation hypotheses. These issues are considered in the context of salient differences and similarities between women's employment conditions in the former East and West Germany prior to reunification. Regarding differences, most obvious were women's much higher rates of employment and labor-force participation in East Germany, facilitated by the near universal availability of publicly funded child care. East Germany differed not only from the West Germany in this regard, but also from other Eastern Bloc countries. As for similarities, the gender earnings gap did not differ greatly between East and West Germany, and neither did patterns of job segregation by occupation and industry.

With reunification came the question of the extent to which women's labor-force participation rates between East and West would converge. Though women's participation rates in the East remained high throughout the 1990s, they slowly but steadily declined, especially for younger women. East German women's labor-force participation came under downward pressure from two sources: the rapidly declining availability of affordable child care, and the greater unemployment and job loss experienced by East German women than East German men. The difference in total unemployment rates between East and West following reunification was very disproportionately driven by the unemployment of East German women, whose unemployment rates were much higher than East German men's, twice as high in the years just after reunification. It was in these tumultuous years that the East also experienced plummeting marriage and birth rates, demographic shocks of mammoth proportions.

The most definitive studies indicate that the greater job loss experienced by East German women resulted in large measure from the disproportionate loss of lower wage jobs, with men and women's probability of job loss being similar for jobs paying a similar wage. That the burden of post-reunification job loss fell more on East German women than men was partly a legacy of the pre-reunification pattern of job segregation, for these women had been long over-represented in lower wage jobs.

1   Unemployment, labor market flexibility, and women as a buffer workforce

Introduction: defining labor market flexibility

Since the early 1970s, various notions of labor flexibility have come to play a central and even dominating role in discussions of unemployment and economic performance. Two causes, not obviously related, appear most important.

First, the weight given to labor market flexibility in accounting for high unemployment marked a widespread retreat from the postwar Keynesian consensus and a resurgence of theories of unemployment rooted in marginalist, neo-classical principles. The Keynesian consensus had enjoyed considerable influence and provided the framework for public policies aimed at lowering unemployment through the stimulation of effective demand. The retreat from the consensus occurred in the face of dramatically rising unemployment in most of the advanced capitalist countries since the early 1970s, which traditional Keynesian policies seemed at a loss to counter. As important as the rise in unemployment was the variation in unemployment experience among the advanced economies, with some countries faring considerably worse than others. The variation among countries led economists to seek out country-specific causes of rising unemployment and its persistence.

Combined with the opening created by the collapse of the Keynesian consensus, it seemed natural that many economists would look to differences among countries in wage rigidity, and labor market rigidity in general. For the neo-classical theory and its offshoots, it is these rigidities that are held to be the causes of persistent unemployment. The theory of the natural rate of unemployment and efficiency wage theory share the fundamental premise of the unadorned neo-classical theory of unemployment: that persistent unemployment results from wages being above a market-clearing level defined by the intersection of upward sloping supply and downward sloping demand curves for labor. Job search theory is also a variant of the neo-classical theory of unemployment, in which the social wage – which includes unemployment insurance benefits – is argued to be the relevant determinant of unemployment. Thus labor market flexibility as it relates to unemployment is more than just another term for wage flexibility, encompassing as it does a broad range of factors. Not least among these is flexibility in hiring and firing workers in the face of economic fluctuations.

The second cause of labor flexibility's prominence is the interest in flexible production techniques, often associated with the just-in-time production system developed in the postwar years at Toyota Motors. Much of the interest in flexible production originated in the business community, as US and European manufacturers witnessed, at their expense, the competitive successes of Toyota and many other Japanese firms. Within academic circles, the interest in flexible production took off after the 1984 publication of Piore and Sabel's *The Second Industrial Divide*, which initiated a wide-ranging debate about the virtues and significance of what the authors refer to as "flexible specialization." An integral aspect of flexible production is labor flexibility, in most respects a different notion of labor flexibility than in the unemployment debates, involving flexibility in job definition and design and the mobility of workers among tasks.

It is worth asking whether there is anything to be gained from considering these quite different notions of labor flexibility together, for in a sense they are mere homonyms. Yet the full range of labor flexibility definitions has been employed to explain differences in unemployment performance among the advanced capitalist economies, justifying a broad view. Consider an editorial from the May 30 1986 *Financial Times*, reflecting a commonly held view regarding differences in comparative unemployment performance: "Japan's low unemployment is primarily a reflection of very high internal mobility, America's a reflection of high external mobility. Europe suffers high unemployment because it lacks either sort of mobility" (Quoted in Metcalf 1987: 51–2). Here "external" refers to the mobility of workers in the labor market at large, and "internal" refers to the mobility of workers within firms. Mobility is only one aspect of labor market flexibility, but low rates of unemployment in Japan and the US are also argued to result from greater internal and external labor market flexibility more generally, as will be noted in some detail.

This chapter undertakes two tasks, both addressing the view that the relatively favorable employment performance of Japan and the US is attributable to greater labor market flexibility.

First, the chapter surveys the empirical literature on the relationship between labor market flexibility and unemployment. Results from recent research suggest rather strongly that labor market flexibility cannot be the primary cause of differences in employment performance among the advanced countries, particularly among Germany, Japan, and the US.

Second, the chapter argues that the internal labor flexibility on which Japanese firms rely heavily requires a good deal of external flexibility, particularly flexibility in hiring and firing. Such external flexibility is provided, in large measure, by women workers, who are largely excluded from the so-called lifetime employment system. These women serve as a buffer workforce, generally leaving the labor market upon losing their jobs. As such, they do not figure in unemployment statistics. Japanese women's importance to the basic workings of the economy is suggested by a number of empirical studies, as well as by the writings of those most responsible for the development of just-in-time production at Toyota Motors, from which the system spread to a great many firms in Japan and elsewhere.

In 1994, then US Secretary of Labor Robert Reich spoke of the term labor market flexibility going "directly from obscurity to meaninglessness without any intervening period of coherence" (in Brodsky 1994: 53). Before proceeding to the two tasks of this chapter, then, it seems worthwhile to consider some definitions and distinctions in common use regarding labor market flexibility. Distinctions are typically made by dichotomizing: flexibility in employment versus flexibility in work; numerical versus functional flexibility; and external versus internal flexibility. Different writers make these distinctions somewhat differently, but one can provide a clear enough sense of what they are about. Here is James Curry's definition of flexibility in work:

> Flexibility in work refers essentially to flexibility within the firm or within the production process. This is the notion that flexible technologies enable a more rapid transfer of machines and processes between production functions or types. . . . Coupled with more flexible forms of work organisation, such as flextime, group and team approaches, or more general job definitions, the new technologies enable a firm to produce variations of products, even completely different products, cheaply in smaller batches. This makes it possible for firms to respond easily and quickly to ever rapidly changing markets.
>
> (Curry 1993: 100)

This describes key aspects of just-in-time production as practiced at Toyota, and is in essence the same as the functional flexibility. The definition of internal flexibility encompasses the definitions of flexibility in work and functional flexibility, but also refers more broadly to the mobility of workers among a firm's facilities and to the flexibility of payment systems within a firm (Brodsky 1994: 59).

Curry writes:

> Flexibility in employment, is essentially a labour market concept. As markets and the business cycle go through their usual changes, managers of firms find it desirable to shift the size of their work forces. This sort of flexibility has characterised the entire history of capitalism.
>
> (Curry 1993: 101)

This definition is similar to that used by an OECD study to describe numerical flexibility. Associating numerical flexibility with Fordism, the study refers to such flexibility as "controlling the number of hours worked and the organization of working time, regulation of hiring and dismissals, and the use of part-time and temporary workers" (in Brodsky 1994: 59). External flexibility encompasses flexibility in employment and numerical flexibility but also includes a host of issues related to the functioning of the labor market at large. This includes, most obviously, labor mobility across regions, sectors, and occupations, as well as wage flexibility, meaning downward wage flexibility.

It is worth mentioning that the characterization of Europe as having high unemployment is crude and potentially misleading. Unemployment rates varied a great deal across Europe, particularly long-term unemployment of more than one year in duration (Nickell 1997: 56). More than that, average annual unemployment rates were actually higher in the US than in Germany in both the 1983 to 1988 period and the 1989 to 1994 period. Yet *long-term* unemployment rates were a good deal higher in Germany in the 1983 to 1988 period, the 1989 to 1994 period, and also in 1996 (Table 1.1). (Through nearly all of this book, when Germany is referred to it means the former West Germany or, for the 1990s, the regions of the former West Germany. The exceptions are Tables 1.2, 3.1, and 4.6 and Figures 4.1, 4.2, and 4.4, where some data for the 1990s are only available for unified Germany. Chapter 5, a comparison of the former East and West Germany, is the other exception.) It is long-term unemployment that is particularly relevant regarding the relationship between labor market flexibility and unemployment, for it is only unemployment for longer periods of time that reflects hitches in the process of labor market adjustment and not simply changing market conditions themselves.

A robust measure of labor market performance is private sector employment growth relative to the growth of the working-age population (aged 15 to 64).[1] Here too Germany performed more poorly than the US or Japan. From 1973 to 1990, the average annual percent growth of this measure was 0.77 for the US, 0.14 for Japan, and –0.35 for Germany. Much of this difference is accounted for by the rapid decline of agricultural employment in Germany, but Germany was also outperformed in the service, industrial, and manufacturing sectors (Table 1.2). The growth of the working-age population was nearly twice as high in the US as in Germany over these years, and thus the differences in total job creation between the two countries are all the larger.[2]

It is also worth considering the change in unemployment rates from the years prior to the economic turmoil of the 1970s. After all, the notion of labor market rigidity as a cause of unemployment implies rigidity in the face of change, and no changes were as tumultuous as the oil crises and the breakdown of the Bretton Woods system of fixed exchange rates. From 1968 to 1972, average annual unemployment rates were 4.6 percent in the US, 1.2 percent in Japan, and 0.8 percent in Germany; from 1991 to 1995, average annual unemployment rates were 6.5 percent in the US, 2.6 percent in Japan, and 7.1 percent in Germany (Table 1.3). That is, unemployment increased by 41 percent in the US, somewhat more than doubled in Japan, and increased well over eightfold in Germany. The patterns of increase are very similar using the 1986 to 1990 years as the end period.

Differences in unemployment among the advanced economies, particularly between continental Europe and the US, are often overstated.[3] Yet the above data suggest that there are real and sizeable differences in employment performance between Germany, the US, and Japan. Employment performance was if anything worse in France than Germany, as measured by unemployment rates, long-term unemployment rates, and total and non-agricultural private sector

Table 1.1 Unemployment rates in twenty OECD countries

	[1] 1983–96	[2] 1983–8	[3]	[4]	[5] 1989–94	[6]	[7]	[8] 1996: Long-term unemployment rates	[9]	[10]
	Total	Total	Short-term	Long-term	Total	Short-term	Long-term	Male & female	Male	Female
Australia	8.7	8.4	5.9	2.4	9.0	6.2	2.7	2.4	2.7	2.0
Austria	3.8	3.6	n/a	n/a	3.7	n/a	n/a	1.4	1.3	1.6
Belgium	9.7	11.3	3.3	8.0	8.1	2.9	5.1	5.8	4.4	7.8
Canada	9.8	9.9	9.0	0.9	9.8	8.9	0.9	1.3	1.5	1.1
Denmark	9.9	9.0	6.0	3.0	10.8	7.9	3.0	1.8	1.6	2.1
Finland	9.1	5.1	4.0	1.0	10.5	8.9	1.7	5.2	5.5	4.8
France	10.4	9.8	5.4	4.4	10.4	6.5	3.9	4.5	3.6	5.5
Germany	6.2	6.8	3.7	3.1	5.4	3.2	2.2	3.2	3.3	3.0
Ireland	15.1	16.1	6.9	9.2	14.8	5.4	9.4	6.8	7.4	5.8
Italy	7.6	6.9	3.1	3.8	8.2	2.9	5.3	7.9	6.0	11.0
Japan	2.6	2.7	2.2	0.5	2.3	1.9	0.4	0.7	0.8	0.4
Netherlands	8.4	10.5	5.0	5.5	7.0	3.5	3.5	2.9	2.5	3.4
New Zealand	6.8	4.9	4.3	0.6	8.9	6.6	2.3	1.2	1.3	0.9
Norway	4.2	2.7	2.5	0.2	5.5	4.3	1.2	0.8	0.8	0.7
Portugal	6.4	7.6	3.5	4.2	5.0	3.0	2.0	3.6	3.0	4.2
Spain	19.7	19.6	8.3	11.3	18.9	9.1	9.7	12.1	8.5	18.0
Sweden	4.3	2.6	2.3	0.3	4.4	4.0	0.4	1.3	1.5	1.1
Switzerland	1.8	0.8	0.7	0.1	2.3	1.8	0.5	0.9	0.7	1.2
United Kingdom	9.7	10.9	5.8	5.1	8.9	5.5	3.4	3.3	4.4	1.8
United States	6.5	7.1	6.4	0.7	6.2	5.6	0.6	0.5	0.6	0.5

Sources: Columns 1–7: Nickell (1997) (from OECD *Economic Outlook*, *UK Employment Trends*, US Bureau of Labor Statistics); Columns 8–10: *ILO Key Indicators of the Labour Market* (1999).

Notes

Long-term employment rates include those unemployed for longer than one year. Columns 1–7, from Nickell, use standardized unemployment rates according to OECD definitions, with these exceptions: for Austria and Denmark, official national rates used; for Italy, unemployment rates are constructed by the US Bureau of Labor Statistics to correspond to US definitions; Columns 8–10 do not use standardized unemployment rates.

Table 1.2 Per capita employment growth by sector in twenty OECD countries

	Total civilian		Services		Industry		Manufacture	
	1973–90	1973–95	1973–90	1973–95	1973–90	1973–95	1973–90	1973–95
Australia	0.11	0.07	1.31	1.15	-1.94	-1.89	-2.98	-2.76
Austria	0.35	0.54	1.15	1.59	-0.36	-0.57	-0.38	-0.98
Belgium	-0.35	-0.35	1.02	0.86	-2.52	-2.30	-2.68	-2.63
Canada	0.85	0.50	1.58	1.18	-0.36	-0.76	-1.00	-1.12
Denmark	0.29	0.01	1.40	0.95	-1.29	-1.20	-0.49	-0.58
Finland	0.39	-0.55	1.87	0.88	-0.45	-1.65	-0.19	-1.08
France	-0.50	-0.50	1.14	1.06	-2.18	-2.31	-2.55	-2.45
Germany[a]	*-0.35*	*-0.47*	*0.99*	*0.97*	*-1.36*	*-1.68*	*-1.05*	*-1.75*
Ireland	-0.78	-0.35	0.66	1.11	-1.35	-0.93	-1.14	-0.65
Italy	-0.03	-0.09	1.93	1.62	-1.17	-1.04	-1.33	-1.17
Japan	*0.14*	*0.20*	*1.18*	*1.17*	*-0.37*	*-0.25*	*-0.61*	*-0.67*
Netherlands	-0.07	0.25	1.03	1.41	-1.93	-1.90	-1.88	-1.98
New Zealand	-0.53	-0.19	0.32	0.48	-2.15	-1.29	-1.49	-0.67
Norway	0.56	0.45	1.98	1.71	-1.26	-1.20	-1.93	-1.60
Portugal	-0.18	-0.63	1.79	1.74	0.62	-0.36	0.31	-0.61
Spain	-1.02	-1.14	0.92	0.84	-1.33	-1.85	-1.54	-2.21
Sweden	0.55	-0.17	1.64	0.91	-0.84	-1.71	-1.02	-1.76
Switzerland	-0.09	-0.34	1.10	0.78	-1.48	-1.79	-2.02	-2.35
United Kingdom	0.03	-0.16	1.14	1.00	-1.46	-2.08	-1.98	-2.41
United States	*0.77*	*0.60*	*1.52*	*1.35*	*-0.58*	*-0.91*	*-1.08*	*-1.32*
G7	0.31	0.25	1.41	1.31	-0.94	-1.05	-1.24	-1.37
Total OECD[b]	0.14	0.02	1.32	1.18	-1.04	-1.24	-1.32	-1.54

Source: OECD *Historical Statistics, 1960–1995*.
Notes
Derived from the difference between the average annual growth of employment in respective sectors and the average annual growth of the working-age (15–64) population.
a For the regions of the former West Germany prior to the 1992 and unified Germany thereafter, with the change from 1990 to 1991 not included in the OECD dataset.
b Excluding the Czech Republic, Hungary, South Korea, and Poland.

Table 1.3 Unemployment rates and changes in unemployment rates in twenty OECD countries

	[1]	[2]	[3]	[4]	[5]
	Unemployment rates: five-year averages			*Change from 1968–72 to 1986–90*	*Change from 1968–72 to 1991–95*
	1968–72	*1986–90*	*1991–95*	*Col. [2]/Col. [1]*	*Col. [3]/Col. [1]*
Australia	1.9	7.1	9.9	3.67	5.12
Austria	1.5	3.4	3.8	2.21	2.47
Belgium	2.2	10.2	11.5	4.57	5.13
Canada	5.3	8.3	10.5	1.56	1.97
Denmark	1.0	6.8	8.8	6.76	8.76
Finland	2.6	4.3	14.7	1.64	5.57
France	2.6	9.8	11.0	3.78	4.24
Germany	*0.8*	*7.2*	*7.1*	*8.84*	*8.72*
Ireland	5.6	16.2	14.7	2.91	2.64
Italy	5.6	11.5	11.3	2.05	2.00
Japan	*1.2*	*2.5*	*2.6*	*2.08*	*2.15*
Netherlands	1.4	9.0	6.8	6.51	4.90
New Zealand	0.4	5.7	8.9	14.89	23.32
Norway	1.1	3.5	5.5	3.28	5.23
Portugal	2.5	6.1	5.7	2.46	2.26
Spain	2.8	18.6	20.6	6.68	7.40
Sweden	2.2	1.8	6.4	0.84	2.94
Switzerland	—	0.6	3.1	—	—
United Kingdom	2.4	8.4	9.2	3.43	3.78
United States	*4.6*	*5.8*	*6.5*	*1.27*	*1.41*
G7	3.1	6.4	6.9	2.04	2.20
Total OECD[a]	3.2	6.9	7.3	2.14	2.25

Sources: OECD *Historical Statistics, 1960–1995*, Bundesministerium für Arbeit und Sozialordnung: *Arbeits und Sozialstatistik Hauptergebnisse.*
Notes
German unemployment rates in this table are constructed to include the self-employed, as per the standard definition of the unemployment rate. They are consistently lower than official German unemployment rates.
a Excluding the Czech Republic, Hungary, South Korea, and Poland.

employment growth relative to the growth of the working-age population (Tables 1.1 and 1.2). That brings us to the first task of this chapter, assessing the empirical evidence regarding the relationship between labor market flexibility and unemployment. This section considers evidence on nominal and real wage flexibility, the role of wage-setting institutions, the hypothesized trade-off between unemployment and inequality, social policy as a source of inflexibility, and the Beveridge curve as a summary indicator of labor-market inflexibility. These are all issues of external labor-market flexibility, most of which have received a good deal of attention in recent debates about the causes of high unemployment.

Part 1: evidence on the relationship between labor market flexibility and unemployment

Nominal wage flexibility

A general consensus has emerged from recent empirical studies regarding the response of nominal wages to demand fluctuations. In short, there is no solid evidence that countries with higher unemployment also have greater nominal wage rigidity. A study by Robert Gordon looks at data from the 1960s to the mid-1980s for the US, Japan, and a bloc of eleven Western European countries including Germany. Since Gordon examines manufacturing, non-manufacturing, and the aggregate economy, he evaluates nominal wage flexibility in relation to output changes in respective sectors, rather than unemployment. At the aggregate level, that relevant to comparative employment performance, Gordon describes differences between the US, Japan, and Europe as "minimal" (Gordon 1987: 689). Gordon describes comparative results for the manufacturing and non-manufacturing sectors as follows:

> The sectoral division between manufacturing and non-manufacturing displays the expected result that there is little cyclical responsiveness of wage rates in US manufacturing, but the unexpected result that there is also less cyclical responsiveness in Japanese manufacturing than in Europe, and more cyclical responsiveness in both the US and European non-manufacturing sectors than in Japan. These results suggest that the emphasis in my own past research on the greater nominal wage rigidity in the US than in Japan may be limited in applicability to the manufacturing sector, and that differences in nominal wage flexibility in the aggregate economy (and in the nonmanufacturing sector) may be much less than is commonly supposed.
>
> (Gordon 1987: 689)

Gordon's findings are consistent with those observed by David Blanchflower and Andrew Oswald regarding the elasticity between local (within country) unemployment rates and wages for a range of countries. Blanchflower and Oswald find that elasticities are remarkably similar across the range of countries, including the US, Germany, and Japan (though they rely on other studies for estimates for Japan). The authors summarize their findings as follows:

> This uniformity [across countries] was probably not expected by any researcher and seems remarkable. By the standards of modern economics, the picture of a wage curve where the elasticity of wages with respect to unemployment is –0.1 seems to be a consistent one.
>
> (Blanchflower and Oswald 1995: 157)

In his review article on European unemployment, Charles Bean summarizes studies that consider whether differences in unemployment among the advanced capitalist economies can be attributed to differences in nominal wage rigidity in the face of commonly-experienced demand shocks. Bean concludes that these studies do not support the view that greater nominal wage rigidity accounts for the greater unemployment increases in the European Community countries. There are studies that provide evidence of differences in nominal wage rigidity among the advanced capitalist economies, but none of these studies provide evidence that nominal wage rigidity was greater in the European Community countries (Bean 1994: 585).

Real wage flexibility

In the 1980s, Michael Bruno and Jeffrey Sachs undertook cross-country studies that examined changes over time in the "real wage gap." Their method involved comparing observed real wages with theoretically market-clearing real wages, with the difference between the two defined as the real wage gap. The determination of the real wage gap was argued to enable the distinction between unemployment resulting from excessive real wages, called classical unemployment (based on marginalist principles), and unemployment resulting from a lack of aggregate demand, called Keynesian unemployment (Bean 1994: 577).

One measure used to proxy the real wage gap is the ratio of the real wage to labor's average real output, providing a measure of labor's share in the economy. Bruno and Sachs argue that the measure increased in the US less rapidly than in Europe but also, it is noteworthy, less rapidly than in Japan (Gordon 1987: 686). An increasing wage gap indicates that real wage growth is outstripping labor productivity growth, squeezing profitability and potentially constraining growth. Robert Gordon argues that the increase in Europe and Japan of the real wage gap is overstated, a result of measurement error. In contrast with Bruno and Sachs and most other studies, Gordon argues that the income of not just employees but also the self-employed should be used to derive the ratio of the real wage to labor's average real output. Partially this is a question of data consistency, for data on employment and worker-hours, also used to construct the wage gap, include the self-employed. But it also sensible on its own terms to classify self-employment income as part of labor's share in the economy. By including self-employment income, the trend increase in the real wage gap in Europe and Japan basically disappears for the years considered (the 1960s through the mid-1980s) (ibid.: 707).[4]

Bean argues that there is more evidence that real rather than nominal wage flexibility played a role in accounting for Germany's and much of Europe's relatively poor employment performance. Bean summarizes a number of studies looking at the relationship between real wage flexibility and unemployment. Just as important, Bean emphasizes the differences in labor market institutions among countries that might plausibly account for differences in real wage flexibility. He writes:

> All these studies point to the conclusion that the responsiveness of real wages to unemployment is markedly lower in the United States and the

European Community than in Japan, Austria, Switzerland, and the Nordic countries . . . [W]e have here a potential explanation for why the disinflation of the early eighties was so much more painful for the European Community and for the United States than for Japan and non-EC Europe. *The fact that the latter group of countries have markedly different labor market structures from the European Community and the United States has led a number of authors to focus on institutional differences as a key factor in understanding the heterogeneity of unemployment experience.*

(Bean 1994: 600–1, emphasis added)

It is worth emphasizing that these studies find real wage rigidity greater not just in the European Community but also in the US. In fact, most studies indicate that real wage rigidity is greater in the US than in the European Community (Bean 1994: 600). As noted, though, the US had significantly better employment performance than the two largest European Community economies, Germany and France, even prior to the 1990s. Just as important, it is worth emphasizing that the studies to which Bean refers evaluate the relationship between real wages and *unemployment*, rather than some other cyclic indicator. The problem is, Japanese unemployment rates are notoriously underestimated, in terms of both levels and fluctuations (Hamada and Kurosaka 1984: 92). This point is discussed in detail in a subsequent section (Unemployment and labor flexibility in Japan). Cross-country studies evaluating the relationship between real wages and *output* (rather than unemployment) find that Japan does not have comparatively high real wage flexibility, for either the manufacturing sector or for the economy as a whole (Hamada and Kurosaka 1986: 290–1; Hashimoto and Raisian 1992: 85–8). These findings are consistent with Robert Gordon's regarding comparative nominal wage flexibility at the aggregate level (Gordon 1987: 689).[5] These cautions noted, the relationship between wage-setting institutions and unemployment, mediated by real wage flexibility, is the subject of several influential studies.

Real wage flexibility and wage-setting institutions

As part of their study of the real wage gap, Bruno and Sachs emphasize the degree of corporatism in labor-management relations, as indicated primarily by the degree of centralization of wage-setting arrangements. According to Bruno and Sachs, Austria, West Germany, the Netherlands, and the Scandinavian countries rank high by this measure, Japan and the rest of Europe rank in the mid-range, and the US and Canada rank low. Bruno and Sachs argue that more corporatist systems of labor-management relations are better able to adjust real wages to the market-clearing level in the face of demand shocks. As a consequence, the authors argue, more corporatist economies had had, on average, lesser unemployment rate increases since the early 1970s as well as lower rates of unemployment in the 1980s (Bruno and Sachs 1985). In a similar study by the OECD, an inverse relation was found between the degree of consensus (measured again primarily by the degree of centralization of wage-setting) and the Okun misery index: the sum of inflation and unemployment rates (Metcalf 1987: 59).

Calmfors and Driffil argue against the simple monotonic relation between the degree of corporatism and economic performance. They argue, rather, that both highly-corporatist and weakly-corporatist economies have performed well in recent decades compared with economies in the middle range. As with Bruno and Sachs, corporatism is measured largely by the degree of centralization of wage-setting institutions, particularly unions. The logic underlying their argument is that

> large and all-encompassing trade unions naturally recognize their market power and take into account both the inflationary and unemployment effects of wage increases. Conversely, unions operating at the individual firm or plant level have very limited market power. In intermediate cases, unions can exert some market power but are led to ignore the macroeconomic implications of their actions.
>
> (Calmfors and Driffil 1988: 13)

In systems of highly-centralized bargaining, it is argued, wages are determined through a calculated consideration of macroeconomic consequences; in systems of highly-decentralized bargaining, on the other hand, wages are argued to be determined by the unfettered workings of the labor market itself. In either case (but not the intermediate case), the end results in terms of unemployment are similar. It is on these grounds that Japan, Switzerland, and the US, classified by Calmfors and Driffil as decentralized, are argued to have performed relatively well.

Calmfors and Driffil test their hypotheses by looking at correlations between, first, rankings of countries by centralization of wage-setting, with countries with greater and lesser centralization both given higher rankings; and second, rankings of measures of macroeconomic performance, including unemployment and employment rates and the Okun misery index, all in terms of both levels (based on annual averages from the mid-1970s to mid-1980s) and change (the difference between annual averages from the mid-1960s to mid-1970s and annual averages from the mid-1970s to mid-1980s). Their hypothesis is supported by consistently significant correlations between high–low rankings of the centralization of wage setting and rankings of economic performance, with signs of coefficient estimates as hypothesized (Calmfors and Driffil 1988: 22).[6]

As noted by Bean, though, most studies indicate that real wage rigidity is greater in the US than the European Community (Bean 1994: 600). This is at odds with Calmfors and Driffil's argument that low US unemployment results from real wage flexibility, itself resulting from decentralized wage setting. A more clear-cut characteristic of decentralized wage-setting is that it allows a greater dispersion of wages across the economy, particularly in the absence of high minimum wages and other wage floors (Blau and Kahn 1995). It is reasonable to think that a greater dispersion of wages combined with low wage floors would be associated with higher levels of employment. Such thinking is reflected in the widely held view that there is an inverse relationship between inequality and unemployment, that higher unemployment in much of Europe is the flip side of greater inequality in the US and Japan in the face of similar relative demand shifts away from less-skilled workers. This view follows directly from theories of unemployment rooted in the neo-classical view of the labor market (in the absence of sufficiently offsetting supply shifts of less-skilled workers). Leaving aside any shortcomings of the neo-classical view, it is surely reasonable to think that certain jobs can only be profitable at the very low wage levels enabled by decentralized wage-setting and low wage floors.

David Soskice provides a fundamental criticism of Calmfors and Driffil, arguing that their ranking scheme is at odds with their theory, at least for certain key countries. Soskice writes that

> The Calmfors-Driffil theory relates to coordination, but the empirical measure they use – the degree of centralization of bargaining institutions – relates to the actual location of bargaining. . . . The problem which arises is that less centralized systems (at least on a formal level) may in fact be highly coordinated. Critically, the two countries which do most empirical work in Calmfors-Driffil as examples of well-performing decentralized economies fall into this category: Japan and Switzerland.
>
> (Soskice 1990: 41)

Soskice describes the manner in which wage setting is coordinated in Switzerland and Japan, in spite of being set formally at the company level (ibid.: 41–2). In Switzerland, coordination occurs through employer organizations. In Japan, coordination occurs through the annual Spring Offensive (*Shunto*), with employers' organizations and union federations negotiating a percentage increase in base pay for strategic large firms. This percentage increase is emulated throughout the economy, at other unionized firms, non-unionized firms, and for government employees. Soskice also argues that Calmfors and Driffil misrank Germany, for which wage setting is highly coordinated for the economy as a whole in spite of formally occurring at the regional level by industry. Among the coordinating mechanisms in Germany are industry agreements extending to all companies within an industry, and the federations of employer organizations and industry unions, all of which cross regional boundaries (ibid.: 44).

In some sense, the answer to whether wage setting in Japan is centralized is both yes and no, depending on why one asks the question. An economy-wide percentage increase in base pay is certainly the relevant measure if one is interested in the relationship between real wage flexibility and macroeconomic performance, and thus Soskice's criticism of Calmfors and Driffil is valid. A percentage increase in base pay has no effect, though, on lessening the dispersion of wages throughout the economy, as is typical of centralized wage setting. In fact, inter-industry wage inequality in Japan is highest among the OECD countries, as is male–female wage inequality (Tachibanaki 1987: 662–3; Blau and

Kahn 1995: 106). Regarding Switzerland, Blau and Kahn indicate that male–female wage differences are also among the highest for the advanced economies. In spite of Soskice's criticism, it is nonetheless plausible that the relatively favorable employment performance of the US and Japan results, at least in part, from a common cause: not because of real wage flexibility resulting from decentralized wage setting (for the US does not have the former and – at least in terms of macroeconomic adjustment – Japan does not have the latter) but because of wage inequality, making possible the creation of jobs that would otherwise be unprofitable. Yet however plausible the notion of an unemployment and inequality trade-off, there is a lack of solid empirical support for it.

The trade-off between unemployment and inequality

The possibility of a trade-off between unemployment and inequality is suggested by many authors, among them Andrew Glyn, who writes:

> During the 1980s most countries displayed either increased joblessness, with more long-term unemployment and more concentration on women or youths (many EC countries), or greater earnings inequality (the Anglo-Saxon economies, Japan). Even the high employment/egalitarian earnings distribution typical of the Nordic countries was fraying.
>
> (Glyn 1995: 13)

The basic logic underlying the trade-off is that all countries experienced similar relative demand shifts away from less-skilled workers that were not sufficiently offset by supply shifts of less-skilled workers. The prevalent view is that these demand shifts resulted from skill-biased technical change, though the expansion of trade with low-wage countries is also argued to have been a cause (Wood 1994; Burtless 1995: 801). From marginalist principles follows the prediction that wage differences must rise in order for labor markets to clear. An economy will experience increasing inequality or increasing unemployment, the former if wages are downwardly flexible, the latter if wages are downwardly inflexible. This view of the trade-off between unemployment and inequality has been tagged the "unified theory" (Blank 1997: 14).

Particularly relevant to the unified theory are wages for lower-paid workers, for whom wage floors are created by collective bargaining agreements, minimum wage regulations, and unemployment insurance benefits (high levels of unemployment insurance benefits are argued to raise the reservation wage, the wage at which a labor-force participant is indifferent between working and not working). In this view, relatively favorable employment growth in the US and Japan is associated with growing inequality, with both argued to result from greater wage flexibility, itself resulting from lower wage floors. On the flip side, the less favorable employment growth of many European countries, among them Germany and France, is argued to be associated with lesser changes in inequality, with both resulting from lesser wage flexibility and higher wage floors.

As noted, the evidence on employment performance in the Japan, the US, Germany, and France is consistent with the unified theory. The finding of growing earnings inequality is robust for the US but less so for the other countries, depending on the measures of inequality and datasets used. *The OECD Jobs Study* provides evidence on earnings distributions over the 1980s consistent with the unified theory. These measures are based on "the ratio of the lower limit of earnings received by the top 10 per cent (9th decile) of all male workers relative to the upper limit of earnings received by the bottom 10 per cent (1st decile)" and show growing inequality for Japan and especially the US, and declining inequality for France and Germany (OECD 1994a: 19). For the manufacturing sector, measures of inter-industry earnings inequality over the 1980s show strongly increasing inequality in the US, a small decline in inequality in Japan, little change in France, and a small increase in inequality in German till 1984 and smaller decrease thereafter (based on "a group-wise decomposition of Theil's T statistic") (Galbraith, Darity, and Lu 1998: fig. 1). Summarizing recent studies of inequality in Germany, Beissinger and Moeller write that "A closer look at the evidence reveals that no consensus about the prevailing trends of wage dispersion in Germany exists" (Beissinger and Moeller 1998: 2). The one uncontroversial finding the authors note is that there is less inequality in the lower tail of earnings distribution in Germany and other European countries than in US (Beissinger and Moeller 1998: 2; Blau and Kahn 1994). Consistent with this, wage floors do appear a good deal lower in the US and Japan than in Germany and France, a result of wage-setting institutions, minimum wages, and unemployment insurance benefits, which are now considered in turn.

First, regarding the cases of Japan and the US, decentralized wage-setting institutions made possible a wide dispersion of wages. Wage setting was much more centralized in Germany and France, with collective bargaining at the industry level and with extension mechanisms resulting in nine-tenths of workers, unionized and non-unionized, being covered by collective agreements (OECD 1994b: 173).

Second, the ratio of the minimum wage to average hourly compensation of production workers in manufacturing was 0.26 in both the US and Japan in 1992, compared with 0.38 in France (Card and Krueger 1995: 241). Adjusted by GDP purchasing power parities, the minimum wage in the US was 55 percent lower than in France, with 26 percent of the US workforce employed at below the French minimum wage. Though there is no minimum wage for Germany as a whole, the US minimum wage is less than 50 percent of the minimum wage in the retail industry in Hamburg (McKinsey Global Institute 1997: 5).

Third, regarding unemployment insurance benefits, there was not a large difference in the share of income replaced by unemployment benefits, at 60 percent for Japan, 50 percent for the US, 57 percent for France, and 63 percent in Germany as of the early 1990s. What did differ a great deal, though, was the duration of unemployment benefits, from six months in Japan and the US to three years in France and four years in Germany (Nickell 1997: 61). The duration of unemployment benefits might lengthen the period for which a labor-force participant's reservation wage is high, contributing to long-term unemployment.

This evidence, though suggestive, is not sufficient to vindicate the unified theory. Even the strongest and most robust cross-country correlations between employment performance and inequality do no provide direct evidence for the unified theory.[7] Direct evidence requires showing that the employment growth of workers on the low end of the pay scale is relatively high in countries with growing inequality compared with countries with lesser inequality, for it is the experience of this group of workers that is argued to drive the relationship between unemployment and inequality. The most definitive recent studies provide little evidence, though, that this is so. Particularly valuable are studies by David Card, Francis Kramarz, and Thomas Lemieux on the US, France, and Canada (1995); Alan Krueger and Jörn-Steffan Pischke on the US and Germany (1997); Beissinger and Moeller on Germany (1998); and Francine Blau and Lawrence Kahn on the US and Germany (1997).

The US, Canada, and France are often held to rank in order of descent by degree of labor-market flexibility, a result of differences in wage-setting institutions, minimum wage laws, and government social policy. Card, Kramarz, and Lemieux address the evidence that differences in employment growth in these countries in the 1980s can be attributed to differences in labor market flexibility. Focusing on the employment growth of less-skilled workers, the authors consider the argument that, in recent years, less demand for these workers relative to more-skilled workers for all countries was manifested differently in each of the countries: in the US by growing income inequality, stagnant real wage growth, and stronger employment growth, and conversely, by smaller changes in income inequality, more rapid real wage growth, and weaker employment growth in Canada and, especially, France.

The empirical evidence regarding the patterns of wage growth and income inequality in the US, Canada, and France is not the source of much controversy, the authors note, arguing that these patterns are consistent with the view that the greater restrictiveness of labor markets impedes downward wage flexibility (Card, Kramarz, and Lemieux 1995: 2–3). For different age and education groups, the authors examine correlations between initial wages, and changes in wages and employment-to-population rates.[8] These correlations provide no evidence in support of the unemployment–inequality trade-off. The authors summarize their results as follows:

> Consistent with the view that French labor market institutions restrict relative wage flexibility, we find that wage differentials between skill groups held constant or narrowed slightly over the 1980s. As in Canada, however, we find little evidence that this apparent rigidity in relative wages translated into greater employment losses for less-skilled workers. Indeed, the pattern of employment-population growth rates across age-education cells in France is almost identical to the pattern in the United States. Taking the evidence for the United States, Canada, and France as a whole, we conclude that it is very

difficult to maintain the hypothesis that the "wage inflexibility" in Canada and France translated into greater employment losses for less-skilled workers in these countries.

(Card, Kramarz, and Lemieux 1995: 3)

In their study of Germany and the US from 1979 to 1991, Krueger and Pischke (1997) use similar methods to Card, Kramarz, and Lemieux. The authors examine initial wages and changes in wages and employment-to-population rates for twenty groups of workers of both sexes, classified by age and education. Regarding patterns of inequality, the evidence is consistent with the unified theory, with relative and absolute declines in wages for workers in the lowest wage groups in the US but no such declines in Germany. There is no evidence, however, that employment growth was lower in Germany than in the US for workers with the lowest initial wages. On the contrary, there is a more strongly positive relationship between initial wages and employment growth in the US than in Germany for both men and women, evidence that employment growth was relatively low for lower-paid workers in the US. This is just the opposite of what the unified theory predicts. Summarizing their results and those of similar studies, the authors write that

the slow growth in employment in many European countries appears too uniform across skill groups to result from relative wage flexibility alone. Furthermore, a great deal of labor market adjustment seems to take place at a constant real wage in the US.

(Krueger and Pischke 1997: abstract)

Beissinger and Moeller (1998) undertook a study of Germany in the 1980s similar to Krueger and Pischke's but with considerably more detailed data. The authors made use of a micro dataset enabling them to evaluate 420 groups of workers of both sexes, categorized by two education, seven age, and thirty industry classifications (with price and output composition controls for industries and labor supply controls for education and age groups). In contrast with Krueger and Pischke, the authors found evidence of growing earnings inequality for men. Consistent with Krueger and Pischke, the authors found no evidence of slower employment growth for men with lower initial wages. That is, there is essentially zero correlation between initial wages and employment growth for men across the 420 worker groups, a result at odds with the unified theory. In Krueger and Pischke's study, however, results for Germany are broadly similar for men and women. This is in decided contrast with Beissinger and Moeller's study, where results for women are roughly the opposite as for men, of which the authors conclude that "the general picture obtained for female workers is in line with the two-sides-of-the-same-coin hypothesis" (that is, the unemployment–inequality trade-off) (Beissinger and Moeller 1998: 19). Given the quality of data used, Beissinger and Moeller's study of Germany seems more definitive than Krueger and Pischke's, and the results should be interpreted as such. Since German women are paid less than German men, a greater number of them are likely to be affected by high wage floors. Perhaps this accounts for some of the differences observed between men and women's patterns of earnings and employment.

Blau and Kahn compare Germany and the US, looking at employment and wages for young workers with the least education: those aged 18 to 29 who were high-school dropouts in the US and without an apprenticeship qualification or higher education in Germany (Blau and Kahn 1997). Real wages for young workers with the least education were higher in absolute terms in Germany than in the US (adjusted for purchasing power) and also rising in Germany and declining in the US. At the same time, employment-to-population rates were a good deal higher in Germany than in the US for these least-educated workers, particularly for women, providing anecdotal evidence against the unified theory. It should be noted that these results do not contradict those of Beissinger and Moeller for German women, since Blau and Kahn look at employment rates in a given year, not at changes in employment over time. Moreover, Blau and Kahn note that employment rates within Germany were higher for more educated women.[9]

There have not as yet been comparable studies done for Japan, but a cross-country study by the OECD suggests that the cases noted here of the US, Canada, France, and Germany are broadly representative of the experience of the advanced economies (OECD 1996: 75–6). The OECD study examined cross-country correlations between what it calls "incidence of low pay" and unemployment rates, or employment-to-population, rates for several demographic groups.[10] Consistent with the results of the studies by Card, Kramarz, and Lemieux, and Krueger and Pischke, correlation coefficients are all statistically insignificant and often the opposite sign to that hypothesized by the unified theory.

Minimum wage levels have received a good deal of attention regarding the relationship between unemployment and inequality, partly because they provide so direct an impediment to downward wage flexibility. From theories of unemployment based on marginalist principles follows the expectation that higher minimum wages will result in less employment for less-skilled workers. In their recent volume, *Myth and Measurement: The New Economics of the Minimum Wage* (1995), David Card and Alan Krueger present the results of empirical studies that address the employment effects of minimum wage increases. Card and Krueger's studies provide no robust evidence of an inverse relation between minimum wages and employment of minimum wage workers (ibid.: 1). The authors' analyses are based on cross-state and time series data for the US. Card and Krueger also present the results of analogous studies done for Puerto Rico, Canada, and the United Kingdom. The authors summarize these findings as follows:

> This book presents a new body of evidence showing that recent minimum-wage increases have not had the negative employment effects predicted by the textbook model. . . . Moreover, a reanalysis of previous minimum wage studies finds little support for the prediction that minimum wages reduce

employment. If accepted, our findings call into question the standard model of the labor market that has dominated economists' thinking for the past half century.

(Card and Krueger 1995: 1)

The "standard model of the labor market" to which the authors refer is, of course, the neo-classical model, with its upward sloping supply and downward sloping demand curves for labor.

Social policy as a source of inflexibility

Various social policies have been argued to contribute to unemployment by impeding labor market flexibility. (Minimum wage legislation and unemployment insurance benefits were briefly considered earlier, in light of the hypothesized trade-off between inequality and unemployment.) *The OECD Jobs Study*, for example, argued that relatively generous social policies acted to lessen labor market flexibility in continental Europe. Within the context of the destabilizing effects in the 1970s and 1980s of the oil crises, the breakdown of the Bretton Woods system of fixed exchange rates, financial market liberalization, the increased globalization of production, and the rapid pace of technical change, the *Study* writes:

> [I]n the midst of this tumultuous period when so many forces were testing the flexibility of economies, policies to achieve social objectives were extended, with the unintended side-effect of making markets, including importantly labour markets, more rigid. This erosion of the ability to adapt to change was probably most pronounced in continental Europe and Oceania.
>
> (OECD 1994c: 30)

The National Bureau of Economic Research (NBER) undertook an ambitious research project in the 1990s, the primary objective of which was to examine the hypothesized trade-off between protective social policies and economic flexibility, particularly labor market flexibility. This project resulted in a collection of essays titled *Social Protection versus Economic Flexibility: Is There a Trade-off?* (Blank 1994). Comparative studies were conducted for the advanced capitalist economies on a wide range of social policies. Among these were employment protection programs (a study of West Germany, France, and Belgium); regional labor mobility (Japan and the US); housing market policies (the US, West Germany, and Japan); health insurance policies (the US and West Germany); public pensions (the US, Japan, and Sweden); relative size of public sectors (the US and the United Kingdom); income assistance programs (the US and France); and child care and maternity provisions (the US, the Netherlands, and Sweden).

In her introduction to the volume, Rebecca Blank writes, "When the authors of this volume came together to present their research to one another, all of us were struck by the correspondence in results and inferences across these papers" (Blank 1994: 15). The correspondence to which Blank refers is that none of the studies found any evidence that social policies had a substantial adverse impact on labor market flexibility, and that social policies often had favorable social outcomes, the latter of which tend to be neglected by economists in the debates on comparative economic performance. The harmony of conclusions occurred in spite of the range of datasets and methods used, as well as countries considered. As Blank writes, "these papers give little evidence that labor market flexibility is substantially affected by the presence of social protection programs, nor is there evidence that the speed of labor market adjustment can be enhanced by limiting these programs" (ibid.: 15).

Other empirical studies examine the effects on employment performance of employment protection legislation and payroll taxes (Jackman, Layard, and Nickell 1996: 15–26); non-employment benefits, such as for sickness and invalidity (Blöndal and Pearson 1995: 163–7); and social policy expenditures as a share of gross domestic product (Scherer 1994: 44–7; Scharpf 1997). These studies make use of country-level data for the OECD countries, comparing measures of these social policy provisions with measures of employment and unemployment rates. Consistent with the results of the NBER project, these studies do not find that more generous social policies are associated with higher levels of unemployment, particularly long-term unemployment. As noted, it is primarily the variation in long-term unemployment that drives the variation in unemployment rates among the advanced economies, and that is of particular relevance regarding labor market flexibility (Nickell 1997: 57).

The strongest evidence that protective social policies have adverse effects on unemployment comes from studies of unemployment insurance benefits, yet even here the evidence is mixed. Bean summarizes these studies in his survey article on European unemployment, and notes that increases in the duration of, and share of, income replaced by unemployment benefits do not appear directly to have caused increases in unemployment (Bean 1994: 594). This is an important point, for one of the striking characteristics of Germany as well as France is how much unemployment rates increased between the pre-oil shock and recent periods as compared with Japan and especially the US (ibid.: 574). Bean argues, though, that in the face of commonly-experienced demand shocks, unemployment benefits of longer duration lead to longer spells of unemployment, and thus partly account for the differences in unemployment rates among the advanced capitalist economies. Bean notes that though the share of income replaced by unemployment insurance benefits is relatively high in the non-European Community countries of Europe (such as the Scandinavian countries), the duration of these benefits is relatively short, typically less than a year, and these countries had low unemployment compared with the European Community countries (ibid.: 592). In summarizing several studies on this issue, Bean writes as follows:

> [T]hese studies . . . find a very significant relationship between the length of time for which unemployed workers are eligible for benefits (generally much

longer in the European Community than elsewhere) and the degree of persistence in the unemployment process across countries.

(Bean 1994: 610)

Nickell notes that microeconometric evidence indicates that "at least part of the observed cross-country correlation" between the duration of unemployment insurance benefits and the duration of unemployment results from the former acting upon the latter (Nickell 1997: 67). Yet it is also plausible, as Nickell suggests, that the direction of causality runs both ways, as governments extend benefits to protect the long-term unemployed (ibid.). More generous unemployment insurance benefits need not have an adverse effect on unemployment provided that they are accompanied by active labor market policies, requiring the unemployed to participate in programs assisting their return to employment. Jackman, Layard, and Nickell refer to this as the Swedish model, which they argue played a key role in Sweden's low unemployment in the 1980s (Jackman, Layard, and Nickell 1996: 6–10). At the same time, such active labor market policies require that jobs are available, and it is here the authors argue that Sweden faltered in the 1990s: not because of its labor market policies but because of macroeconomic mismanagement.

There is one last point worth making regarding the relationship between social policy and unemployment. From the 1950s through the mid-1970s, unemployment rates were lower in every year in Germany and France than in the US, often much lower (OECD 1994a: 36). Yet expenditures on social policy were a good deal higher in Germany and France than in the US over these years. In 1960, public expenditures on social protection policies as a percentage of gross domestic product were 18.10 percent in Germany, 13.42 percent in France, and 7.26 percent in the US; in 1970, the measures were 19.53 in Germany, 16.68 in France, and 10.38 in the US (OECD 1994d: 57–8). Thus the relatively generous social policies of Germany and France were long-standing features of these economies, firmly established in the early postwar years. Measured in this manner, it is clear that generous social policies are entirely consistent with very low rates of unemployment, or at least that this was once so.

The Beveridge curve as a summary indicator of labor market inflexibility

The 1997 British Academy Keynes Lecture given by Robert Solow was titled "What is Labor-Market Flexibility? What is it Good For?" Solow argues that labor market flexibility and rigidity are never defined with much rigor, but rather by listing various possible sources of rigidity: trade union influence, unemployment insurance benefits, restrictions on hiring and firing and number of hours worked, high rates of overtime compensation, and health and safety regulations. Solow writes that

This sort of definition by example is far from satisfactory. Not that the examples are irrelevant: each of the restrictions I have mentioned certainly contributes its mite to labor-market rigidity in the very broad sense that it limits the possible responses to any exogenous change in circumstances. Nevertheless there are . . . important reasons to look for something more systematic.

(Solow 1997)

Solow argues for the need for a "summary indicator of labor-market rigidity," which would strengthen the analytical foundations of the study of labor market flexibility and unemployment. Just as important, a summary indicator could enable policy makers to evaluate trade-offs among various possible sources of rigidity in the context of overall labor market flexibility.

Solow argues on behalf of the Beveridge curve as a summary indicator of labor market inflexibility. (The Beveridge curve was developed by William Beveridge in the 1940s to provide a measure of how far the economy was from full employment (Bleakley and Fuhrer 1997: 3).) The curve is the negatively sloped relation between the vacancy rate (the number of unfilled jobs as a proportion of the labor force) on a vertical axis and the unemployment rate on a horizontal axis. An increase in labor market rigidity would be reflected in a rightward shift of the curve, with unemployment rates higher for any given vacancy rate. There are, Solow notes, data availability problems in deriving the Beveridge curve, particularly in the way that vacancies are estimated. That said, the Beveridge curve brings coherence and concreteness to the way one thinks about labor market flexibility and its relationship to unemployment. More to the point, Beveridge curves constructed for recent decades provide no evidence that the differences in unemployment among the advanced economies can be explained by differences in labor market flexibility.

Solow presents Beveridge curves for the US, the United Kingdom, Germany, and France, with data spanning from mid-1960s to the 1990s. For the US and the United Kingdom, the curve shifted strongly to the right in the early 1970s and then shifted back left in the late 1980s, consistent with the view that there was an increase and then subsequent decrease in labor market inflexibility. In Germany and France, by contrast, there were no such decisive shifts. Rather, the curves indicate a vertical wall from the mid-1960s to early 1970s, at about 1 percent unemployment for Germany and 2 percent unemployment for France, suggesting a minimal level of frictional unemployment. Thereafter, the Beveridge curves for Germany and France indicate a fairly stable inverse relation between vacancy and unemployment rates.[11] Solow argues that this is just the opposite of what one would expect if labor market flexibility were the primary cause of high and persistent unemployment. Solow writes:

[T]he main message transmitted by the Beveridge curves . . . goes squarely against the cliche that high and persistent European unemployment is entirely or mainly a matter of "labor-market rigidities." It is precisely in France and Germany, where unemployment has been higher and more persistent, that there is no sign of a big adverse shift in the Beveridge curve. It is precisely in the US and the UK, where unemployment has been at least more variable and, in the case of the US, lower, that one can detect a substantial adverse shift, followed by a favorable one. To the extent that the location of the Beveridge curve is a reasonable summary for the degree of labor-market rigidity, the large continental economies do not seem to have suffered from noticeably more rigid labor markets during the during the high-unemployment 1980s than they did in the low-unemployment 1970s. *In fact what stands out from the pictures for France and Germany is the depressed level of the vacancy variable.*

(Solow 1997, emphasis added)

What distinguishes Germany and France from Japan and the US is not a shortage of labor market flexibility, but rather a shortage of jobs. It may be simplistic to argue that high European unemployment can be overcome with a return to the old macroeconomic policies of the Keynesian consensus. The world is perhaps too changed for that. Yet there is no strong empirical support for the prevailing view that high unemployment results from labor market rigidities. The main causes of high unemployment appear to lie elsewhere.

Especially in the 1990s, the relatively rapid growth and low unemployment of the US economy was the envy of much of Europe as well as Japan, with many attributing the difference to the greater flexibility of US labor markets. Regarding high German unemployment, the *Financial Times* summarizes the views of Manfred Neumann, economics professor at Bonn University, as follows: "The biggest problem, he says, is rigid labour markets" (Atkins 1999). Others argue that the deregulation of Japanese labor markets, particularly regarding the lifetime employment system, is needed for Japan to overcome its current deep recession (Nakamoto 1999). In the wake of the East Asian financial crisis, such views led the International Monetary Fund to advocate the reform of labor laws and the liberalization of labor markets in East Asian countries (Singh 1998: 15). In a January 2000 address to the Industrial Relations Research Association, Joseph Stiglitz, Chief Economist of the World Bank, expressed his concern on these issues, in which he associates Japanese labor-management relations with the "high road":

I worry that one of the more adverse consequences of the East Asian crisis may be the abandonment of the "high road," as firms are being encouraged to break long standing implicit contracts with workers, to "downsize" in response to the new economic realities – even if downsizing implies forcing long term workers into unemployment.

(Stiglitz 2000)

A few things should be said regarding the determinants of the US economic growth in the 1980s and 1990s. For one, the focus on labor market flexibility does not give due credit to the competitive successes of many US firms. This held in a wide range of industries both mature (automobiles) and more high-tech (computer components and software, pharmaceuticals), and was based in large measure on innovations in product design and production processes and the successful marketing of these innovations. US firms were also highly successful in the advanced services, particularly financial services. The expansion of the advanced service sector in the US is argued by Saskia Sassen (1988) to be a key factor in what she calls "the rise of global cities": New York and Los Angeles. Sassen argues that the of rise of global cities facilitated the movement of traditional high-wage manufacturing jobs away from the developed economies, but at the same time generated a rapidly growing labor demand for high-income employment in the advanced service sector. This generated in turn a secondary labor demand in the low-wage service sector, in which many jobs were filled by recent immigrants into the US. Sassen summarizes her view as follows:

> The consolidation of such global centers [as New York and Los Angeles] generates a restructuring of labor demand. The job supply is shaped by several key trends, notably (a) the growth of the advanced service sector, including the financial system, and (b) the shrinking of traditional manufacturing industries and their replacement with a downgraded manufacturing sector and high technology industries, in both of which sweatshops are mushrooming. The evidence shows that the result is an expansion of very high-income professional and technical jobs, and a vast expansion of low-wage jobs. The expansion of the low-wage job supply is in good part a function of growth sectors and only secondarily of declining industries in need of cheap labor for survival. It is in the expansion of the low-wage job supply that we find the conditions for the absorption of the immigrant influx.
>
> (Sassen 1988: 22)

One source of concern for the US economy is that a growing share of employment and income depends on the continued growth of financial services and rise in the value of financial assets. Since the time of Sassen's writing to date, the trend on Wall Street has been stunningly upward. But the history of financial speculation strongly suggests this will not continue. Another source of concern is revealed by examining the key components of aggregate demand in the US: foreign trade, and the government and private sectors. From 1992 to the present, the US foreign trade deficit has steadily increased and the government deficit declined, the latter turning into a surplus by 1998. Both components thus acted as increasing drains on aggregate demand. The mirror image of these movements was the steady decline since 1992 of the private sector financial surplus, becoming a deficit in 1996 (Godley 1998: 12). That is, private sector expenditures grew faster than incomes, such that the former now exceed the latter. This decline in the private sector financial surplus was driven largely by households (Eatwell and Taylor 2000). An expansionary fiscal policy does not seem likely in the current political climate, and neither does a significant sustained improvement in the trade deficit. Thus the question arises as to whether the current US expansion is sustainable. Wynne Godley thinks otherwise, writing,

> As the private sector's deficit is now at a level where large injections of finance are needed just to maintain it where it is, it can hardly go on growing much longer. . . . This means that the motor which has driven the US economy through one "Goldilocks era" – namely the expansion of private spending financed by loans – cannot possibly drive it through another.
>
> (Godley 1998: 12)

If and when the downturn comes and depending on its duration and severity, the temptation to emulate the US will lessen. As with the upturn, the downturn will be driven by the competitive strategies of US firms and broader macroeconomic forces, for which US labor markets can be neither credited nor blamed.

Part 2: unemployment and labor flexibility in Japan

Internal and external labor markets and women as a buffer workforce

The second part of this chapter argues that internal labor market flexibility in Japan is not an alternative to, but is rather closely complemented by, external labor market flexibility. In particular, it is argued that impediments to hiring and firing resulting from the lifetime employment system, which applies almost exclusively to men, are accommodated by the flows of women into and out of employment and the labor force.

In making adjustments to fluctuating demand conditions, Japanese firms are often regarded as exceptional in their heavy reliance on internal labor markets. This view is expressed by Toshiaki Tachibanaki, who writes,

> Japanese firms prefer internal work forces rather than external work forces when they adjust labour input. For example, reallocation or transfer of workers to other establishments within a firm or to other sections within an establishment are frequently used, and also labour hoarding is quite common. *In other words, the internal labour market dominates the external labour market.*
>
> (Tachibanaki 1987: 652, emphasis added)

In their comparison of Japanese and US labor markets, Robert Bednarzik and Clinton Shiells make a similar point. For Japan, they write, "Employment adjustments are mainly done internally through intra- and inter-company transfers or retraining programs, often with government financial assistance" (Bednarzik and Shiells 1989: 41). This greater reliance on internal labor markets is argued to be an important determinant of Japan's low unemployment rates. This was noted in the introduction of this chapter, with a *Financial Times* editorial attributing low US unemployment to "high external mobility" and low Japanese unemployment to "high internal mobility." Similar arguments are made by others (Tachibanaki 1987: 652; Hashimoto 1993: 158).

Japan's reliance on internal adjustment is reflected in comparatively high employment stability in the face of demand fluctuations. The stability of employment is supported by various measures. For data from 1970 to 1983, ratios of the standard deviations of growth rates of employment to production at the aggregate level are 0.63 in the US, 0.56 for Germany, and only 0.32 in Japan (Tachibanaki 1987: 654). Very similar results are observed for the manufacturing sector for the years 1950 to 1983. Regressing the growth rate of employment on the growth rate of output for the manufacturing sector, coefficient estimates are 0.58 for the US, 0.57 for Germany, and 0.33 for Japan (Hashimoto and Raisian 1992: 86. Cf. Houseman and Abraham 1993: 47 for similar results for US and Japanese manufacturing from 1970 to 1989). Moreover, employment stability increased in Japan from the mid-1970s, with firms relying more on adjustment through working hours (Brunello 1985: 177; Hashimoto 1993: 156–7). Consistent with the increase in employment stability, the average length of job tenure increased from nine years in the early 1970s to nearly thirteen years by the late 1980s (Clark and Ogawa 1992: 337). In the 1990s, average length of job tenure was somewhat shorter in Germany than Japan but quite long in both countries compared with the predominately English-speaking OECD countries, Australia, Canada, the US, and the United Kingdom (Table 1.4). And job turnover rates were considerably lower in Japan than in Germany, indeed a good deal lower than in the eleven OECD countries for which recent data are available (OECD 1996: 168–9).

Several reasons have been advanced for Japan's high stability of employment. Most obvious is Japan's lifetime employment system, based on informal understandings and protecting an estimated third of the labor force. Various rationales are offered for the existence of both Japan's lifetime employment system and greater employment stability. Among these are Japanese firms' greater reliance on firm-specific human capital (Mincer and Higuchi 1988: 98), unemployment laws that encourage adjustment through hours of work rather than employment (Hashimoto 1993: 149), and the high cost of adjustment through new hires compared with adjustment through overtime payments (Tachibanaki 1987: 655). Lifetime employment protection is often associated with employment in larger Japanese firms. Consistent with this view, Clark and Ogawa note that job tenure tends to be longer at larger Japanese firms. They write:

> Tenure is much greater in large and medium-size firms. For example, tenure in firms with 1,000 or more employees was 16 years during 1986–1988, up from 12 years in 1971. In firms with 10–99 employees, tenure was 10 years during 1986–1988, up from slightly over six years in 1971.
>
> (Clark and Ogawa 1992: 337)

Table 1.4 Average length of job tenure in nineteen OECD countries

	Late-70s to mid-80s		Around 1990				Mid-1990s			
	Year	Total	Year	Total	Male	Female	Year	Total	Male	Female
Australia	85	6.6	91	6.8	7.8	5.4	96	6.4	7.1	5.5
Austria	—	—	—	—	—	—	95	10.0	11.0	8.6
Belgium	78	9.6	—	—	—	—	95	11.2	11.7	10.4
Canada	85	7.8	91	7.8	8.9	6.5	95	7.9	8.8	6.9
Denmark	78	7.7	—	—	—	—	95	7.9	8.3	7.5
Finland	84	8.3	91	9.0	9.4	8.5	95	10.5	10.5	10.4
France	78	9.5	91	10.1	10.6	9.6	95	10.7	11.0	10.3
Germany	78	10.0	90	10.4	12.1	8.0	95	9.7	10.6	8.5
Ireland	79	8.9	—	—	—	—	95	8.7	9.8	7.2
Italy	78	9.4	—	—	—	—	95	11.6	12.1	10.6
Japan	82	9.4	90	10.9	12.5	7.3	95	11.3	12.9	7.9
Netherlands	79	8.4	90	7.0	8.6	4.3	95	8.7	9.9	6.9
Norway	—	—	89	9.4	10.2	8.4	—	—	—	—
Portugal	—	—	—	—	—	—	95	11.0	11.1	10.9
Spain	—	—	92	9.8	10.6	8.2	95	8.9	9.8	7.2
Sweden	—	—	—	—	—	—	95	10.5	10.7	10.4
Switzerland	—	—	91	8.8	10.4	6.6	95	9.0	10.4	7.1
United Kingdom	84	8.5	91	7.9	9.2	6.3	95	7.8	8.9	6.7
United States	83	7.2	91	6.7	7.5	5.9	96	7.4	7.9	6.8

Sources: OECD (1986); OECD Economic Outlook (1993, 1997).

Though job tenure does tend to be shorter in smaller Japanese firms, it is nonetheless quite long by international standards (Hashimoto and Raisian 1985: 726–7).[12]

Significantly, women workers have overwhelmingly been excluded from lifetime employment protections (Tachibanaki 1987: 669). Takafusa Nakamura asks, "Is it perhaps true that without a cushion against business slowdowns in the form of some kind of labor force that can be readily sacrificed, Japan's employment system is untenable?" (Nakamura 1995: 162). Several studies provide evidence in the affirmative to Nakamura's question, suggesting that the impediments to labor flexibility imposed by the predominately male lifetime employment system are accommodated by the role of Japanese women as a buffer workforce. Houseman and Osawa, for example, write that "Many Japanese companies were hurt by their inability to shed excess workers during the severe recession in the mid-1970s, and in subsequent years moved to increase their use of part-time workers, who could be easily dismissed" (Houseman and Osawa 1995: 13, 16). As of 1992, fully 95 percent of Japanese part-timers were women.[13] Japanese women's employment and labor-force participation is much more procyclical than Japanese men's, with women typically withdrawing from the labor force in downturns rather than being counted as unemployed (Hamada and Kurosaka 1986: 285–6). In this sense, it seems reasonable to argue that the internal flexibility for which Japan is noted requires the external flexibility provided by women serving as a buffer workforce. At the very least, internal and external labor market flexibility play complementary roles in maintaining Japan's exceptionally low rates of unemployment. The latter argument is made by Hamada and Kurosaka, who also emphasize the gender distinction between internal and external labor market flexibility in Japan (ibid.).

Data on discouraged workers in Japan are worth examining in some detail, for they provide a clear sense of the effect on unemployment rates of women serving as a buffer workforce. Discouraged workers "are defined as persons without work who want a job, but who are not looking for work because they believe that their search will be unsuccessful" (Sorrentino 1995: 32). Regarding the early 1970s economic crisis, Hamada and Kurosaka describe the remarkable gender differences in the growth of discouraged workers in Japan as follows:

> During 1973–75 unemployed men increased from 430 thousand to 650 thousand, raising the unemployment rate merely from 1.3% to 1.9%. However, discouraged workers also increased by 350 thousand during this period. This implies that the unemployment rate for men would have climbed to 3.0%, had it not been for those discouraged workers. For women, this tendency was even stronger. During the same period, unemployed women increased from 240 to 340 thousand, the unemployment rate from 1.2% to 1.7%. However, the unemployment rate would have climbed to 5.7%, had it not been for 830 thousand who were discouraged at that time.
>
> (Hamada and Kurosaka 1984: 82)

In short, if discouraged workers are counted as unemployed, then unemployment rates for Japanese women would have been well over threefold higher in 1975.[14] In this and a later paper, Hamada and Kurosaka summarize several other studies indicating that unemployment rates for the late 1970s are similarly underestimated for Japanese women, from which they conclude that "the main burden of employment adjustment is on the female population" (Hamada and Kurosaka 1986: 285). It is worth emphasizing that no other OECD country had anywhere near such high proportions of discouraged to unemployed workers as did Japan (for which evidence will be provided in the next chapter).

The continued importance of Japanese women serving as a buffer workforce is indicated by data on discouraged workers for the 1980s and 1990s. Were discouraged workers counted as unemployed in Japan, the average annual rate of unemployment in Japan over the 1983 to 1991 period would be well over double the official rate. That is, the average unemployment rate over these years would be 5.5 percent rather than 2.5 percent, providing a significantly different view of the success of the Japanese economy in adjusting to the post early 1970s period of slower world economic growth (OECD 1993a: 35; 1993b: 23, 33).[15] Fully 80 percent of discouraged workers over the 1983 to 1991 period were women, a remarkably high number. Additional evidence for the role of women as a buffer workforce is provided by considering the countercylical movement of discouraged workers over recent Japan's most recent up- and downswings. From 1987 to 1991, upswing years, the number of discouraged workers declined steadily, year by year, from 1.98 million to 1.23 million. From 1991 to 1993, downswing years, the number of discouraged workers increased to 1.38 million. The movement of discouraged women workers was closely parallel, declining steadily from 1.57 million to 959,000 from 1987 to 1991, and increasing to 1.05 million in 1993 (OECD 1995: 88). Changes in the number of discouraged workers run in the opposite direction to changes in Japanese women's labor-force participation over these up- and downswings, suggesting that Japanese women continued to bear the brunt of labor market adjustment in the Japanese economy into the 1990s.[16] More than that, the strongly countercylical movement in the number of discouraged women workers suggest that this phenomena is another manifestation of the role of Japanese women as a buffer workforce.

Just-in-time production and temporary and part-time workers

The lifetime employment system and seniority-based earnings originated in the face of a shortage of skilled labor in the interwar years but did not become prevalent until the postwar years (Hamada and Kurosaka 1986: 287). Consistent with this, the employment stability for which Japan is now noted is not observed in data prior to the 1950s (Mincer and Higuchi 1988: 99; Hashimoto and Raisian 1992: 79). Thus there is a real sense in which Japan's reliance on internal labor market flexibility precedes, and is more fundamental than, the flexibility associated more specifically with just-in-time production, developed at Toyota

Motors in the 1960s and after (Shingo 1989: 106–7, 167). Yet just-in-time production evolved within the context of the lifetime employment system, adapting to the constraint of employment stability for the core – predominately male – workforce. Not only that, just-in-time production and internal labor markets in Japan more generally are both characterized by flexibility in the definition and design of jobs and the rotation of workers among these jobs. This is suggested by Mincer and Higuchi, who argue that Japan's seniority-based earnings system and long job tenure are made viable by such flexibility and the resulting enhancements to firm-specific human capital. They write as follows:

> By gradual adjustments in continuous training, with emphasis on flexibility and job rotation, potential obsolescence [of human capital] is overcome without changing much of the workforce in the firm. If the new cycle of training builds on the partially obsolete previous cycle, and both contain elements of firm specificity, skills adjustments are accomplished at lesser cost using the existing workforce than new hires.
>
> (Mincer and Higuchi 1988: 116)

Just-in-time production originated at Toyota Motors and diffused throughout a wide range of industries in Japan after the early 1970s. During the 1980s, just-in-time techniques were also implemented by US producers, among them Ford, General Motors, and Westinghouse. Two important developers of the system were Taiichi Ohno, a former vice president at Toyota, and Shigeo Shingo, a consultant for Toyota. Much of this account is derived from their writings (Ohno 1988; Shingo 1989).

A key objective of just-in-time production is waste reduction, achieved through a wide-ranging set of principles and practices. The system is particularly focused on waste resulting from overproduction, whether of finished products or parts and subassemblies. The ideal is to produce without an accumulation of inventory, requiring that products be produced just in time for delivery and in just the right number. In this sense, overproduction is defined to include not only products that exceed sales or orders, the conventional sense of overproduction, but also products that match the desired quantity but are produced too early. Similarly, the ideal of eliminating parts inventories requires that parts be available just in time and in just the right number for any given operation in the production process (Shingo 1989: 165). What distinguishes just-in-time mass production from traditional mass production is not the number of automobiles produced, but rather that a greater number of models or model types (for example, coupes, sedans, and station wagons) are produced in a very short period, as short as a single day. As Shingo put it, "The Toyota production system is the antithesis of large-lot production, *not* mass production" (ibid.: 84). It is only with small lot production that automobiles could be produced to order in a timely fashion and that the need for inventories could thereby be eliminated, or at least greatly reduced. Just-in-time production not only minimizes the costs associated with inventory storage. Perhaps even more important, it offers a decided non-price marketing advantage, since it dramatically lessens the delivery time of made-to-order products (ibid.: 86–7).

In the view of Toyota management, the relative costs of labor versus machinery make it preferable to have a machine complete an operation and sit idle until a worker reactivates it, than for a worker to wait for a machine to complete its operation. Thus in times of average capacity utilization, workers typically operate a number of machines, with these machines commonly performing different operations. Higher levels of production are met by raising the operating rates of machinery, increasing the number of workers, and having any given worker operate fewer machines. In this sense, the ability to readily vary output to accommodate just-in-time deliveries requires a great deal of flexibility in job definition and design. The desire for stockless production flows in the face of demand fluctuations is complicated when machines with higher operating capacities work alongside machines with lower operating capacities. A relay system was devised to facilitate the smooth flow of operations, involving workers at any work station helping workers at any adjacent work station whenever one group falls behind. The relay system thus requires that a worker typically be trained to operate at least three types of machinery, and also requires that machinery be installed to accommodate the movement of workers among operations. This further illustrates the importance for just-in-time production of flexibility in job definition and design (Ohno 1988: 14, 25; Shingo 1989: 155–9).

At Toyota and other Japanese firms, temporary non-union employees commonly work alongside regular union employees (Cole 1971: 145–6, 229; Shingo 1989: 85; Brown *et al.* 1997: 51). In a section titled "Excess capacity and temporary workers," Shingo describes the central role played by temporary workers at Toyota as follows:

> During average demand periods, many workers manage ten machines loaded at 50 percent of capacity. When demand increases, temporary workers are hired. This makes it possible to operate at 100 percent capacity, having each worker handle only five machines. To do this effectively, of course, machines had to be improved so that even temporary workers could work independently after no more than three days of training.
>
> (Shingo 1989: 85. Cf. 74–5 for a similar view of the central role of temporary workers in accommodating demand fluctuations.)

The Toyota production system makes extensive use of both internal and external flexibility, with the latter provided in large measure by temporary but also part-time workers. In this regard, Brown *et al.* write:

> In Japan, temporary, part-time, and seasonal workers, as well as employees of subcontractors, know that they provide the buffer stock when adjustments are required in severe recessions. Even though they often work alongside regular union workers, such workers' status is marked by a stripe on a hat or sleeve.
>
> (Brown *et al.* 1997: 51)

It was noted that in recent years about 95 percent of Japanese part-timers have been women (Houseman and Osawa 1995: 13; Brown *et al.* 1997: 52). And as of 1991, 72.3 percent of temporary employees in Japan were women, highest among the sixteen OECD countries for which such data are available (OECD 1993a: 24). These measures provide additional anecdotal evidence that Japanese women serve as a buffer workforce. It is the aim of the subsequent chapters to provide systematic evidence for this view.

As with the Japanese system of labor-management relations more generally, it does not seem particularly meaningful to argue as some have that internal flexibility is more important than external flexibility in Japan. The two types of flexibility function as complements, each facilitating the other, both serving to keep Japanese unemployment rates low.

Conclusion

This chapter examines the relationship between unemployment and labor market flexibility. The latter is considered in the broadest sense, as it relates to labor markets at large (external flexibility) and to practices within firms (internal flexibility). The first part of the chapter addresses the argument that differences in employment performance among the advanced economies result largely from differences in labor market flexibility. Empirical evidence was considered on nominal and real wage flexibility, wage-setting institutions, the trade-off between unemployment and inequality (the so-called unified theory), social policy, and Beveridge curves. With the exception of ambiguous evidence on the duration of unemployment insurance benefits, there is little solid evidence that high unemployment results from labor market rigidities. Regarding the hypothesized trade-off between inequality and unemployment, it was argued that the idea has plausibility on the face of it. It makes sense that certain jobs can only be profitable at low wages and thus that high wage floors would tend to lessen the number of such jobs. The notion of a trade-off is relatively new, and few studies test it directly. Perhaps newer studies, using different methods or looking at different countries, will provide supporting evidence. But at present, the evidence is largely contrary. The one exception is Beissinger and Moeller's study as regards German women (1998).

The second part of this chapter addresses the argument that Japan's low rates of unemployment result from high internal labor market flexibility. This assertion is suspect, or at least overstated, for several reasons. Japanese firms' reliance on internal flexibility is not an alternative to, but rather is complemented by, external flexibility. This external flexibility is provided disproportionately by women workers, who serve as a buffer workforce. Rather than being counted as unemployed, Japanese women who lose their jobs tend to leave the labor force altogether. This is manifested in the remarkably high proportions of discouraged workers in Japan, the vast majority of them women. Thus Japanese unemployment rates are deceptively low, much more so than for the other advanced economies.

Taken together, the first and second parts of this chapter provide a critical view of commonly-offered reasons that unemployment rates and employment growth vary among the advanced economies, particularly among Germany, Japan, and the US. At the same time, the role of Japanese women as a buffer workforce, reflecting their highly procyclical labor-force participation, provides a critical insight into the first part of the chapter regarding the empirical evidence on comparative wage flexibility. Most studies examining wage flexibility in relation to *unemployment* conclude that wage flexibility is comparatively high in Japan. Yet both the level and volatility of Japanese unemployment rates are greatly underestimated by official unemployment statistics, largely a result of Japanese women leaving the labor force upon losing their jobs. That the volatility of Japanese unemployment rates is underestimated is evidenced by both the role of Japanese women as a buffer workforce, and the related phenomenon of the countercyclial movement of discouraged women workers. Studies that examine the relationship between changes in nominal or real wages and *output* conclude that Japan does not have comparatively high wage flexibility (Hamada and Kurosaka 1986; Gordon 1987; Hashimoto and Raisian 1992). The point is of relevance not only to the literature on comparative wage flexibility but also to that on wage-setting institutions and unemployment. There is controversy over how to characterize Japan's wage-setting institutions, whether they are centralized or decentralized, and whether centralization is an appropriate measure of corporatism. Yet both sides of the debate assume – wrongly it seems – that Japan has comparatively high wage flexibility (Calmfors and Driffil 1988: 14–15; Soskice 1990: 41–2).

Regarding internal and external labor markets, the unemployment rate, and wage flexibility, the Japanese economy is quite different from how it is commonly depicted. These insights are revealed by considering the way in which women serve as a buffer workforce in Japan, and the way in which this affects the perception of employment performance, something unique among the advanced economies. Moreover, these insights suggest the value of studying differences between men and women workers, which provides a significantly different view of the basic workings of Japanese labor markets and the economy more generally.

2 Women's integration into the workforce

Introduction: the buffer, job segregation, and substitution hypotheses

In his article "Global Feminization through Flexible Labor," Guy Standing argues that women's integration into the workforce in recent years was generally associated with their providing forms of labor market flexibility. He writes that the 1980s "marked a renewed surge of feminization of labor activity . . . increasing (women's) use as workers but weakening their income and employment security in both low-income industrializing and industrialized countries" (Standing 1989: 1077). While the increase in women's labor force participation was universal among the advanced economies in recent decades, the qualitative manner in which women were integrated into the workforce varied considerably among different countries, certainly between Germany and Japan. The possibility that women's integration into the workforce might well vary – not only among countries but also among sectors and over time within countries – is taken into account by the three hypotheses set forth by Jill Rubery in the introduction to *Women and Recession*, a collection of country studies (Rubery 1988). These are the buffer, job segregation, and substitution hypotheses.

Rubery defines the buffer hypothesis as follows: "According to the *buffer* hypothesis women are a flexible reserve, to be drawn into the labour market in upturns and expelled in downturns; women's employment moves thus *procyclically*" (Rubery 1988: 3). The issue is not just that women's employment moves procyclically, however, but that women's employment moves significantly more procyclically than men's. This is embodied in the econometric tests of the buffer hypothesis used in *Women and Recession*, which are also used here. These tests examine the relationship between women's employment volatility and total (men's and women's) employment volatility, providing measures of *women's relative employment volatility*.

Rubery defines the job segregation hypothesis as follows:

> According to the *job segregation* hypothesis, there is rigid sex-typing of occupations . . . hence demand for female labour is dependent on demand in female-dominated sectors: employment trends will thus be related more

to secular trends in sectoral and occupational structures than to cyclical
factors.

(Rubery 1988: 3, emphasis added)

In her definition, Rubery emphasizes the long-run aspects of job segregation,
but there is also the possibility of interaction between job segregation and the
buffer hypotheses. It may be that employment in the sectors in which women
are concentrated is less vulnerable to cyclic volatility, providing women with a
measure of protection in the face of downswings. In the US, for instance,
women lost fewer jobs than men in past recessions, a result of their being
concentrated in the service sector which tends to be less affected by job loss in
downswings than goods-producing sectors (Goodman, Antczak, and Freeman
1993: 27). For analogous reasons, it may be that the extent to which women
serve as a buffer workforce, indicated by measures of women's relative
employment volatility, depends on the extent to which they are integrated into
a sector. There is evidence for the US and Germany, for instance, that women's
relative employment volatility is lower in manufacturing industries in which
women's share of employment is also low. The explanation is that women are
not integrated into production in these industries and are rather concentrated in
clerical occupations, for which employment volatility is less (Humphries 1988:
26–7). Both these possible relationships between the job segregation and buffer
hypotheses are explored. Comparisons are also made using the dissimilarity
index, a commonly-used measure of job segregation.

Rubery describes the substitution hypothesis as follows: "[T]he *substitution*
hypothesis predicts *counter-cyclical*" patterns of women's employment, for
"the search for cost-saving induces substitution towards cheaper forms of
labour, such as women" (Rubery 1988: 3). Rubery emphasizes the cyclical
aspects of substitution, but the long-run aspects may be of equal importance,
with the "search for cost-saving" reflected in substitution of women for men
not over cycles but over a longer period. This is, of course, entirely consistent
with women serving as a buffer workforce, with their employment being not
only procyclical but significantly more procyclical than men's. The long-run
substitution of women for men – resulting in part from firms' cost-cutting
considerations – combined with women serving as a buffer workforce
describes, in fact, the pattern observed in Japan in recent decades.

Rubery's *Women and Recession* includes studies of workers in the US, the
United Kingdom, France, and Italy. In her summary of these studies, Rubery
sought a balance between what she regarded as two problematic tendencies:
overgeneralizing by attributing too much weight to the more abstract processes
of capitalist development; and, the flip side, attributing too much weight to idio-
syncrasies and ignoring more general systematic factors. She wrote as follows:

[A]lthough no society can be regarded as an isolated, internally coherent
and protected system, there is a need to redress the balance of the debate
in comparative analysis which so far has tended towards the universalist

type, stressing the similarities in women's role even if a neoclassical framework is not explicitly adopted. Our approach here is thus to emphasize the current differences in women's role in the four countries, to relate these differences to a country-specific system of economic and social organization, and to stress the differences as well as the similarities in each country's response to current recessionary conditions.

(Rubery 1988: 254)

A shortcoming not of Rubery's summary but of the studies themselves is that their lack of standardization makes it difficult to find the proper balance between more general and country-specific factors. This chapter attempts to address this problem by matching data over the same years (and thus broadly similar patterns of macroeconomic growth and women's integration into the workforce), matching aggregate, sectoral, and manufacturing-industry employment categories, and using confidence intervals to test for the significance of cross-country differences. Overall, the data for Germany and Japan are sufficiently consistent to permit such standardization. While the use of standardized tests is a modest improvement over the studies in *Women and Recession*, it allows more definitive conclusions. Most important, these tests provide strong evidence that Japanese women functioned more as a buffer workforce than did German women, particularly at more aggregate levels.

Just as important, Germany and Japan merit careful comparison. For the postwar experience of these countries was broadly similar, from the rebuilding of devastated economies to rapid output and productivity growth and eventual world economic leadership. These factors motivate other recent books comparing the economies of Germany and Japan (Fukui, Merkl, Müller-Groeling, and Watanabe 1993; Ifo Institute for Economic Research and Sakura Institute of Research 1997). Both Germany and Japan are also characterized as "high-road" economies, noted by relatively cooperative labor-management relations that are argued to be key determinants of these countries' high real wage and productivity growth (Gordon 1996: 63). At the firm level, the cooperativeness of labor-management relations is manifested in works councils in Germany and enterprise unions and quality circles in Japan. It is also noteworthy that women's labor force participation increased in a nearly identical manner in Germany and Japan since the mid-1970s.

In spite of these similarities, unemployment rates increased much more dramatically in Germany than in Japan in recent decades. This chapter seeks to attribute a substantial part of the difference in unemployment rates in recent years to differing patterns of women's relative labor force and employment volatility combined with the extremely high proportions of discouraged workers in Japan, the vast majority of them women. Also relevant in this regard is that changes in the number of discouraged women workers in Japan are strongly countercyclical. From 1987 to 1991 in Japan, upswing years, the number of discouraged women workers declined by an average annual rate of 11.6 percent. From 1991 to 1993, downswing years, this pattern was reversed, with the number of discouraged workers increasing at an average annual rate of 4.8 percent (OECD 1995: 88).[1] This countercyclical pattern of discouraged workers held just as strongly in earlier years and suggests that the phenomena of discouraged women workers and of women serving as a buffer workforce are closely linked.[2]

The role of women as a buffer workforce in Japan is relevant not only to the perception of Japanese unemployment rates but also to the causes given for Japan's low unemployment rates (as is argued in the previous chapter). Among the most commonly-noted reasons for Japan's low unemployment are its reliance on internal labor market flexibility and its comparatively high wage flexibility. Regarding the first of these reasons, the striking role of Japanese women as a buffer workforce suggests that Japan relies heavily on both internal and external labor markets, the latter provided in large measure by the hiring and firing of Japanese women in the face of up- and downswings. The importance of such external labor market flexibility is also suggested by a recent report by the Bank of Japan, arguing for the viability of the Japanese employment system. The report states:

> [A]n overnight breakdown of the lifetime employment system and other Japanese employment practices seems unlikely. Some argue that Japanese labor practices are causing the prolonged economic adjustment, by making it difficult for companies to undertake comprehensive restructuring. Therefore, these practices must be changed if companies are to remain competitive. In considering these issues, it is necessary to recognize the following characteristics of the Japanese employment system . . . *Fixed-term workers and part-time workers not covered under the system of lifetime employment function as a buffer in maintaining Japanese employment practices.*
>
> (Bank of Japan 1994: 70, emphasis added)[3]

A large majority of both fixed-term (or temporary) and part-time workers in Japan are women. In 1991, for example, 72 percent of temporaries in Japan were women, highest among the sixteen OECD countries for which data are available. As of 1992, 95 percent of part-timers in Japan were women (based on firms' definition of part-time employment) (Houseman and Osawa 1995: 12). That is, the buffer to which the Bank of Japan report refers is largely made up of women workers.

Regarding wage flexibility, studies examining the relationship between changes in wages and unemployment derive estimates suggesting that Japan has comparatively high wage flexibility. But studies examining the relationship between changes in wages and output do not find comparatively high wage flexibility in Japan (Hamada and Kurosaka 1986; Gordon 1987; Hashimoto and Raisian 1992). This difference appears to result from the underestimation of not only the levels but also the volatility of Japanese unemployment rates, reflected in the role of Japanese women as a buffer workforce and the strongly countercyclical patterns of discouraged workers. Thus studies of the relationship between wages and unemployment overstate wage flexibility in Japan.

Many observers of Japanese labor-management relations focus excessively on the core employment system, commonly characterized by the so-called "three pillars" of the system: lifetime employment, seniority-based earnings, and enterprise unions. Others note that Japanese labor markets are deeply dualistic, with employment in the core almost exclusively male and employment in the periphery disproportionately (though by no means exclusively) female (e.g. Brinton 1993). This dualism is reflected in the distinction between internal and external labor market flexibility, with the former associated more with core employment and the latter more with peripheral employment. What distinguishes this study then is not the emphasis on the dualistic nature of Japanese labor markets. Rather, this study is distinguished by the emphasis on the relationship between internal and external labor markets, between core and peripheral employment, in both the perception and causes of Japan's low unemployment rates and macroeconomic performance more generally. The point is developed in the next chapter, which argues that large Japanese firms simultaneously pursue both high- and low-road labor-management strategies, obtaining the productivity advantages of the high road and the cost and flexibility advantages of the low road. Broadly speaking, the high road in Japan is associated more with men employees and the low road more with women employees.

The chapter's structure is as follows. Measures of women's relative labor force and employment volatility are considered at the aggregate level for Germany and Japan. The chapter then examines women's relative labor force volatility and patterns of discouraged workers for the G7 and Scandinavian economies, including – in addition to Germany and Japan – Canada, France, Italy, the United Kingdom, the United States, Denmark, Finland, Norway, and Sweden. For the G7, these results suggest that women function least strongly as a buffer workforce in Canada, France, and Germany, with the United Kingdom and the US in the middle range, and that women function most strongly as a buffer workforce in Italy and Japan. For the Scandinavian countries, evidence is found that women serve strongly as a buffer workforce in Norway. Overall, the evidence on the role of women as a buffer workforce is strongest and most consistent for Japan. More important, it is only in Japan that one observes the combination of women serving strongly as a buffer workforce and very high proportions of discouraged to unemployed workers (with women making up four-fifths of discouraged workers in Japan). It is only in Japan, in other words, that the role of women as a buffer workforce provides a dramatically different view of Japan's unemployment patterns and macroeconomic performance more generally.

There are a large number of foreign workers in Germany, and they are disproportionately male, so it seems worth asking whether foreign workers function as a buffer workforce in a manner analogous to women workers in Japan. Some evidence (though not conclusive) is found that this is so. Given that German data typically include foreign workers, and that such workers are disproportionately male, it also seems worth asking whether this might mask the extent to which German women function as a buffer workforce. Thus measures of women's relative employment volatility are derived first with and then without the inclusion of foreign workers. This makes no sizeable or significant difference in results. Either way, there is little evidence that German women function as a buffer workforce in the economy as a whole. Such evidence is found, though, for individual sectors of the economy.

The role of women as a buffer workforce is considered for seven basic non-agricultural sectors of the economy: finance and insurance; wholesale and retail trade; transport and communication; services (other); manufacturing; construction; and utilities and mining. Sectoral results for Japan are broadly similar as for the aggregate level, in that there is evidence that women served as a buffer workforce in most of these sectors. For Germany, there is evidence of women functioning as a buffer workforce in certain sectors, particularly in finance and insurance, transport and communication, and to a lesser extent, manufacturing. Yet only a small share of German women's employment is in the first two of these three sectors, indicating that these sectors do not play a large role in driving aggregate level results. Regarding the comparison between Germany and Japan, it is only for the manufacturing sector that there is consistent evidence of women serving more strongly as a buffer workforce in Japan. Results were also examined for sixteen manufacturing industries. For three-quarters of these industries, measures of women's relative employment volatility are larger in Japan than in Germany.

The data used in most of these regressions cover a rather long period of time, from the 1950s through the 1990s, and it is worth asking whether the role of women as a buffer workforce changed over this period. Thus different sample periods are considered, as are tests of structural change considering alternative and multiple turning-point years. For Germany, there is evidence that women served more strongly as a buffer workforce during the 1990s, the period after reunification. For Japan, there is evidence that women served more strongly as a buffer workforce after the mid-1950s, following the consolidation of the lifetime employment system. Tests of structural change do not, however, provide robust evidence of more persistent long-run changes in measures of women's relative labor force and employment volatility for either Germany or Japan.

For the sixteen German and Japanese manufacturing industries, measures of women's relative employment volatility are used as dependent variables in cross-sectional regressions in an effort to identify industry characteristics associated with measures of women relative to employment volatility. The independent variables tested are female union propensity (percent female unionized divided by percent female employed); the ratio of hours worked by females to hours worked by males; the ratio of female-to-male hourly earnings; and female percentages of employment. Results were considered both for a broad span of postwar years and for the post-1973 years, the latter period marked by both women's increasing integration into the labor force and a slowdown in output and employment growth. The most striking finding from these cross-sectional regressions is the significant negative correlation for Japanese manufacturing industries between estimates of women's relative employment volatility and female percentages of employment. That is, Japanese women tended to function less as buffer workforce in those industries in which they were more strongly represented, and more in those industries in which their share of employment was lower.

Regarding the job segregation hypothesis and its relation to the buffer hypothesis, correlations are examined between female percentages of employment, and measures of both women's relative employment volatility and total (male and female) employment volatility, for both the seven non-agricultural sectors of the economy and for sixteen manufacturing industries. There is little correlation to speak of between these measures, except for manufacturing industries in Japan, consistent with the cross-sectional results noted earlier. That is, there is a significant negative correlation between female percentages of employment and measures of women's relative employment volatility. In her study of the US, Humphries finds that for manufacturing industries with low female percentages of employment (below 20 percent), there is little evidence of women serving as a buffer workforce (Humphries 1988: 26–7). Humphries argues that this results from women in these industries being concentrated in non-production occupations, such as clerical work, for which employment tends to be less cyclically volatile. A similar pattern is observed for German, though not for Japanese, manufacturing industries. For both German and Japanese manufacturing industries, then, there is evidence of a relationship between the buffer and job segregation hypotheses, though in rather different ways.

Last, dissimilarity indices are considered based on data for the sixteen German and Japanese manufacturing industries. Levels and movements of these indices are quite similar between Germany and Japan, evidence of similar patterns of gender segregation among these industries. In both countries, there were fairly steady declines in dissimilarity indices over the postwar years. Movements in the dissimilarity index can be decomposed into two main effects: movements driven by changes in the relative size of industries (measured by employment) and movements driven by changes in women's share of employment within industries. These decompositions suggest that a good deal more of the decline in the dissimilarity index in Japan was driven by changes in women's share of employment within industries.

Consistent with the evidence provided by the decomposition of the dissimilarity index, it is also argued that in Japan women were substituted for men since the mid-1970s as part of a long-term strategy by firms to cut costs and maintain flexibility in the face of slower growth, increased international competition, and an aging workforce (of particular importance given Japan's system of seniority-based earnings). But this is supported as much by historical and anecdotal as statistical evidence, and is one of the main themes of the next chapter.

Women as a buffer workforce at the macro level and the discouraged worker effect

In order to focus on the possibility that women's role in labor markets differs between Germany and Japan, this chapter applies techniques used in Rubery's *Women and Recession*. Following the methodology of *Women and Recession*, this chapter uses econometric estimation to compare the volatility of women's labor-force participation and employment relative to total (men's and women's) labor-force participation and employment in Germany and Japan, spanning from formal independence for both in 1952 to the 1990s. The main regression results generally run to 1996 but the period to just 1991 is also considered, as for other recent studies on Germany, "to avoid any impact of reunification" (Krueger and Pischke 1997: 12. Cf. Blau and Kahn 1997).[4] All data refer to the former West Germany or, for more recent years, to the regions of the former West Germany.

In order to derive measures of women's relative labor-force and employment volatility, regressions are based on ordinary-least-squares estimates of the following equation:

$$\log F_t - \log F_{t-1} = \alpha + \beta(\log T_t - \log T_{t-1}) + \gamma TIME + \varepsilon \qquad (1)$$

where F is defined as the number of female employees or labor-force participants, T, the number of male and female employees or labor-force participants (with both F and T evaluated in terms of logarithmic growth rates), *TIME*, a linear time trend, and ε, an error term. Primary data are drawn directly from Japanese and German government publications and use annual data.

In addition to logarithmic growth rates, data is filtered using the Hodrick-Prescott non-linear trend filter.[5] As the filter more thoroughly detrends data than logarithmic growth rates, a linear time trend is not included. The equation is as follows (with a smoothing parameter of 100):

$$\log F_t - \log F_{t(HP)} = \alpha + \beta(\log T_t - \log T_{t(HP)}) + \varepsilon \qquad (2)$$

Results from both methods are presented, though they generally differ but slightly.

The key issue in both models is whether estimates of β are significantly greater than 1, in which case it can be said that there is evidence of women functioning as a buffer workforce. More generally, for αs, θs, and γs, the null hypothesis is that these estimates equal 0 and the non-null hypothesis that they do not; for estimates of βs, the null hypothesis is that these equal 1 and the non-null hypothesis that they are greater than 1, with two-tailed tests for estimates of αs, θs, and γs and one-tailed tests for estimates of βs as well as for confidence intervals comparing women's relative labor-force and employment volatility. All results referred to as significant indicate significance at at least the 5 percent level, unless stated otherwise. Augmented Dickey-Fuller tests (including a linear time trend) were run on $(\log T_t - \log T_{t-1})$ and $(\log T_t - \log T_{t(HP)})$, and these and dependent variables are differenced when significant evidence of unit roots is found. Autocorrelation corrections (ARMA) are used as suggested by Durbin-Watson statistics. Regression results are presented in a stripped-down manner, since the buffer hypothesis depends only on estimates of β and not on any other statistics. Thus only estimates of β, associated standard errors, results from confidence interval tests, and adjusted R^2s are presented.

Since female labor-force participation and employment is a component of total labor-force participation and employment, the above equations suffer from a degree of simultaneity bias by construction. Thus, alternative methods are used to access the role of women as a buffer workforce. First, equations (1) and (2) are modified by substituting the number of male employees or labor-force participants for the number of total (male and female) employees or labor-force participants as the key independent variable. For the G7 and Scandinavian economies, percent changes in men and women's labor force participation are regressed – separately – on percent changes in gross domestic product (these data are provided by the OECD in the form of percent changes). In addition, standard deviations of percent changes of men and women's labor force participation are compared. These methods, combined with the results from the equations, all point to the same conclusion: that Japanese women serve strongly as a buffer workforce while this is not so for German women, with evidence for Japan also stronger and more consistent than for any of the other countries considered.

Econometric estimates of the buffer hypothesis are examined at a number of levels: at the aggregate level for all workers, all employees (all workers minus self-employed and unpaid family workers), and non-agricultural employees, as well as for labor-force participants; at the sectoral level for seven basic non-agricultural sectors; and for sixteen industries within the manufacturing sector. It should be noted that when this chapter mentions "sectors" or "sectoral level" hereafter, it is these seven basic sectors that are referred to; when "industries" are mentioned, it is the sixteen industries within the manufacturing sector that are referred to.

Table 2.1 provides data on the number of total, male, and female labor-force participants and female percentages for these categories: total, male, and female unemployment rates; and the G7 unemployment rate. The numbers of labor-force participants increased significantly overall in the postwar years, for both men and women. The growth in the total number of labor-force partici-pants is particularly striking in Japan. Unemployment rates did not differ greatly between men and women within each country, but unemployment rates for Japanese women are problematic, a result of the very high proportions of discouraged women workers in Japan. The female percentage of labor-force participants and non-agricultural employees are plotted in Figures 2.1 and 2.2. The similar movement in these measures between Germany and Japan is apparent, with the pattern for labor-force participants particularly striking from the mid-1970s to 1990. The decline in Japan prior to the mid-1970s of the

42   *Gender, growth, and trade*

Table 2.1 Japan and Germany: labor-force participants and unemployment rates (annual averages, with number of labor-force participants in 1,000s)

Year	Japan Labor-force participants				Unemployment rates		
	Total	Male	Female	% Fem.	Total	Male	Female
1952	37,740	22,710	15,030	39.8	1.2	1.3	1.1
1953	39,690	23,480	16,210	40.8	1.1	1.1	1.2
1954	40,730	24,230	16,500	40.5	1.4	1.4	1.5
1955	41,550	24,410	17,140	41.3	1.6	1.6	1.6
1956	42,350	24,940	17,410	41.1	1.5	1.4	1.6
1957	43,360	25,590	17,770	41.0	1.2	1.1	1.4
1958	43,880	25,860	18,020	41.1	1.5	1.4	1.6
1959	44,330	26,260	18,070	40.8	1.5	1.3	1.7
1960	45,110	26,730	18,380	40.7	1.1	0.9	1.4
1961	45,620	27,080	18,540	40.6	1.0	0.8	1.3
1962	46,140	27,530	18,610	40.3	0.9	0.7	1.2
1963	46,530	27,910	18,620	40.0	0.9	0.7	1.1
1964	47,100	28,310	18,790	39.9	0.8	0.6	1.1
1965	47,870	28,840	19,030	39.8	1.2	1.1	1.3
1966	48,920	29,420	19,500	39.9	1.3	1.3	1.4
1967	49,830	29,920	19,910	40.0	1.3	1.2	1.4
1968	50,610	30,580	20,030	39.6	1.2	1.2	1.1
1969	50,990	30,910	20,080	39.4	1.1	1.2	1.1
1970	51,530	31,290	20,240	39.3	1.1	1.2	1.0
1971	51,860	31,820	20,040	38.6	1.2	1.3	1.1
1972	51,980	32,160	19,820	38.1	1.4	1.5	1.3
1973	53,250	32,780	20,470	38.4	1.3	1.3	1.2
1974	53,110	33,120	19,990	37.6	1.4	1.4	1.3
1975	53,230	33,360	19,870	37.3	1.9	2.0	1.7
1976	53,780	33,680	20,100	37.4	2.0	2.2	1.7
1977	54,520	33,810	20,710	38.0	2.0	2.1	1.8
1978	55,320	34,060	21,260	38.4	2.2	2.4	2.0
1979	55,970	34,370	21,600	38.6	2.1	2.2	2.0
1980	56,500	34,650	21,850	38.7	2.0	2.0	2.0
1981	57,070	34,980	22,090	38.7	2.2	2.3	2.1
1982	57,740	35,220	22,520	39.0	2.4	2.4	2.3
1983	58,880	35,640	23,240	39.5	2.6	2.7	2.6
1984	59,280	35,810	23,470	39.6	2.7	2.7	2.8
1985	59,630	35,960	23,670	39.7	2.6	2.6	2.7
1986	60,190	36,250	23,940	39.8	2.8	2.7	2.8
1987	60,840	36,550	24,290	39.9	2.8	2.8	2.8
1988	61,650	36,930	24,720	40.1	2.5	2.5	2.6
1989	62,700	37,370	25,330	40.4	2.3	2.2	2.3
1990	63,830	37,900	25,930	40.6	2.1	2.0	2.2
1991	65,050	38,540	26,510	40.8	2.1	2.0	2.2
1992	65,780	38,990	26,790	40.7	2.2	2.1	2.2
1993	66,160	39,350	26,810	40.5	2.5	2.4	2.6
1994	66,450	39,510	26,940	40.5	2.9	2.8	3.0
1995	66,670	39,660	27,010	40.5	3.1	3.1	3.2
1996	67,100	39,920	27,180	40.5	3.4	3.4	3.3

Sources: Japan Ministry of Labour: *Yearbook of Labour Statistics;* Bundesministerium für Arbeit und Sozialordnung: *Arbeits- und Sozialstatistik. Hauptergebnisse;* OECD *Historical Statistics, 1960–1995.*

Table 2.1 (continued)

Year	Germany Labor-force participants				Unemployment rates			G7 unemployment rate
	Total	Male	Female	% Fem.	Total	Male	Female	
1952	22,685	14,610	8,075	35.6	6.1	6.3	5.8	—
1953	23,075	14,850	8,225	35.6	5.5	5.7	5.0	—
1954	23,620	15,155	8,465	35.8	5.2	5.3	4.9	—
1955	24,165	15,435	8,730	36.1	3.9	3.7	4.1	—
1956	24,595	15,670	8,925	36.3	3.1	3.0	3.2	—
1957	25,025	15,835	9,190	36.7	2.7	2.7	2.7	—
1958	25,288	15,933	9,355	37.0	3.0	3.1	2.9	—
1959	25,324	15,959	9,365	37.0	2.1	2.2	2.0	—
1960	26,518	16,678	9,839	37.1	1.0	1.1	0.9	3.3
1961	26,772	16,879	9,893	37.0	0.7	0.7	0.6	3.5
1962	26,845	16,968	9,877	36.8	0.6	0.6	0.5	3.0
1963	26,930	17,035	9,894	36.7	0.7	0.8	0.6	3.1
1964	26,922	17,083	9,839	36.5	0.6	0.7	0.6	2.8
1965	27,034	17,190	9,845	36.4	0.5	0.6	0.4	2.7
1966	26,962	17,218	9,745	36.1	0.6	0.7	0.5	2.5
1967	26,409	16,901	9,508	36.0	1.7	2.0	1.3	2.8
1968	26,291	16,791	9,500	36.1	1.2	1.4	0.9	2.7
1969	26,535	16,958	9,577	36.1	0.7	0.7	0.6	2.6
1970	26,817	17,197	9,620	35.9	0.6	0.5	0.6	3.1
1971	26,957	17,201	9,756	36.2	0.7	0.6	0.9	3.6
1972	27,121	17,168	9,954	36.7	0.9	0.8	1.1	3.7
1973	27,434	17,256	10,178	37.1	1.0	0.9	1.2	3.3
1974	27,412	17,142	10,270	37.5	2.1	1.9	2.5	3.7
1975	27,184	16,884	10,301	37.9	4.0	3.7	4.4	5.3
1976	27,034	16,709	10,326	38.2	3.9	3.4	4.8	5.4
1977	27,038	16,664	10,374	38.4	3.8	3.1	4.9	5.3
1978	27,212	16,724	10,488	38.5	3.6	2.9	4.8	5.0
1979	27,528	16,880	10,648	38.7	3.2	2.5	4.3	4.9
1980	27,948	17,081	10,867	38.9	3.2	2.5	4.3	5.5
1981	28,305	17,242	11,062	39.1	4.5	3.8	5.6	6.3
1982	28,558	17,399	11,159	39.1	6.4	5.9	7.3	7.7
1983	28,605	17,436	11,169	39.0	7.9	7.3	8.8	8.1
1984	28,659	17,476	11,183	39.0	7.9	7.3	8.8	7.4
1985	28,897	17,576	11,321	39.2	8.0	7.3	9.0	7.3
1986	29,188	17,705	11,483	39.3	7.6	6.8	9.0	7.3
1987	29,386	17,783	11,602	39.5	7.6	6.8	8.8	6.9
1988	29,608	17,815	11,793	39.8	7.6	6.7	8.8	6.3
1989	29,799	17,831	11,968	40.2	6.8	6.0	8.1	5.8
1990	30,369	17,965	12,404	40.8	6.2	5.4	7.4	5.7
1991	30,662	18,012	12,651	41.3	5.5	5.0	6.3	6.4
1992	30,943	18,086	12,858	41.6	5.8	5.4	6.4	7.2
1993	30,927	17,969	12,958	41.9	7.3	7.1	7.7	7.2
1994	30,872	17,804	13,068	42.3	8.3	8.2	8.4	7.0
1995	30,648	17,983	12,665	41.3	8.4	8.1	8.7	6.7
1996	30,578	17,916	12,663	41.4	9.1	9.0	9.3	—

Note German unemployment rates in this table are constructed to include the self-employed, as per the standard definition of the unemployment rate. They are consistently lower than official German unemployment rates.

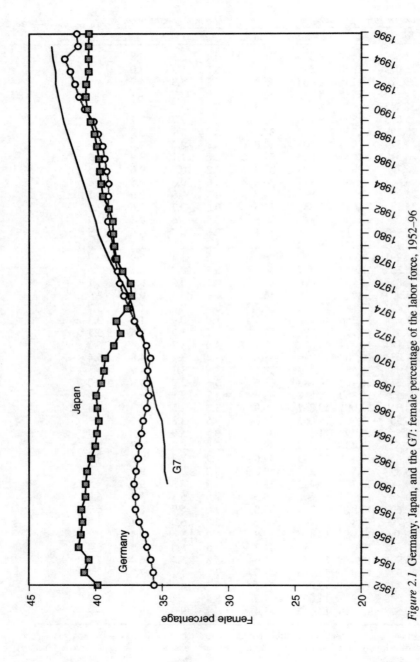

Figure 2.1 Germany, Japan, and the G7: female percentage of the labor force, 1952–96

Sources: Bundesministerium für Arbeit und Sozialordnung: *Arbeits- und Sozialstatistik Haupterbnisse;* Japan Ministry of Labour: *Yearbook of Labour Statistics;* OECD *Historical Statistics, 1960–1995.*

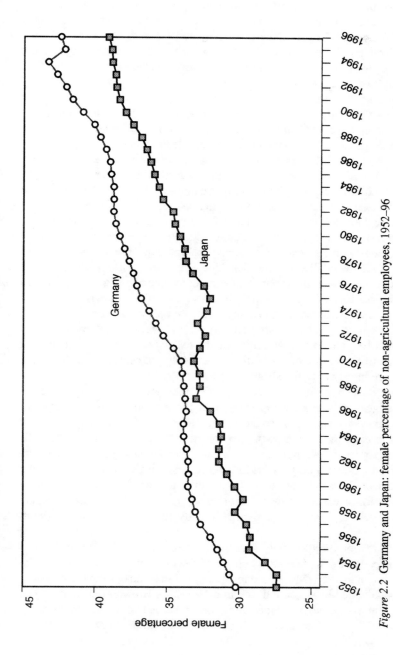

Figure 2.2 Germany and Japan: female percentage of non-agricultural employees, 1952–96

Sources: Bundesministerium für Arbeit und Sozialordnung: *Arbeits- und Sozialstatistik. Hauptergebnisse*; Japan Ministry of Labour: *Yearbook of Labour Statistics*.

female percentage of labor-force participants results in large part from the decline of self-employment and unpaid family work in agriculture, in which Japanese women were heavily represented. Figure 2.1 also shows that the levels and increase of the female percentage of labor-force participants since the mid-1970s were fairly similar in Germany and Japan to the average for G7 countries. Graphs of female percentages for all workers and all employees, not shown, are nearly identical to those for labor-force participants and non-agricultural employees, respectively.

Aggregate level regression results reveal that women served considerably more strongly as a buffer workforce in Japan than in Germany, with, most strikingly, a β estimate of 1.83 in Japan compared with 1.19 in Germany at the labor-force level, based on logarithmic growth rates for the span of years from 1952 to 1996 (Table 2.2, upper half). For Japan, β estimates are significantly greater than 1 at all four levels of aggregation based on equations (1) and (2). For Germany, β estimates are significantly greater than 1 only at the labor-force level. Confidence interval results indicate that estimates for Japan are significantly greater than for Germany for labor-force participants and all workers.

The strongly countercylical movement of discouraged workers in Japan, 80 percent of them women, leads one to suspect that Japanese women's unemployment is less cyclically volatile than Japanese men's. That is, the effect of Japanese women leaving the labor force altogether upon losing their jobs is to dampen the volatility of their unemployment rates. This is clearly the case in Japan and to a lesser extent in Germany.[6] Since employment moves procyclically and unemployment countercyclically, this suggests that estimates of women's relative labor-force volatility ought to be greater than estimates of women's relative employment volatility. As expected, β estimates at the labor-force level are higher than for all workers.

It is worth mentioning that β estimates for Germany are consistently somewhat larger for the 1952 to 1996 years than the 1952 to 1991 years, but more or less the same in Japan.[7] This suggests that German women served more as a buffer workforce in the slow growth years of the 1990s, the period after reunification. Comparing the shorter span of years provides stronger evidence that women served more as a buffer workforce in Japan than Germany. Based on the Hodrick-Prescott filter for data to 1991, for example, confidence interval tests provide evidence that β estimates are significantly larger for Japan than Germany at all four levels of aggregation, though at only the 10 percent level for all employees.

The period from 1958 to 1996 is also considered separately. Partly this is a matter of expediency, to facilitate comparison with sectoral-level results, for which data begin in 1958. More fundamentally, the lifetime employment system was not consolidated in Japan until the mid-1950s. As Brown *et al.* write, "The system of lifetime employment became more prevalent after the Productivity Accord of 1955, which spurred the importation of new technology while it protected workers' jobs" (Brown *et al.* 1997: 38). This system is argued, in the next chapter, to be one of the key reasons that Japanese women served so

Table 2.2 Japan and Germany: aggregate-level regression results

Eq. (1) $\log F_t - \log F_{t-1} = \alpha + \beta(\log T_t - \log T_{t-1}) + \gamma TIME + \varepsilon$

Eq. (2) $\log F_t - \log F_{t(HP)} = \alpha + \beta(\log T_t - \log T_{t(HP)}) + \varepsilon$

1952–96

	Eq. (1) Japan β	adj.R²	Eq. (1) Germany β	adj.R²	C.I.	Eq. (2) Japan β	adj.R²	Eq. (2) Germany β	adj.R²	C.I.
Labor force	1.825** (0.120)	0.85	1.186* (0.109)	0.79	**	1.733** (0.105)	0.86	1.259* (0.111)	0.89	*
All workers	1.685** (0.114)	0.84	1.081 (0.084)	0.84	**	1.611** (0.105)	0.85	1.116 (0.090)	0.92	**
All employees	1.258* (0.117)	0.80	1.123# (0.081)	0.88	—	1.338** (0.122)	0.77	1.146# (0.087)	0.93	—
Non-agric. employees	1.316** (0.110)	0.83	1.088 (0.078)	0.90	—	1.410** (0.109)	0.81	1.105 (0.082)	0.93	#

1958–96

	Eq. (1) Japan β	adj.R²	Eq. (1) Germany β	adj.R²	C.I.	Eq. (2) Japan β	adj.R²	Eq. (2) Germany β	adj.R²	C.I.
Labor force	1.939** (0.126)	0.87	1.115 (0.110)	0.78	**	1.880** (0.118)	0.87	1.253* (0.117)	0.88	**
All workers	1.777** (0.117)	0.87	1.060 (0.090)	0.82	**	1.722** (0.111)	0.86	1.118** (0.094)	0.91	*
All employees	1.519** (0.085)	0.89	1.088 (0.088)	0.85	**	1.543** (0.087)	0.89	1.137# (0.090)	0.93	*
Non-agric. employees	1.535** (0.090)	0.90	1.057 (0.084)	0.85	**	1.535** (0.093)	0.89	1.104 (0.086)	0.93	*

Sources: Japan Ministry of Labour: *Yearbook of Labour Statistics*; Bundesministerium für Arbeit und Sozialordnung: *Arbeits- und Sozialstatistik. Hauptergebnisse*.

Notes

F = female, T = total (male and female), and $TIME$ = linear linear time trend. Below coefficient estimates are standard errors. #, *, and ** indicate significance at the 10, 5, and 1 percent levels, respectively, with one-tailed tests throughout. For β estimates, significance tests for $\beta > 1$. For confidence interval tests (C.I.), significance tests for β estimates for Japan being > Germany.

strongly as a buffer workforce.[8] Coefficient estimates differ only slightly for Germany but are consistently larger in Japan, and significantly larger than for Germany at all four levels of aggregation (Table 2.2, lower half).[9] Equations (1) and (2) are modified by substituting male labor-force participation and employment for total male labor-force participation and employment. Results are consistent with those noted above. Based on data for 1958 to 1996 and using the Hodrick-Prescott filter, for example, β estimates are less than 1 for Germany at all four levels of aggregation, ranging between 0.78 and 0.87. For Japan, these estimates are considerably larger, ranging between 1.37 and 1.56.[10]

Equations (1) and (2) were modified using dummy variables to test for change over time in estimates of women's relative labor-force and employment volatility, considering several and multiple turning-point years. Of particular concern was whether women's relative labor-force and employment volatility changed as women were increasingly integrated into the workforce during the slower growth years after the mid-1970s. However, there is little robust evidence of persistent shifts in these measures over time.[11]

Tests of whether women served as a buffer workforce are conducted at the labor-force level for the G7 and Scandinavian countries making use of an OECD dataset, in which data are provided as percent changes. The Scandinavian countries are examined as they are often taken as models of gender equity. For example, the Scandinavian countries ranked highest among all countries in the mid-1990s by the "Gender Development Index," a measure developed in the United Nations Development Programme's *Human Development Report* (1995).[12] To address the problem of simultaneity bias, results based on equation (1) (except using percent changes) are supplemented by estimates of the following equations:

$$(F_t - F_{t-1})/F_t * 100 = \alpha + \beta_f ((Y_t - Y_{t-1})/ Y_t * 100) + \gamma TIME + \varepsilon \qquad (3)$$

$$(M_t - M_{t-1})/M_t * 100 = \alpha + \beta_m ((Y_t - Y_{t-1})/ Y_t * 100) + \gamma TIME + \varepsilon \qquad (4)$$

where M is defined as the number of male labor-force participants, Y as gross domestic product, and other variables as above. Confidence intervals are then used to test whether β_f is significantly greater than β_m, providing evidence that women serve as a buffer workforce at this level of aggregation. Ratios are also constructed by dividing the standard deviation of percent changes in female labor-force participation by the standard deviation of percent changes in male labor-force participation. The span of years considered is 1960 to 1995, except as noted in Tables 2.3 and 2.4. For each country, the female percentages of labor-force participants in 1960 and 1990 are noted under the country headings in Table 2.3. All OECD labor-force participation and GDP data are differenced, to eliminate unit roots in the case of regressions and for the sake of comparability in the case of standard deviation ratios.

Based on equation (1), Japan has the highest estimate of β among the G7 and Scandinavian countries, at 1.93, but the estimate is nearly as high in Italy and

Norway (Table 2.3), with countries ranked by the magnitude of β estimates, separately for the G7 and Scandinavian countries.[13] Estimates of β are significantly greater than 1 for six of eleven countries – the exceptions being Canada, Denmark, Finland, Germany, and Sweden – with estimates lowest in Finland and Germany, and with the estimate for Japan significantly greater than that for Germany at the 1 percent level. Based on equations (3) and (4), the difference between estimates of β_f and β_m is greatest for Japan, and only in Japan is the difference statistically significant (Table 2.4). For France, Germany, and Sweden,

Table 2.3 G7 and Scandinavia: labor-force regression results and discouraged workers, 1960–95[a]

$$(F_t - F_{t-1})/F_t * 100 =$$
$$\alpha + \beta((T_t - T_{t-1})/T_t * 100) + \gamma TIME + \varepsilon$$

	β	adj.R^2	Discouraged workers as % of unemployed: 1991	Female % of discouraged workers: 1991
Japan	1.926**		90.8	78.0
(1960: 41%; 1990: 41%)	(0.116)	0.89		
Italy	1.799**		23.7	78.9
(1960: 31%; 1990: 37%)	(0.250)	0.62		
United States	1.419**		12.1	57.6
(1960: 33%; 1990: 45%)	(0.138)	0.78		
United Kingdom	1.366*		4.8	38.4
(1960: 33%; 1990: 43%)	(0.178)	0.63		
France	1.220*		1.5	82.9
(1960: 33%; 1990: 43%)	(0.110)	0.79		
Canada	1.209#		6.5	52.2
(1960: 27%; 1990: 44%)	(0.143)	0.68		
Germany	1.003		—	—
(1960: 37%; 1990: 41%)	(0.125)	0.70		
Norway	1.893**		24.8	58.6
(1960: 28%; 1990: 45%)	(0.149)	0.85		
Sweden	1.208		54.1	52.7
(1960: 34%; 1990: 48%)	(0.166)	0.61		
Denmark	1.203		2.4	71.4
(1960: 31%; 1990: 46%)	(0.164)	0.62		
Finland	0.787 (*)		24.3[b]	55.9
(1960: 44%; 1990: 47%)	(0.110)	0.60		

Sources: OECD *Historical Statistics, 1960–1995;* OECD *Employment Outlook* (1993).
Notes
F = female, T = total (male and female), and $TIME$ = linear time trend. Below coefficient estimates are standard errors. #, *, and ** indicate significance at the 10, 5, and 1 percent levels, respectively, with one-tailed tests throughout. ( ) around the above significance symbols indicates significance in the opposite direction as hypothesized. For β estimates, significance tests for $\beta > 1$. Percentages under country headings are female percentages of labor-force participants in 1960 and 1990, respectively.

a To 1990 for Germany, 1992 for Italy, and 1993 for the US.
b Data are for 1987.

the difference between β_f and β_m is actually negative, though small in all three cases. Canada, France, and Germany are the three countries for which there is evidence that men served as a buffer workforce, with estimates of β_m significantly greater than 0.

These tests reveal that Japan, Italy, and Norway are exceptional in the role of women serving as a buffer workforce, with the United Kingdom and US in the middle range of these eleven countries. These patterns are confirmed again by considering the female-to-male standard deviation ratios of percent changes in labor-force participation, with the measures highest in Japan and lowest in Finland and Germany (Table 2.4).

One should perhaps not make too much of these estimates based on the OECD

Table 2.4 G7 and Scandinavia: labor-force regression results, 1960–95[a]

$$\text{Eq. (3) } (F_t - F_{t-1})/F_t * 100 =$$
$$\alpha + \beta_f((Y_t - Y_{t-1})/Y_t * 100) + \gamma TIME + \varepsilon$$
$$\text{Eq. (4) } (M_t - M_{t-1})/M_t * 100 =$$
$$\alpha + \beta_m((Y_t - Y_{t-1})/Y_t * 100) + \gamma TIME + \varepsilon$$

	Eq. (3) β_f	adj.R^2	Eq. (4) β_m	adj.R^2	C.I.	(S.D. $\Delta((F_t - F_{t-1})/F_t))$/ (S.D. $\Delta((M_t - M_{t-1})/M_t))$
Japan	0.267** (0.085)	0.19	0.004 (0.028)	−0.06	*	3.44
Italy	0.198 (0.138)	0.00	0.020 (0.056)	−0.06	—	2.52
United States	0.046 (0.064)	−0.03	0.040 (0.035)	−0.01	—	1.80
United Kingdom	0.142 (0.097)	0.00	−0.011 (0.057)	−0.06	—	1.74
France	0.088 (0.083)	−0.02	0.132 * (0.054)	0.12	—	1.42
Canada	0.228** (0.071)	0.20	0.189 ** (0.043)	0.36	—	1.49
Germany	0.116# (0.064)	0.06	0.127 * (0.054)	0.13	—	1.14
Norway	0.186 (0.193)	−0.04	0.021 (0.067)	−0.07	—	2.94
Sweden	−0.036 (0.129)	−0.06	0.153 # (0.086)	0.04	—	1.43
Denmark	0.000 (0.143)	−0.07	−0.106 (0.081)	0.00	—	1.71
Finland	0.047 (0.073)	−0.05	0.018 (0.096)	−0.06	—	0.77

Source: OECD *Historical Statistics, 1960–1995.*

Notes

F = female, M = male, Y = GDP, and $TIME$ = linear time trend. Below coefficient estimates are standard errors. #, *, and ** indicate significance at the 10, 5, and 1 percent levels, respectively. For β estimates, significance tests for βf and $\beta m > 0$ using two-tailed tests. For confidence interval tests (C.I.), significance tests for $\beta f > \beta m$ using one-tailed tests. The right-hand column shows female-to-male standard deviation ratios of differenced percent changes in labor-force participation.

a To 1990 for Germany, 1992 for Italy, and 1993 for the US.

data in and of themselves, for they are sensitive to the level of aggregation and the span of years examined. For instance, most other studies focus on relative employment volatility, not relative labor force volatility.[14] Still, it is worth emphasizing that the simultaneity bias resulting from equations (1) and (2) does not affect the basic conclusion that women served strongly as a buffer workforce in Japan but not in Germany. Particularly instructive, as regards simultaneity bias, is the near perfect linearity for the G7 and Scandinavian countries between β estimates based on equation (1) and the female-to-male standard deviation ratios of logarithmic growth rates of labor-force participation. That is, the correlation coefficient between these measures is 0.97. One observes a similar degree of linearity based on the same measures compared across the sixteen manufacturing industries. Also noteworthy is the consistency with Houseman and Abraham's study of Japanese women as a buffer workforce in manufacturing, for which results are not effected by simultaneity bias (or at least simultaneity bias by construction) (Houseman and Abraham 1993).[15]

Though Italy, Japan, and Norway appear alike regarding the role of women as a buffer workforce, Italy and Norway do not have the very high rates of discouraged workers in relation to unemployed workers, men or women, that one observes in Japan. It is worth noting, in this regard, the definition of discouraged workers in Japan, which accords with that in most countries. For the 1985 to 1993 Special Survey of the Labour Force, discouraged workers were defined as follows:

> 1. Had not looked for work during the survey week but; 2. wished to have a job for pay and profit if there were any or conditions were favorable and; 3. the reason for not looking for work was that there was no prospect of finding a job either, in the area, suitable for own knowledge or skill [or] under the current economic situation or in the current season.
>
> (OECD 1995: 83)

In Germany, data for discouraged workers are not collected, for, as Buchele and Christiansen write, "In Germany . . . individuals need not be actively seeking work to be registered" as unemployed (Buchele and Christiansen 1996: notes to table 6). The point is supported by Nickell, who writes:

> It is worth noting that, for some countries, OECD standardised unemployment rates differ quite substantially from domestically produced registered unemployment rates [such as those referred to in this study, unless noted otherwise]. Thus in (West) Germany, for example, registered unemployment rates are considerably higher because they include numbers of individuals who are not seeking work and the unemployed are normalised on a measure of the labour force which excludes the self-employed.
>
> (Nickell 1997: 39)[16]

Table 2.3 shows 1991 data on both discouraged workers as a percent of unemployed, and the female percentage of discouraged workers, for the G7 and

Scandinavian economies. Both measures are quite high in Japan, 90.8 and 78.0 percent respectively, and are higher yet for earlier years, particularly for the early 1980s (OECD 1993a: 35). It should be noted that 1991 was a business cycle peak year, during which the number of discouraged workers was at a low point in Japan, indeed lower than in any year from 1983 to 1993. It should also be noted that at no time from the mid-1980s to 1993 did Italy or any other OECD country have such high rates of discouraged workers in relation to unemployed workers as did Japan (OECD 1995: 52). Among the eighteen OECD countries for which data on discouraged workers are available, Japan and, to a lesser extent, Sweden are truly anomalous. These are also the two OECD countries with the lowest official rates of unemployment in 1991, with unemployment rates of 2.1 percent in Japan and 2.7 percent in Sweden, compared with the OECD average of 7.1 percent (for twenty OECD countries). The proportion of discouraged to unemployed workers was 54.1 percent in Sweden in that year, compared with the OECD average of 14.3 percent (including Japan and Sweden). In no other countries did the proportion of discouraged to unemployed workers exceed 25 percent (OECD 1993a: 10). The cases of Japan and Sweden are emphasized by Sorrentino in her ten-country study (the G7 plus Australia, the Netherlands, and Sweden) of alternative unemployment measures, which considers discouraged workers and those working part-time for economic reasons.[17] In regards to this and an earlier study of hers, she writes:

> In general, this article reinforces the findings of the 1993 one. The principal finding of that study was that Japan and Sweden, the countries with the lowest unemployment rates as conventionally measured, had by far the largest increases when the definition was expanded to include persons working part time for economic reasons and discouraged workers. This continued to be the case. The current study shows that, in times of recession and recovery alike, the Japanese unemployment rate consistently tripled when these additional measures of underutilization of labor were incorporated. For Sweden, the most inclusive indicator more than doubled until 1992–93, when labor market conditions deteriorated drastically and the conventional rate jumped sharply, resulting in some closing of the differential between the conventional and expanded rates.
>
> (Sorrentino 1995: 31)

In the case of Japan, the discouraged worker effect was far more important than the effect of part-time work for economic reasons, while the opposite was true of Sweden (Sorrentino 1995: 34).[18] Japan is exceptional among the G7 and Scandinavian economies in the way that women serving as a buffer workforce affect the perception of unemployment and macroeconomic performance more generally. Over the 1983 to 1991 years, for example, the average rate of unemployment was 7.2 percent in Germany and 2.5 percent in Japan. Counting discouraged workers as unemployed over these same years (in both numerator and denominator) would increase the Japanese unemployment rate by 120 percent, to 5.5 percent (OECD 1993a: 35; 1993b: 32–3). On average, fully 80 percent of the discouraged workers over these years were women. And though there is an element of subjectivity in the determination of discouraged workers, the evidence on the role of Japanese women as a buffer workforce, combined with the strongly countercyclical movement of discouraged women workers, suggests that the discouraged-worker phenomenon in Japan is real.

This is not to argue that the superiority of Japanese over German macroeconomic performance in the 1980s was mere illusion. For more robust measures of employment performance (such as private sector employment growth relative to the growth of the working-age population) also reveal that Japan outperformed Germany (Table 1.2). Still, the convergence between unemployment rates when one accounts for discouraged workers is striking, with an average gap of only 1.7 percent between Germany and Japan for the years 1983 to 1991, providing a significantly different view of Japanese unemployment and macroeconomic performance more generally.

Foreign workers in Germany as a buffer workforce

There are a significant number of foreign workers in Germany, and they are disproportionately male. In 1991, for example, foreign workers made up 8.6 percent of employees in the seven sectors considered here. Fully 67.9 percent of foreign workers were male, compared with 59.1 percent of non-foreign workers in the seven basic non-agricultural sectors of the economy.[19] Foreign workers are included in all the above regressions for Germany. Thus it seemed worthwhile to consider whether foreign workers might function as a buffer workforce and, being disproportionately male, might mask to some extent the role of women as a buffer workforce. A dataset spanning from 1975 to 1993 was available at the seven-sector level that distinguished between foreign and all workers, enabling a test of this hypothesis. Regressions were run on the following equations:

$$\log A_t - \log A_{t-1} = \alpha + \beta(\log T_t - \log T_{t-1}) + \gamma TIME + \varepsilon \tag{5}$$

$$\log A_t - \log A_{t(HP)} = \alpha + \beta(\log T_t - \log T_{t(HP)}) + \varepsilon \tag{6}$$

A is defined as the number of total (men and women) foreign workers and the remaining variables are defined as in the previous equations, with T including both foreign and non-foreign workers. The hypothesis of interest is whether β is significantly greater than 1, providing evidence that foreign workers serve as a buffer workforce. Based on equation (5), estimates of β are quite large, ranging between 1.16 and 2.93, with an estimate of 1.53 for employment in the sum of the sectors. Yet standard errors are also quite large, and thus there is mixed evidence of statistical significance that foreign workers served as a buffer workforce. Results are roughly similar based on equation (6) (Table 2.5). Still, there is enough evidence to suspect that foreign workers might mask to some extent the role of German women as a buffer workforce. To address this

Table 2.5 Sectoral-level regression results for Germany: foreign workers as a buffer work-force, 1975–93

	Eq. (5) log A_t – log A_{t-1} = $\alpha + \beta(\log T_t - \log T_{t-1}) + \gamma TIME + \varepsilon$		Eq. (6) log F_t – log $F_{t(HP)}$ = $\alpha + \beta(\log T_t - \log T_{t(HP)}) + \varepsilon$	
	β	adj.R^2	β	adj.R^2
Finance and insurance	2.929 (1.650)	0.29	4.094 * (1.666)	0.37
Wholesale and retail trade	1.340 (0.651)	0.48	1.577 (0.753)	0.17
Other services	1.293 (0.643)	0.48	1.320 (0.888)	0.14
Manufacturing	1.940 ** (0.336)	0.67	1.545 # (0.347)	0.61
Construction	1.528 * (0.233)	0.72	1.384 (0.321)	0.71
Utilities and mining	1.591 ** (0.204)	0.81	1.610 ** (0.186)	0.81
Transport and communication	1.160 (0.311)	0.37	0.908 (0.447)	0.77
Total	1.531 # (0.386)	0.63	1.270 (0.565)	0.29

Source: Statistisches Bundesamt: *Statistisches Jahrbuch für die Bundesrepublik Deutschland.*
Notes
A = foreign workers (men and women), T = total (male and female, including foreign), and *TIME* = linear time trend. Below coefficient estimates are standard errors. #, *, and ** indicate significance at the 10, 5, and 1 percent levels, respectively, with one-tailed tests throughout. For β estimates, significance tests for $\beta > 1$.

possibility, regressions were run using equations (1) and (2), which include foreign and non-foreign workers on both sides of the equations, and also on the following equations:

$$\log NF_t - \log NF_{t-1} = \alpha + \phi(\log NT_t - \log NT_{t-1}) + \gamma TIME + \varepsilon \qquad (7)$$

$$\log NF_t - \log NF_{t(HP)} = \alpha + \phi(\log NT_t - \log NT_{t(HP)}) + \varepsilon \qquad (8)$$

where *NF* is defined as the number of non-foreign female employees, *NT* the number of non-foreign male and female employees, and the remaining variables defined as in the earlier equations. The question of interest is whether ϕ from equations (7) and (8) is significantly greater than β from equations (1) and (2) respectively, which would provide affirmative evidence of the masking effect of disproportionately male foreign workers. Yet there is no such evidence, with estimates of β and ϕ between the equations nearly identical, for individual sectors and for the sum of employment seven sectors (Table 2.6). In short, data that includes foreign workers do not appear to understate the role of

Table 2.6 Sectoral-level regression results for Germany: women as a buffer workforce with and without foreign workers, 1975–93

| | Eq. (1) $\log F_t - \log F_{t-1} =$ $\alpha + \beta(\log T_t - \log T_{t-1}) + \gamma TIME + \varepsilon$ Eq. (7) $\log NF_t - \log NF_{t-1} =$ $\alpha + \phi(\log NT_t - \log NT_{t-1}) + \gamma TIME + \varepsilon$ | | | | |
| | Eq. (1) | | Eq. (7) | | |
	β	*adj.R²*	ϕ	*adj.R²*	*C.I.*
Finance and insurance	1.319** (0.095)	0.96	1.324** (0.103)	0.95	—
Wholesale and retail trade	1.069 (0.063)	0.95	1.062 (0.063)	0.95	—
Other services	0.902(#) (0.069)	0.92	0.905 (#) (0.070)	0.92	—
Manufacturing	1.168* (0.069)	0.90	1.167* (0.080)	0.88	—
Construction	0.370(**) (0.180)	0.03	0.373 (**) (0.194)	0.03	—
Utilities and mining	0.617(**) (0.096)	0.70	0.609 (**) (0.101)	0.67	—
Transport and communication	1.458** (0.180)	0.81	1.458** (0.186)	0.80	—
Total	0.972 (0.070)	0.89	0.976 (0.081)	0.88	—

| | Eq. (2) $\log F_t - \log F_{t(HP)} =$ $\alpha + \beta(\log T_t - \log T_{t(HP)}) + \varepsilon$ Eq. (8) $\log NF_t - \log NF_{t(HP)} =$ $\alpha + \phi(\log NT_t - \log NT_{t(HP)}) + \varepsilon$ | | | | |
| | Eq. (2) | | Eq. (8) | | |
	β	*adj.R²*	ϕ	*adj.R²*	*C.I.*
Finance and insurance	1.486** (0.123)	0.96	1.453** (0.137)	0.94	—
Wholesale and retail trade	1.102# (0.069)	0.95	1.092 # (0.068)	0.95	—
Other services	0.922 (0.064)	0.92	0.899 (#) (0.061)	0.93	—
Manufacturing	1.187** (0.047)	0.96	1.183** (0.055)	0.95	—
Construction	0.461(**) (0.171)	0.27	0.457 (**) (0.188)	0.22	—
Utilities and mining	0.587(**) (0.092)	0.70	0.583 (**) (0.096)	0.68	—
Transport and communication	1.462** (0.139)	0.93	1.453** (0.153)	0.91	—
Total	1.017 (0.065)	0.94	1.004 (0.083)	0.92	—

Table 2.6 (Source and notes)

Source: Statistisches Bundesamt: *Statistisches Jahrbuch für die Bundesrepublik Deutschland.*
Notes
F = female including foreign, T = total (male and female) including foreign, and $TIME$ = linear time
trend. NF = female excluding foreign, NT = total (male and female) excluding foreign. Below coefficient estimates are standard errors. #, *, and ** indicate significance at the 10, 5, and 1 percent
levels, respectively, with one-tailed tests throughout. ( ) around the above significance symbols indicates significance in the opposite direction as hypothesized. For β and ϕ estimates, significance tests
for $\beta, \phi > 1$. For confidence interval tests (C.I.), significance tests for $\beta < \phi$.

women as a buffer workforce in Germany. It is also worth noting that there are
three sectors for which there is consistent evidence of German women serving
as a buffer workforce: finance and insurance; transport and communication;
and manufacturing. For the sum of employment in the seven sectors considered,
β estimates are very near 1.

Women as a buffer workforce and the job segregation hypothesis in sectors and manufacturing industries

Results based on equations (1) and (2) for seven basic non-agricultural sectors
are shown in Table 2.7. For this and the table on manufacturing industries (2.8),
sectors and industries are ranked by the female percentage of employment in
Japan as of 1990, with these measures for both Germany and Japan noted under
sector and industry headings. The span of years considered is 1958 to 1996.
Based on equation (1), β estimates are greater in Japan than Germany for four
of the seven sectors, with finance and insurance, wholesale and retail trade, and
transport and communication the exceptions. Based on equation (2), β
estimates are greater in Japan than Germany for five of seven sectors, with
finance and insurance and wholesale and retail trade the exceptions. But the
large β estimates for wholesale and retail trade for Germany are almost entirely
a result of the inclusion of years 1991 to 1996. Restricting the sample to 1958
to 1991, β estimates for Germany on wholesale and retail trade are not significantly greater than 1, and estimates for Japan are larger than for Germany for
five of seven sectors based on equation (1) and six of seven sectors based on
equation (2).[20] Regardless of the span of years considered, though, estimates of
β are significantly greater in Japan than in Germany only for the manufacturing
sector (at the 5 percent level based on equation (2) but only the 10 percent level
based on equation (1)). For utilities and mining in Germany, estimates of β are
significantly less than 0, for both these regressions and those considering the
role of foreign workers as a buffer workforce (Table 2.6). This may reflect one
aspect of the job segregation hypothesis, with women in utilities and mining
concentrated in clerical occupations for which employment is less volatile in
the face of up- and downswings.

Though there is little evidence of German women serving as a buffer workforce at the aggregate level, it is worth emphasizing that such evidence exists
rather strongly for certain sectors. Combined with the sectoral-level results for

Table 2.7 Japan and Germany: sectoral-level regression results, 1958–96

Eq. (1) $\log F_t - \log F_{t-1} =$
$\alpha + \beta(\log T_t - \log T_{t-1}) + \gamma TIME + \varepsilon$

	Japan		*Germany*		
	β	*adj.R²*	β	*adj.R²*	*C.I.*
Finance and insurance (J: 50%; G: 51%)	1.087 (0.079)	0.91	1.289** (0.093)	0.82	—
Wholesale and retail trade (J: 46%; G: 60%)	1.181 ** (0.073)	0.93	1.305* (0.168)	0.66	—
Other services[a] (J: 45%; G: 63%)	1.158 # (0.097)	0.85	1.058# (0.042)	0.95	—
Manufacturing (J: 33%; G: 28%)	1.350 ** (0.094)	0.87	1.116* (0.052)	0.94	#
Construction (J: 15%; G: 11%)	1.187 * (0.078)	0.83	0.970 (0.233)	0.50	—
Utilities and mining (J: 13%; G: 11%)	1.057 (0.246)	0.35	0.114(#) (0.569)	0.21	—
Transport and communication (J: 12%; G: 25%)	1.557 * (0.302)	0.41	1.687** (0.271)	0.68	—

Eq. (2) $\log F_t - \log F_{t(HP)} =$
$\alpha + \beta(\log T_t - \log T_{t(HP)}) + \varepsilon$

	Japan		*Germany*		
	β	*adj.R²*	β	*adj.R²*	*C.I.*
Finance and insurance (J:50%; G:51%)	1.041 (0.069)	0.88	1.321 ** (0.096)	0.87	(*)
Wholesale and retail trade (J:46%; G:60%)	1.167* (0.071)	0.88	1.472 ** (0.137)	0.86	(#)
Other services[a] (J:45%; G 63%)	1.165 * (0.091)	0.87	1.114 ** (0.045)	0.97	—
Manufacturing (J:33%; G:28%)	1.441** (0.095)	0.91	1.158 ** (0.050)	0.97	*
Construction (J:15%; G:11%)	1.065 (0.069)	0.86	1.007 (0.142)	0.56	—
Utilities and mining (J:13%; G:11%)	1.042 (0.217)	0.37	0.438 (*) (0.324)	0.14	—
Transport and communication (J:12%; G:25%)	1.824** (0.322)	0.68	1.607 ** (0.183)	0.77	—

Sources: Japan Ministry of Labour: *Yearbook of Labour Statistics*; Bundesministerium für Arbeit und Sozialordnung: *Arbeits- und Sozialstatistik. Hauptergebnisse*.

Notes

F = female, T = total (male and female), and *TIME* = linear time trend.. Below coefficient estimates are standard errors. #, *, and ** indicate significance at the 10, 5, and 1 percent levels, respectively, with one-tailed tests throughout. ( ) around the above significance symbols indicates significance in the opposite direction as hypothesized. For β estimates, significance tests for $\beta > 1$. For confidence interval tests (C.I.), significance tests for β estimates for Japan being > for Germany. Percentages under sector headings are female percentages of employment in 1990 for Japan and Germany, respectively.

a Data for Japan begin in 1971.

Germany noted earlier regarding the role of foreign workers as a buffer work-force, there is consistent evidence of women serving as a buffer workforce for three sectors in Germany: finance and insurance, transport and communication, and manufacturing, with β estimates particularly large in the first two sectors. A large proportion of German women are employed in manufacturing. As of 1990, 26 percent of the German women employed in the seven non-agricultural sectors were employed in manufacturing. Yet relatively few German women were employed in finance and insurance and transport and communication, with women's combined employment in the two sectors making up less than 10 percent of the women's employment for all seven sectors (as of 1990). Thus women's employment in these two sectors appears too small to drive aggregate level results.

The female percentage of manufacturing employment for Germany and Japan is shown in Figure 2.3. For Germany, women's employment declined fairly steadily relative to men's from the late 1950s on. For Japan, in contrast, there was a trend increase in the female percentage of manufacturing employment from the mid-1970s to about 1990. There is a sense, then, in which women were substituted for men in Japanese manufacturing over these years, much as one observes for both Germany and Japan at more aggregate levels. That the measure for Japan is several percentage points lower for larger firms (with thirty or more employees) demonstrates that Japanese women are dispro-portionately employed in smaller firms.

Regression results for sixteen manufacturing industries are shown in Table 2.8, evaluating the span of years from 1952 to 1996. In both Germany and Japan, there was statistically significant evidence of women serving as a buffer workforce in a number of industries. Estimates of β are greater in Japan for thirteen of sixteen industries based on equation (1) and twelve of sixteen based on equation (2). Confidence interval results indicate that β estimates are signif-icantly greater in Japan than Germany for only a few industries, and are not significantly greater for the manufacturing sector as a whole. Regarding the latter, this results from the broader span of years under consideration than for the sectoral-level results noted above. While the estimate of β for Germany is nearly the same regardless of the span of years considered, the estimate of β for Japan is larger for the shorter span of years. Restricting the sample to years 1958 to 1996, results are similar to those noted at the sectoral level, with esti-mates for Japan significantly greater than for Germany at the 10 percent level (Table 2.8, bottom row).

Cross-sectional regressions were done using as a dependent variable measures of women's relative employment volatility for individual manufac-turing industries. These regressions were done in an effort to determine whether women's relative employment volatility might be associated with other characteristics of women's employment. The technique is similar to that used by Green and Weisskopf in their 1990 article, "The Worker Discipline Effect: A Disaggregative Analysis." Cross-sectional regressions were estimated for the 1952 to 1991 and 1973 to 1991 periods, using least-squares estimation with White corrections for heteroskedasticity.[21] These periods were used to address

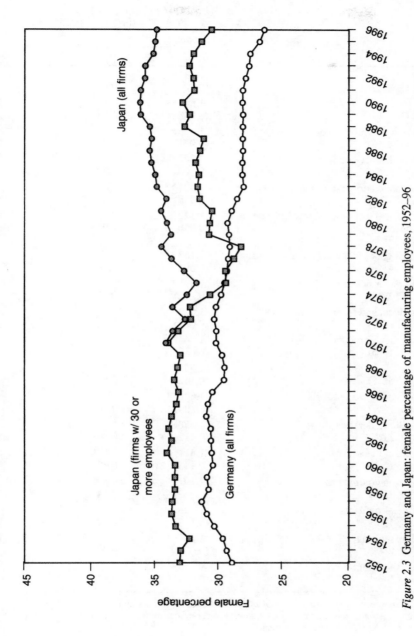

Figure 2.3 Germany and Japan: female percentage of manufacturing employees, 1952–96

Sources: *Arbeits und Sozialstatistik. Hauptergebnisse; Statistisches Jahrbuch für die Bundesrepublik Deutschland; Japan Ministry of Labour: Yearbook of Labour Statistics; ILO Yearbook of Labour Statistics.*

Table 2.8 Japan and Germany: manufacturing industry regression results, 1952–96

	Eq. (1) $\log F_t - \log F_{t-1} =$ $\alpha + \beta(\log T_t - \log T_{t-1}) + \gamma TIME + \varepsilon$	
	Japan	
	β	*adj.R^2*
Apparel (J: 81%; G: 80%)	1.035 (0.029)	0.97
Textiles (J: 55%; G: 49%)	1.382** (0.088)	0.85
Food, beverages and tobacco (J: 52%; G: 45%)	1.095# (0.071)	0.86
Leather and leather goods (J: 52%; G: 57%)	1.242* (0.120)	0.78
Electrical machinery and apparatus (J: 39%; G: 35%)	1.431** (0.072)	0.93
Jewelry, musical instruments, toys and sporting goods, misc. (J: 38%; G: 33%)	1.122* (0.058)	0.91
Professional goods and precision instruments (J: 37%; G: 43%)	1.163* (0.091)	0.89
Paper and paper products (J: 28%; G: 29%)	1.425** (0.112)	0.82
Wood products and furniture (J: 28%; G: 19%)	1.003 (0.061)	0.92
Fabricated metal products (J: 25%; G: 13%)	1.244** (0.079)	0.88
Printing (J: 25%; G: 36%)	1.328* (0.152)	0.64
Chemicals and allied products (J: 25%; G: 28%)	1.428** (0.123)	0.79
Non-metallic mineral products (J: 24%; G: 21%)	1.350** (0.112)	0.83
Non-electrical machinery (J: 20%; G: 16%)	1.314* (0.143)	0.79
Transportation equipment (J: 15%; G: 15%)	1.191 (0.162)	0.64
Primary metal products (J: 12%; G: 15%)	1.728** (0.190)	0.69
Total manufacturing (J: 33%; G: 28%)	1.263** (0.072)	0.90
Total manufacturing 1958–96	1.350** (0.094)	0.87

Sources: Japan Ministry of Labour: *Yearbook of Labour Statistics*; Bundesministerium für Arbeit und Sozialordnung: *Arbeits- und Sozialstatistik. Hauptergebnisse*; Statistisches Bundesamt: *Statistisches Jahrbuch für die Bundesrepublik Deutschland*.
Notes
F = female, T = total (male and female), and *TIME* = linear time trend. Below coefficient estimates are standard errors. #, *, and ** indicate significance at the 10, 5, and 1 percent levels, respectively, with one-tailed tests throughout.

Table 2.8 (continued)

			Eq. (2) $\log F_t - \log F_{t(HP)} = \alpha + \beta(\log T_t - \log T_{t(HP)}) + \varepsilon$				
Germany			Japan		Germany		
β	adj.R^2	C.I	β	adj.R^2	β	adj.R^2	C.I.
1.038 * (0.022)	0.99	—	1.030 (0.031)	0.96	1.063 ** (0.017)	0.99	—
1.056 (0.043)	0.96	**	1.389 ** (0.090)	0.85	1.062 # (0.041)	0.96	**
1.310 ** (0.110)	0.81	—	1.078 (0.068)	0.85	1.721 ** (0.040)	0.94	(**)
0.899 (0.076)	0.81	*	1.255 * (0.116)	0.73	0.953 (0.055)	0.90	*
1.262 ** (0.040)	0.98	#	1.434 ** (0.067)	0.94	1.264 ** (0.040)	0.97	#
1.055 (0.055)	0.93	—	1.232 ** (0.060)	0.91	1.058 (0.054)	0.93	#
1.247 ** (0.064)	0.94	—	1.122 # (0.078)	0.87	1.236 ** (0.025)	0.96	—
1.160 ** (0.036)	0.97	*	1.428 ** (0.136)	0.73	1.161 ** (0.037)	0.96	#
0.887 (0.154)	0.49	—	0.964 (0.061)	0.88	1.305 * (0.140)	0.72	(*)
1.240 ** (0.065)	0.91	—	1.271 ** (0.083)	0.88	1.230 ** (0.066)	0.95	—
1.245 ** (0.068)	0.91	—	1.313 * (0.176)	0.65	1.258 ** (0.074)	0.90	—
1.198 ** 0.041	0.96	#	1.409 ** (0.139)	0.70	1.172 ** (0.044)	0.95	—
1.051 (0.088)	0.86	#	1.412 ** (0.114)	0.82	1.071 (0.106)	0.85	#
1.023 (0.075)	0.86	#	1.248 * (0.111)	0.81	1.067 (0.068)	0.86	—
1.097 (0.082)	0.91	—	1.265 # (0.173)	0.71	1.047 (0.080)	0.85	—
1.136 # (0.087)	0.88	*	1.755 ** (0.181)	0.75	1.157 * (0.079)	0.86	*
1.137 ** (0.044)	0.97	—	1.294 ** (0.077)	0.87	1.168 ** (0.042)	0.96	—
1.126 ** (0.045)	0.97	#	1.344 ** (0.102)	0.82	1.144 ** (0.040)	0.97	#

( ) around the above significance symbols indicates significance in the opposite direction as hypothesized. For β estimates, significance tests for β > 1. For confidence interval tests (C.I.), significance tests for β estimates for Japan being > for Germany. Percentages under industry headings are female percentages of employment in 1990 for Japan and Germany, respectively.

whether the estimates were robust with respect to changes over the more recent years of slower output and employment growth, also the period when women increasingly became integrated into the workforce.

Independent variables were constructed for Germany and Japan for female union propensity (percent female unionized divided by percent female employed); the ratio of hours worked by females to hours worked by males (in an effort to address the extent of part-time female employment); the ratio of female-to-male hourly earnings (including bonuses and premiums); and female percentages of employment.[22] For all variables but the female percentage of employment, it was hypothesized that associated coefficient estimates would be less than 0; for the female percentage of employment, no sign was hypothesized (with two-tailed tests being used throughout). Regarding the hypothesized signs, higher female union propensities are representative of the strength of women's integration into industries, which is expected to be reflected in lower estimates of women's relative employment volatility. The hypothesis for ratios of female-to-male hourly earnings was based on the expectation that high relative employment volatility was likely to be associated with low relative pay, especially in the case of Japan, given the seniority-based system of pay and promotion. The ratios of male-to-female hours worked attempted to address the effect of part-time women's employment, which is characterized by high employment volatility (Kawashima 1987: 606; Houseman and Osawa 1995: 16).

Results are shown in Table 2.9. For Germany, signs for estimates on female union propensity, the ratio of hours worked, and the ratio of hourly earnings are as hypothesized. The only estimate of significance is for the ratio of hourly earnings for the 1952 to 1991 period, but at only the 10 percent level. For Japan, signs are generally as hypothesized, the exception being for the ratio of hours worked for the 1973 to 1991 period. For the 1952 to 1991 period, estimates are significant and negative on both the ratio of hourly earnings and on the female percentage of employment. For the 1952 to 1991 period, estimates are significant and negative on both the female union propensity and the female percentage of employment. Regressions were also done using ordinal rankings of variables, to provide a sense of robustness, and the results are essentially the same.[23]

The result for Japan on the female percentage of employment is most note-worthy, as it holds strongly in both periods. This negative correlation is also suggested by a look at these estimates for Japan in Table 2.8, in which industries are ranked by the female percentage of employment for 1990. Based on equation (1), for instance, five of the six bottom-most industries have β estimates greater than 1.3, compared with only three of the remaining ten industries. This negative correlation is not the result of simultaneity bias, for there is a highly linear relationship between β estimates derived from equation (1) and female-to-male standard deviation ratios of logarithmic growth rates of employment.[24] The case of the apparel industry in Japan is instructive in this regard. As of 1990, 81 percent of employees in the industry were female. One might think that the insignificant β estimate of 1.035 is little more than the result of regressing one variable on itself. However, the female-to-male

Table 2.9 Japan and Germany: cross-sectional regression results for sixteen manufacturing industries using measures of women's relative employment volatility as a dependent variable

C	F UNION	F/M HOURS	F/M WAGES	% F	adj.R²
Japan					
1952–91					
3.888	−0.192	−0.301	−3.593*	−0.011**	0.54
(2.223)	(0.431)	(1.941)	(1.395)	(0.003)	
1973–91					
7.512	−4.035*	0.453	−5.792	−0.015*	0.16
(5.288)	(1.386)	(4.357)	(4.934)	(0.006)	
Germany					
1952–91					
3.810	−0.180	−1.579	−1.495#	0.0004	−0.08
(3.031)	(0.599)	(3.088)	(0.808)	(0.002)	
1973–91					
3.277	−0.642	−0.802	−1.310	−0.003	−0.24
(4.831)	(1.365)	(5.614)	(2.149)	(0.005)	

Sources: Japan Ministry of Labour: *Yearbook of Labour Statistics*;
Bundesministerium für Arbeit und Sozialordnung: *Arbeits- und Sozialstatistik. Hauptergebnisse*;
Statistisches Bundesamt: *Statistisches Jahrbuch für die Bundesrepublik Deutschland.*
Notes
C = constant; *F UNION* = percent female unionized/percent female employed; *F/M HOURS* = ratio of female-to-male hours worked; *F/M WAGES* = ratio of female-to-male wages; *% F* = percent female employed. #, *, and ** indicate significance at the 10, 5, and 1 percent levels, respectively, using two-tailed tests. For all variables, significance tests for estimates < 0. Below coefficient estimates in parentheses are standard errors.

standard deviation ratio of the logarithmic growth rate of employment for the apparel industry in Japan is also very nearly 1, at 0.996.

In her study of the US, Humphries observes that there tends to be less evidence of women serving as a buffer workforce in manufacturing industries with fewer than 20 percent women. Humphries plausibly argues that this results from women in low-female-percentage industries being disproportionately concentrated in clerical work, which is relatively sheltered from job loss in downswings. She writes as follows: "Whatever else may be said about such segregation it does afford some relative protection in the business cycle. . . . [W]hen they [women] have penetrated beyond the clerical and ancillary tasks they tend to occupy the more cyclically volatile operative jobs" (Humphries 1988: 26–7).

The case of Germany is quite similar to that of the US. Based on equation (1), for instance, β estimates are significant for only one of the five manufacturing industries with fewer than 20 percent female employees, with an average estimate of 1.08 (Table 2.8). As noted, Japan is quite distinct from both Germany and the US in this regard. This difference may result from those uniquely Japanese employees referred to as "office ladies." Though these women are classified as clerical workers, the tasks they perform are typically of limited practical value, such that their relative employment volatility seems likely to be considerably higher than for women clerical workers in Germany or the US. Saso describes the role of these "office ladies" as follows:

> Office women's work, which includes a lot of time serving tea and at the copy machine, seems to be quite superficial and indeed wholly non-productive, though it may be conceded that their presence in the office does serve a decorative function and perhaps engenders the much-prized harmony in the workplace.
>
> (Saso 1990: 228–9)

Another way of looking at the relation between the job segregation and buffer hypotheses is to examine the correlation between, first: female percentages of employment (based on annual averages for the period in question) and measures of women's relative employment volatility (in this case, β estimates from equation (1)), and second: female percentages of employment and total (male and female) employment volatility (the standard deviation of the logarithmic growth rate of total employment). Regarding the correlations between female percentages of employment and total employment volatility, the key question of interest is whether those industries or sectors in which women are strongly represented are relatively isolated from business cycles. In the US, for example, one study examining recessions from 1969 to 1991 observes that job loss is less in downturns in the service sectors compared with the goods-producing sectors, and that women tend to be concentrated in the former sectors and men in the latter (Goodman, Antczak, and Freeman 1993: 26). Correlation coefficients are examined for the years 1952 to 1991 and 1973 to 1991 for the sixteen manufacturing industries, and for the years 1958 to 1991 for the seven basic non-agricultural sectors of the economy.

For the seven non-agricultural sectors, correlations for Germany and Japan between female percentages of employment and total employment volatility are negative, consistent with the study of the US, but they are quite small and insignificant, the latter no surprise given the number of observations. Correlations between female percentages of employment and measures of women's relative employment volatility are also small and insignificant.[25] Thus there is little solid evidence, at this level of aggregation, of a relationship between patterns of job segregation and patterns of employment volatility.

For the sixteen manufacturing industries, correlations between female percentages of employment and total employment volatility are negative for Germany and positive for Japan, insignificant for both countries for the 1952 to 1991 years but significant for Japan for the 1973 to 1991 years. That is, there is weak evidence that the manufacturing industries in which German women are more strongly concentrated have lower total employment volatility and stronger evidence, at least for the 1973 to 1991 years, that the manufacturing industries in which Japanese women are more strongly concentrated have higher total employment volatility.[26] Correlations between female percentages of employment and measures of women's relative employment volatility are similar to the results of cross-sectional regressions, which evaluate these same measures. That is, for Germany these measures are near 0 while for Japan these measures are sizeable and negative.[27] For Japan, that is, women tend to serve more strongly as a buffer workforce in industries where their share of employment is low, less so where their share of employment is high.

Comparing patterns of gender segregation

A commonly-used measure of gender segregation is the dissimilarity index. While typically used to measure segregation among occupations, the dissimilarity index is used here to measure job segregation among our sixteen manufacturing industries, and thus follows up directly on the above analyses.[28] The dissimilarity index and its decompositions are defined as follows, with *DI* indicating dissimilarity index; *SEX* indicating sex composition effects; *STR* indicating structural effects; and *INTER* indicating interaction effects:

$$DI \quad = \tfrac{1}{2} \Sigma_{i=1}^{k} ((Nf_i/Nf) - (Nm_i/Nm)) * 100$$

$$SEX \quad = \tfrac{1}{2} \Sigma_{i=1}^{k} D_i^0 * (D_i^1 - D_i^0) * 100$$

$$STR \quad = \tfrac{1}{2} \Sigma_{i=1}^{k} D_i^0 * (S_i^1 - S_i^0) * 100$$

$$INTER \quad = \tfrac{1}{2} \Sigma_{i=1}^{k} (D_i^1 - D_i^0) * (S_i^1 - S_i^0) * 100$$

where $D_i = ((Nf_i/Nf)/(N_i/N)-(Nm_i/Nm)/(N_i/N))$; $S_i = N_i/N$; Nf_i is defined as the number of female employees in a manufacturing industry; Nf is defined as the number of female employees for the sum of manufacturing industries; Nm_i and Nm are defined analogously for male employees and N_i and N for total (male plus female) employees; and superscripts 0 and 1 indicate initial and subsequent year, respectively.

The dissimilarity index is essentially a normalized variance, ranging in value from 0 to 100. If women and men are not employed in any of the same industries, the index will equal 100, and if they are employed among industries in exactly the same proportions as they are employed for the sum of manufacturing industries, then the index will equal 0, in which case there is no gender segregation. Anker describes the intuitive meaning of the dissimilarity index as follows:

> *the proportion of male workers* plus *the proportion of female workers who would need to change occupations in order to have the same proportion of women in every occupation* (and the same proportion of men in every occupation but with a different value).

> (Anker 1998: 90, emphasis in original)[29]

In comparing dissimilarity indices between countries, one of the problems that arises is that the female percentage for total manufacturing employment varies between countries, hindering direct comparison. This is less problematic than it might be in the case of Germany and Japan, for which female percentages of employment are broadly similar over the span of the postwar years, ranging between 27 and 32 percent for Germany and 28 and 34 percent for Japan from 1952 to 1996.

The sex composition (*SEX*) and structural (*STR*) components refer only to *changes* in the dissimilarity index. That is, the dissimilarity index can change both because of sex composition changes within industries and also because the relative size of sectors or industries changes, with the interaction of these two effects captured by the interaction effect (*INTER*). The sex composition component of changes in the dissimilarity index is particularly useful in evaluating the long-run side of the substitution hypothesis.

Dissimilarity indices and female percentages of employment for manufacturing as a whole are shown in Table 2.10 at five-year intervals between 1952 and 1996 and including endpoint years. In the 1950s, dissimilarity indices were a good deal higher in Japan than Germany, indicating greater gender segregation in the former. The dissimilarity index declined by about 20 points overall for Japan between 1952 to 1996, compared with about 12 points overall for Germany. From 1975 to 1996, the measure declined by about 6 points for Japan and 5 points for Germany. In sum, gender segregation in manufacturing at the industry level declined considerably in both countries in the postwar period. For Japan, the decline was particularly rapid in the 1950s, bringing convergence between the two countries such that patterns of gender segregation were quite similar from 1960 on.

Regarding the long-term substitution of women for men employees (as part of a cost-cutting strategy, for instance), what are important are not just changes in the dissimilarity index but changes in the index resulting from changes in sex composition within industries (*SEX*). In this regard, not only did the dissimilarity index decline by more in Japan than in Germany, but a good deal more of the decline in Japan was driven by sex composition changes. From 1975 to 1996 for Japan, for instance, 86 percent of the cumulative year-to-year change in the dissimilarity index is accounted for by changes in sex composition within industries; from 1952 to 1996, the measure is 56 percent. For Germany, only 22 to 26 percent of the change in the dissimilarity index is accounted for by changes in sex composition within industries, for years 1975 to 1996 and 1952 to 1996, respectively.[30] In short, there is much stronger evidence that women were substituted for men *within* manufacturing industries in Japan than in Germany. This is particularly so, and of particular importance, for the years from the mid-1970s, when the female percentage of employment in manufacturing declined overall in Germany but increased in Japan, at least until around 1990. During this period, it is argued that in Japan women were substituted for men as part of a cost-cutting strategy in the face of slower growth, an increasingly competitive international economy, and an aging workforce: the last particularly costly given Japan's seniority-based earnings system. This pattern

Table 2.10 Japan and Germany: dissimilarity indices and female percentage of employment for manufacturing industries (sixteen industries)

	Japan		Germany	
	DI	% female	DI	% female
1952	47.05	33.04	38.30	29.05
1955	43.36	33.36	38.91	30.56
1960	36.33	33.39	37.47	31.44
1965[a]	35.09	33.29	32.61	30.44
1970	32.55	33.92	31.51	30.08
1975	32.11	29.47	30.87	29.06
1980	31.20	30.71	30.70	28.96
1985	32.04	31.81	28.99	27.78
1990	29.31	32.78	27.45	27.77
1995	27.20	31.28	26.40	26.88
1996	26.29	30.57	26.14	26.54

Sources: Japan Ministry of Labour: *Yearbook of Labour Statistics*; Bundesministerium für Arbeit und Sozialordnung: *Arbeits- und Sozialstatistik. Hauptergebnisse*; Statistisches Bundesamt: *Statistisches Jahrbuch für die Bundesrepublik Deutschland*.
Notes
DI = dissimilarity index.
a For Germany, data are for 1966.

of substitution, not over cycles but as part of a more long-term cost-cutting strategy, which was referred to in Japan as "Operation Scale-Down" (Nakamura 1995: 222), is a central theme of the chapter 3.

The substitution of women for men employees in Japan since the 1970s occurred for both the manufacturing sector and for the economy at large, as indicated by the female percentage of employment and the dissimilarity index for manufacturing, and by the female percentage of employment and labor-force participants at the aggregate level. From the mid-1970s to the 1990s, there was also a widening of male–female wage differences in Japan and a decline in female union propensity, for both the manufacturing sector and the economy as a whole. In Germany, these two measures moved in the opposite direction, indicating a degree of convergence in men and women's employment conditions. For Japan, the substitution of women for men employees did not bring a convergence of men and women's employment conditions by these measures, but rather the opposite. Regarding the effects of job segregation, it is worth emphasizing that a decline in such segregation (as indicated by *DI* and *SEX*) is entirely consistent with greater inequality between men and women by other basic measures of employment conditions.[31]

Another way of comparing gender segregation is by examining the correlation between countries of female percentages of employment for manufacturing industries. This gets around the problem of there being different total female percentages of employment among countries as correlation coefficients simply provide measures of linearity. Using different data for Germany and Japan for twenty-two manufacturing industries, the correlation coefficient for 1990 data is very high, at 0.86 (consistent with the similarity in DI between Germany and Japan for the span of years from 1960 to 1996).[32] Table 2.11 shows correlation coefficients for this measure between Germany and Japan and other G7 countries as well as Australia, Denmark, and the Netherlands. The female percentages themselves as well as data years (most often 1990) are shown in Table 2.12. It turns out that similarly high correlation coefficients are observed between all pairs of countries, with coefficients ranging between 0.82 and 0.97 and an average correlation coefficient of 0.90 (with each of the coefficients significant at the 1 percent level). This result is not driven by a few outlier industries, for the average Spearman correlation coefficient is nearly as high, at 0.88. It is truly remarkable that patterns of gender segregation in manufacturing industries could be so similar in the face of so many other fundamental differences among these economies. But the explanation of this striking regularity is left for future research.

In his study of occupational gender segregation (1998), Anker constructed dissimilarity indices for a wide range of countries for the 1970 and 1990 period. Of the six developed economies for which data are exactly comparable (using the international standard classification of occupations, or ISCO, for non-agricultural occupations), Japan had considerably lower dissimilarity indices, regardless of the year or level of occupational disaggregation. The other five of these countries were Finland, France, the Netherlands, Norway, and Switzerland. Dissimilarity indices for Japan held very stable over the 1970 to 1990 period, at about 53 for the 259-occupation level and about 45 for the 75-occupation level. Using data similar to the 75-occupation level for Japan, the dissimilarity index for Germany was also higher than in Japan, at 52 in 1990 (Anker 1998: 112, 117).[33] In short, there was less occupational gender segregation by these measures in Japan than in any of the other countries. Occupational status is generally held to be an important determinant of earnings, and thus the lower levels of occupational gender segregation in Japan might seem surprising in light of the very wide male–female wage differences in Japan compared with the rest of these countries, with Norway representing the extreme opposite of Japan in this regard (Blau and Kahn 1995: 106). Partly in reference to Japan, Anker makes the distinction between horizontal and vertical segregation. He writes:

> Horizontal segregation refers to the distribution of men and women across occupations – for example, women may work as maids and secretaries and men as truck drivers and doctors. Vertical segregation refers to the distribution of men and women in the same occupation but with one sex more likely to be at a higher grade or level – for example, men are more likely to be production supervisors and women production workers, men more likely to be senior managers and women junior managers. . . . [I]t seems likely that vertical segregation is an especially important determinant of Japan's low female-male pay ratio. For example, Japanese women are more or less excluded from the managerial career path in large

Table 2.11 Correlation coefficients for female percentage of manufacturing employment in twenty-two industries for ten OECD countries

Mean: 0.90

	Australia	Canada	Denmark	France	Germany	Italy	Japan	Netherlands	UK
Canada	0.94								
Denmark	0.93	0.91							
France	0.86	0.84	0.91						
Germany	0.93	0.93	0.97	0.88					
Italy	0.86	0.91	0.91	0.86	0.91				
Japan	0.82	0.84	0.86	0.84	0.86	0.90			
Netherlands	0.92	0.92	0.90	0.87	0.87	0.84	0.82		
United Kingdom	0.93	0.93	0.97	0.93	0.96	0.91	0.88	0.94	
United States	0.95	0.94	0.95	0.90	0.93	0.92	0.87	0.90	0.95

Sources: Australia, Denmark, Germany, Italy, and the United Kingdom: UNIDO *Industrial Statistics Database (1999)*; Canada: Statistics Canada, *Labour Force Survey*; France: Ministere de l'economie, des Finances et du Budget, *Annuaire Statistique de la France*, 1990; Japan: Japan Ministry of Labour: *Yearbook of Labour Statistics* (1990); Netherlands: *ILO Yearbook of Labour Statistics* (1988); United States: Bureau of Labor Statistics: *Employment, Hours, and Earnings, United States, 1990–95*.

Note

For Australia, data are for 1989, for France, 1988, for Italy, 1991, and for the Netherlands, 1986.

Table 2.12 Female percentage of manufacturing employment by industry for ten OECD countries

ISIC code and industry		Australia 1989	Canada 1990	Denmark 1990
31	Food, beverages and tobacco	31.0	32.3	43.4
32	Textiles, apparel, leather and leather goods	63.1	66.4	70.6
33	Wood products and furniture	16.6	16.5	24.4
34	Paper, paper products and printing	34.0	30.2	35.7
351+352–3522	Industrial chemicals	25.5	26.2	31.7
3522	Drugs and medicines	46.9	38.6	52.6
353+354	Petroleum and coal products	5.9	21.0	10.7
355+356	Rubber and plastic	30.2	26.1	36.1
36	Non-metallic mineral	10.7	19.1	24.0
371	Iron and steel	7.3	7.7	16.0
372	Non-ferrous metals	7.9	10.7	23.6
381	Fabricated metal products	17.3	17.8	21.7
382–3825	Non-electrical machinery	13.3	19.6	20.5
3825	Office and computing machinery	32.5	32.9	28.8
383–3832	Electrical apparatus, other	31.7	29.8	36.0
3832	Radio, TV and communication equipment	43.3	40.5	43.9
3841	Shipbuilding and repairing	7.7	8.9	9.4
3842+44+49	Other transport	4.2	7.6	20.3
3843	Motor vehicles	15.7	23.0	16.7
3845	Aircraft	10.8	20.7	15.0
385	Professional goods and precision instruments	47.5	40.5	43.2
39	Jewelry, musical instruments, toys and sporting goods, misc.	33.9	41.7	50.3
	Total female percentage of employment	27.1	28.5	33.9
	Male employment (in thousands)	774	1,505	338
	Female employment (in thousands)	288	600	173
	Total employment (in thousands)	1,061	2,105	511
	Manufacturing employment as a share of total civilian employment	14.9	16.0	22.8
	Female percentage of labour force	40.7	44.2	46.1

Sources for male and female employment: Australia, Denmark, Germany, Italy, and the United Kingdom: UNIDO *Industrial Statistics Database*, 1999; Canada: Statistics Canada, *Labour Force Survey*; France: Ministere de l'economie, des Finances et du Budget, *Annuaire Statistique de la France*, 1990; Japan: Japan Ministry of Labour, *Yearbook of Labour Statistics*, 1990; Netherlands: *ILO Yearbook of Labour Statistics*, 1988; United States: Bureau of Labor Statistics, *Employment, Hours, and Earnings, United States, 1990–95*. Source for manufacturing employment as a share of total civilian employment and female percentage of labor force: OECD *Historical Statistics, 1960–1995*.

Table 2.12 (continued)

France 1988	Germany 1990	Italy 1991	Japan 1990	Netherlands 1986	UK 1990	US 1990	Unweighted average
35.6	42.2	26.5	54.5	23.5	39.0	32.5	36.1
65.1	60.5	62.8	68.7	42.2	61.4	66.8	62.8
29.1	20.8	23.3	30.8	9.7	18.8	22.2	21.2
35.6	27.9	24.7	31.4	22.1	33.3	38.1	31.3
21.0	22.9	15.8	26.0	14.9	24.6	26.7	23.5
46.6	51.4	25.1	26.0	25.0	42.8	44.9	40.0
4.9	13.0	8.2	13.3	10.0	10.2	16.3	11.3
28.9	28.6	25.3	38.6	13.8	29.9	35.1	29.2
19.2	21.9	16.6	25.0	6.9	14.2	19.7	17.7
8.4	8.5	6.8	10.9	6.9	6.8	10.1	9.0
14.3	15.2	10.4	20.3	0.0	9.8	18.3	13.0
18.5	22.0	17.3	26.9	8.2	18.1	22.2	19.0
19.2	15.7	13.5	20.5	8.0	16.1	18.4	16.5
32.7	30.1	24.8	41.9	16.0	24.0	34.2	29.8
34.2	31.8	29.3	41.9	16.0	29.2	42.9	32.3
34.2	46.4	32.4	41.9	16.0	30.7	41.7	37.1
14.3	6.0	4.1	18.5	6.3	8.4	13.8	9.7
14.3	11.5	9.8	18.5	6.3	7.5	21.9	12.2
17.7	15.2	14.4	18.5	6.3	11.6	19.4	15.9
14.3	14.1	10.3	18.5	6.3	12.2	22.6	14.5
19.2	40.2	38.0	37.9	22.2	31.9	41.4	36.2
N/A	50.4	54.1	49.6	19.3	44.6	46.4	43.4
30.6	27.1	27.3	36.3	16.2	28.2	32.9	28.8
2,931	5,194	2,000	7,348	804	3,445	12,792	
1,293	1,926	751	4,190	155	1,353	6,285	
4,223	7,102	2,751	11,538	959	4,798	19,077	
21.6	31.6	22.1	24.1	19.3	25.5	18.0	21.6
42.6	40.8	36.9	40.6	34.8	42.9	44.7	41.4

Notes

Year represents year of input-output data from OECD *Input-Output Database*, 1995, or, in the case of France and Italy, nearest available year for which male-female employment data are available. (Input-output data is for 1990 for France and 1985 for Italy.)

"–" under "ISIC code and industry" indicates subtraction; there are duplicate data for some industries in France, Japan, and the Netherlands, when data for these industries is combined in the original data sources.

corporations, so that even when they get a job in a large company, they rarely get into a career track position.

(Anker 1998: 35)

Another way of looking at vertical segregation is in the context of labor market dualism, characterized by core and peripheral employment. Particularly striking in Japan is the sharp dualism along gender lines within firms, a theme of the subsequent chapter.

Conclusion

Three hypotheses are evaluated to characterize women's integration into the workforce in Germany and Japan: the buffer, job segregation, and substitution hypotheses. In Japan, women served strongly as a buffer workforce, much more than in Germany. This was particularly so from 1958 on, the period after the consolidation of the predominately male lifetime employment system in Japan. In comparison with the other G7 and also the Scandinavian economies, Japan is unique in having the combination of high estimates of women's relative labor-force volatility and high proportions of discouraged workers (relative to unemployed workers), 80 percent of them women. That the two phenomena are closely related is suggested by the strongly countercylical movement of discouraged workers, a pattern that dates back to at least the 1973 economic downturn associated with the first oil crisis. Counting discouraged workers as unemployed reveals a substantially different view of the Japanese unemployment rate, increasing by more than twofold for the 1983 to 1991 period, and bringing a substantial convergence with the German unemployment rate, with a gap of only 1.7 percentage points for the period.

Looking at data for seven basic sectors of the economy as well as sixteen manufacturing industries enables one to address the relationship between the buffer and the job segregation hypotheses. The most important conclusions are for manufacturing industries. It turns out that job segregation matters in both Germany and Japan, though in quite different ways. In Germany, women tend to function less as a buffer workforce in industries in which their share of employment is low, the same result as is found for the US. The explanation is that women tend not to be in production jobs in these industries but in clerical and ancillary jobs, the latter less vulnerable to job loss in downturns. In Japan, in contrast, women serve more as a buffer workforce in industries in which their share of employment is low, less so in industries in which their share of employment is high. It was suggested, tentatively, that this may result from the role of Japanese women as "office ladies."

There is little evidence to speak of in support of the short-run aspects of the substitution hypothesis, that women are substituted for men in downswings as part of a cost-cutting measure. That is, there is little evidence that men function as more of a buffer workforce than women in Germany and Japan. The long-run aspects of the substitution hypothesis are more interesting, particularly regarding Japan. There is the obvious sense in which women have been substituted for men in Germany and Japan as well as the other advanced economies, evidenced by the rise in the female percentage of labor-force participants and employees. But the substitution hypothesis addresses whether women were substituted for men as a cost-cutting measure, less as a matter of labor supply than of labor demand, as a competitive strategy undertaken by firms. The supply versus demand effects are difficult to untangle, and one must rely on anecdotal and historical evidence. But in Japan there is a good deal of such evidence, considered in the next chapter. The basic argument is that Japanese women came into increased demand by firms after the early 1970s. Slower growth, an increasingly competitive global economy, and a rapidly aging workforce put increased pressure on the lifetime employment and seniority-based earnings systems in Japan, pressure relieved by the increased use of women as a low-wage peripheral workforce.

The substitution of Japanese women for men is also suggested by the analysis of the dissimilarity and its decompositions for the sixteen manufacturing industries. At this level of aggregation, both countries saw similar declines in gender segregation since the mid-1970s. This analysis revealed that since the mid-1970s most of the decline in gender segregation in Germany was simply the result of changes in the relative size of industries. In Japan, in contrast, the decline in gender segregation since the mid-1970s was largely the result of women's changing share of employment *within* industries. And while the female percentage of manufacturing employment declined in Germany, it increased strongly in Japan from the mid-1970s to about 1990. The lessening of gender segregation in Japan did not bring increased equality of men and women's employment conditions, as one might have expected. Rather the lessening of gender segregation was associated with the opposite, with male–female wage differentials widening and women's union membership declining relative to men's. In Germany, on the other hand, these measures moved in the opposite direction.

The empirical analyses of this chapter reveals striking differences between the role of women in German and Japanese labor markets. The next chapter looks to labor market institutions in Germany and Japan in an effort to account for these differences. Among the institutions considered are the lifetime employment system and seniority-based earnings, temporary and part-time employment, the role of unions, and maternity leave policies and child care provisions.

3 Industrial relations and labor market institutions

Introduction: combining high and low road strategies in Japan

Throughout the postwar years, Japanese women served strongly as a buffer workforce, their labor force and employment volatility considerably greater than Japanese men's. This was not the case for German women, whose labor force and employment volatility was much like German men's. Male–female wage differences were also very large in Japan, with women earning about half what men earned on an hourly basis for manufacturing and non-agricultural employees alike (Figures 3.1 and 3.2). For Germany, male–female wage differences were in the middle range of OECD countries.

Just as important, German and Japanese women's employment conditions relative to men's diverged in certain key respects in recent decades as their labor-force participation grew in a nearly identical manner. From 1973 to 1991, for instance, the female percentage of the labor force increased from 37 to 41 percent in Germany and from 38 to 41 percent in Japan (Figure 2.1).[1] In the face of these similar patterns of integration, male–female wage differences narrowed in Germany, as was typical of the OECD countries, but widened in Japan from the mid-1970s until the 1990s. The patterns of divergence held for both manufacturing and non-agricultural employees in Germany and Japan (the exception is for Japanese manufacturing firms with between five and twenty-nine employees, discussed later). The divergence of women's relative employment conditions is also evidenced by patterns of women's union representation, as measured by their union propensity (the ratio of the percentage of female union members to the percentage of female employees). For both manufacturing and non-agricultural employees, women's union propensity increased in Germany and declined in Japan from the mid-1970s (Figure 3.3). Within both countries, changes in male–female wage differences and women's union propensity seem of a piece, reflections of the more marginal nature of women's integration into the workforce in Japan than Germany.

This chapter aims to account for these different patterns between Germany and Japan and, along with the next chapter, the divergence in these patterns. It is argued that the patterns observed in Japan result from a highly dualistic

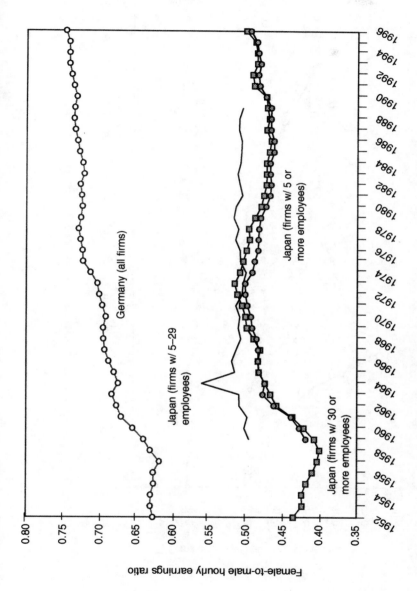

Figure 3.1 Germany and Japan: manufacturing female-to-male hourly earnings ratio, 1952–96

Sources: *ILO Yearbook of Labour Statistics*; *ILO LABORSTA*; Japan Ministry of Labour: *Yearbook of Labour Statistics*.

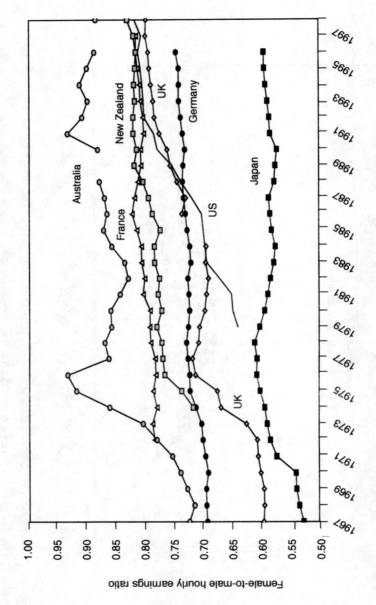

Figure 3.2a OECD countries: non-agricultural female-to-male hourly earnings ratio, 1967–98

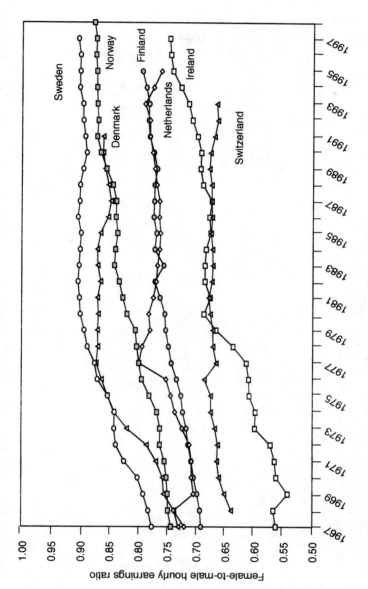

Figure 3.2b OECD countries: non-agricultural female-to-male hourly earnings ratio, 1967–98

Sources: *ILO LABORSTA*; Statistiches Bundesamt: *Statistiches Jahrbuch für die Bundesrepublik Deutschland*; Japan Ministry of Labour: *Yearbook of Labour Statistics*; US B.L.S.: *Current Population Survey*.
Note
Manufacturing for Finland, Ireland, Norway and Sweden and industry for Germany.

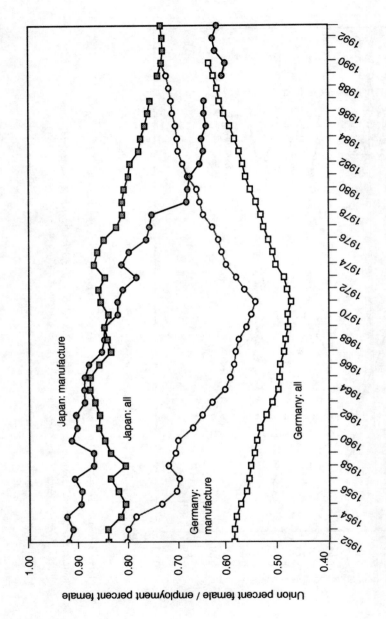

Figure 3.3 Germany and Japan: female union propensity for manufacturing and all employees, 1952–93

Sources: Bundesministerium für Arbeit und Sozialordnung: *Arbeits- und Sozialstatistik. Hauptergebnisse;* Statistiches Bundesamt: *Statististisches Jahrbuch für die Bundesrepublik Deutschland;* Japan Ministry of Labour: *Yearbook of Labour Statistics.*

employment system, with women under-represented in core employment and over-represented in peripheral employment (also referred to as primary and secondary employment, respectively, in dual labor market theory). Core employment in Japan is characterized by its so-called "three pillars": lifetime employment, seniority-based earnings, and membership in an enterprise union, all of which apply almost exclusively to full-time workers with "regular" (that is, not temporary or part-time) employment status. Also important is the extensive use of within-firm training for core employees, facilitated by their long tenure. Peripheral employment includes, in essence, all other employment, of which temporary and part-time employment are of considerable importance. In a sense, this chapter is a direct extension of an argument in Chapter 1. There it was argued that the Japanese economy and individual Japanese firms make use of both internal and external labor market flexibility, and that these function as complements. In a similar manner, internal labor markets are associated more with core employment, in which men are disproportionately represented. Particularly when it comes to hiring and firing, external labor markets are associated more with peripheral employment, in which women are disproportionately represented, but which also includes substantial numbers of men. The association of core employment with internal labor markets and peripheral employment with external labor markets is a long-standing one, as old as dual labor market theory itself (Doeringer and Piore 1971: 167–9). These dichotomies seem particularly suited to describing the Japanese employment system, in which there appears to be scant opportunity for movement from peripheral to core employment, particularly for women.

The employment system in Japan is more simply and deeply dualistic than in either Germany or the US.[2] In his comparison of labor markets in Germany and Japan, Raschke describes the dualistic nature of the Japanese employment system, particularly the dualism within firms, as follows:

> The lifetime employment and seniority-based wage systems as well as intrafirm vocational training are well-established and closely interconnected institutions in Japan. The labour force in a Japanese enterprise is divided, as a rule, into two categories: regular employees and temporary employees. In a private enterprise economy, such as Japan's, which guarantees security of employment (lifetime employment) for a large proportion of employees (i.e. regular workers), there must be some mechanisms to ensure sufficient labour market flexibility with regard to working hours and wages, such as the use of temporary employees. To be sure, segmentation of the labour market is also found in Germany, but it is neither as overt nor as institutionalized as in Japan.
>
> (Raschke 1993: 199–200)

That Japanese women's employment conditions became less like Japanese men's in recent decades is argued to be a reflection of a deepening, increasingly stark dualism, in large part an outcome of measures taken by Japanese firms to cut costs and maintain the core employment system in the face of slower economic growth, an aging workforce, and an increasingly competitive world economy.

In his book *Fat and Mean* (1996), David Gordon discusses the distinction between high road and low road systems of labor-management relations, or cooperative and conflictual systems, respectively. Gordon characterizes both Germany and Japan as high road economies, writing as follows:

> Across the advanced capitalist economies, at a broad level of generalization, two quite distinct types of labor-management systems reflect sharply contrasting approaches to managing production workers and encouraging productive performance. One approach features relatively cooperative labor-management relations, including a fair degree of employment security, positive wage incentives, often with substantial employee involvement and also often with strong unions. The other builds upon much more conflictual labor-management relations, including relatively little employment security, reliance on the threat of job dismissal as a goad to workers, minimal wage incentives, sometimes weak unions. . . . As is commonly recognized, Germany, Sweden, and Japan provide examples of the former kind of approach, even though among their labor-management systems there are also important differences. And, as many have pointed out in recent years, the United States tends more and more to represent the archetype of the latter system, also exemplified by Canada and the United Kingdom.
>
> (Gordon 1996: 63)

In Gordon's view and that of others, the high road emphasizes "rapid productivity growth and innovation, high quality production and higher wages" while the low road emphasizes "cost-cutting and thus low wage growth" (Milberg 1998: 1). Gordon notes that, on average, high road economies – Germany, Japan, the Netherlands, Norway, and Sweden – outperformed the low road economies – the US, the United Kingdom, and Canada – in terms of unemployment, inflation, and productivity growth (though he only considers the period up to 1989) (Gordon 1996: 148, 150, 163). Even though manufacturing wages tended to increase more rapidly in the high road economies over the 1979 to 1989 business cycle, unit labor costs in manufacturing increased less rapidly, a reflection of more rapid productivity growth in the high road economies (ibid.: 27, 166). Gordon goes on to argue that the greater competitiveness of the high road economies in terms of unit labor costs translated into greater trade competitiveness.

In Gordon's view, the key to the success of the high road economies lies in the relationship between co-operation and productivity growth. Gordon argues that the wage increases and job security that characterize the cooperative economies facilitate productivity growth, for workers stand to reap the gains of productivity increases (Gordon 1996: 148–9). This is not a controversial view. As Locke and Kochan write,

> One of the most widely accepted propositions in our field [of industrial relations] is that innovations in work practices or other forms of worker–management cooperation or productivity improvement are not likely to be sustained over time when workers fear that by increasing productivity they will work themselves our of their jobs.
>
> (Locke and Kochan 1995: 368)

In addition, the longer employees work at a firm, the more sense it makes for a firm to invest in job training, in improving workers' skills. In the case of Japan, the employment security provided by the lifetime employment system is commonly argued to be an essential determinant of Japan's high productivity growth and competitiveness over much of the postwar period (Brown *et al.* 1997: 67).

Gordon's characterization of Japan's economic success is valuable. At the same time, it tells only half the story, for one must square Gordon's account with the dualistic nature of the Japanese employment system.[3] This dualism exists along two main lines, and gender distinctions are relevant to both. The first is a dualism by firm size, which many observers have noted, particularly regarding the greater prevalence of lifetime employment and seniority-based earnings at larger firms (Taira 1989: 182; Nakamura 1995). Job tenure, for example, tends to be longer in larger Japanese firms, a reflection of the greater prevalence of lifetime employment (Clark and Ogawa 1992: 337). Wages are also considerably higher in larger Japanese manufacturing firms (Nakamura 1995: 156). Regarding the distribution of men and women in large and small firms, 30 percent of Japanese men worked in firms with 500 or more employees, compared with 24 percent of Japanese women; 53 percent of Japanese men worked in firms with up to ninety-nine employees, compared with 58 percent of Japanese women (as of 1979) (Brinton 1993: 50).

Just as important is the dualism that exists within large Japanese firms. This was suggested in Chapter 1 regarding the manner in which temporary employees play an integral role in the just-in-time system of production at Toyota Motors and, more generally, by Japanese firms' use of temporary and part-time workers alongside regular workers (Shingo 1989: 74–5, 85; Brown *et al.* 1997: 51). The two-fold nature of dualism in Japan is well-described by Brinton, who writes as follows:

> In each industry a dualistic structure of large and small firms developed, with higher wages being paid in the large firms. . . . The other type of dualism has only been implied by the discussion so far: the division *within* large companies between the permanently employed "haves" and the temporarily employed "have nots." Both forms of dualism have exercised a profound effect on the nature of women's working lives in the postwar period.
>
> (Brinton 1993: 130)

One of the keys to the success of large Japanese firms is that they simultaneously pursue both high and low road strategies, reaping the benefits of each. That is, the disproportionately male core workforce representing the high road facilitates "rapid productivity growth and innovation", and the disproportionately female peripheral workforce representing the low road facilitates "cost-cutting and thus low-wage growth" (Milberg 1998: 1). The highly dualistic nature of Japanese firms has been recognized by American firms attempting to incorporate aspects of the Japanese system. The characteristics of the "new labor relations models" implemented by a number of US firms are noted by Locke, Kochan, and Piore. These include greater job security, greater flexibility in the definition and design of jobs, greater worker involvement in production decisions, and systems of bonus payments. The authors describe these characteristics as "highly influenced . . . by various patterns and practices observed in Japan" (Locke, Kochan, and Piore 1995: xxii) and go on to describe the dualism of these "new labor relations models" as follows:

> Companies often conceive of these new arrangements in terms of a core–periphery model, in which the new participatory arrangements and associated employment guarantees (profit-sharing systems, etc.) extend to only a portion of the labor force. Flexibility to adjust to uncertainty is then reintroduced through a peripheral labor force that has no strong company ties and can easily be hired and fired.
>
> (Locke, Kochan, and Piore 1995: xxiii)

The authors' discussion of core and peripheral employment could just as well describe larger Japanese firms. In this sense, the present chapter may be instructive in understanding not only Japanese women's employment but also peripheral employment more generally, suggesting the possible consequences of firms in the US and elsewhere emulating Japanese employment practices. This is not to argue that the core–periphery dualism need play itself out along gender lines, but that the substantial benefits of the "new labor relations models" for some workers may well imply substantial costs for others.

The core of this chapter describes the way in which key labor market institutions influence employment conditions in Germany and Japan. These include, first, institutions specific to Japan: lifetime employment, seniority-based earnings, and the large-scale withdrawal of women from the labor force at ages 25 to 30, after which women typically return after their mid-thirties as peripheral employees. Next are comparisons of temporary and part-time employment, and the role of unions (and, in Germany, works councils). Taken singly, each of these factors is more favorable for women in Germany than in Japan. Taken together, they seem to tell a convincing story of why women workers in Japan fared so differently from their male counterparts, as indicated by both women's relative employment volatility and male–female wage differences. More than that, these institutional factors are argued to be the concrete expressions of Japan's stark and deepening labor market dualism, as well as the means by which Japanese firms simultaneously pursue high and low roads of labor-management relations.

As to why Japanese women serve so strongly as a buffer workforce, the lifetime employment system is of primary importance. For it is the province of men, almost exclusively, and imposes a rigidity in the face of economic fluctuations, a rigidity compensated for by the flexibility of Japanese women's employment and labor-force participation. Japanese women's labor-force participation is volatile not only over business cycles but over lifecycles, indicated by the sharp drop in labor-force participation rates for Japanese women in their mid-twenties to mid-thirties. The two patterns are related, for Japanese women return to the workforce in strong numbers after their mid-thirties, typically as temporary or part-time workers. It is in large part through their employment as temporaries and part-timers that Japanese women so readily flow into and out of employment and the labor force, as several studies confirm the high employment volatility of temporary and part-time work in Japan. Patterns of union representation are relevant for similar reasons, for union members are typically full-time, permanent workers protected under the lifetime employment system.

Regarding the institutional determinants of male–female wage differences, particularly the very large gap in Japan, two factors are emphasized. The first follows directly from the point just made: the volatile nature of Japanese women's employment and labor-force participation has particularly negative consequences within the context of Japan's system of seniority-based earnings, which requires continuous employment within a firm. Second, a cross-country study by Blau and Kahn (1994) provides strong evidence that the overall structure of earnings inequality among firms and industries is an important institutional determinant of male–female wage differences, with greater overall inequality associated with greater male–female wage differences. The overall structure of earnings is highly unequal among industries and firms in Japan, partly the result of enterprise unions and the decentralized manner in which they bargain for wages (in spite of the element of centralization provided by the annual "Spring Offensive," or *Shunto*). A related consideration is that Japanese women are disproportionately concentrated in smaller firms, where wages are lower (Brinton 1993: 50, Figure 2.3).

In the face of these substantial differences between Germany and Japan in women's relative employment, labor-force volatility and male–female wage differences, there was divergence between Germany and Japan after the mid-1970s in the last measure as well as in women's union propensity. The causes of difference are of necessity different from the causes of divergence. But the lifetime employment and seniority-based earnings system, as well as enterprise unions in Japan, are argued to provide the causal context in which the divergence occurred. That is, in the face of slower growth, an increasingly competitive world economy, and a rapidly aging workforce, the inflexibility and costliness of the predominately male lifetime employment and seniority-based earnings system were accommodated by the role of Japanese women as a low-cost buffer workforce. The widening male–female wage differences and the decline in women's union representation are suggestive of the deepening of labor market dualism along gender lines in Japan. At the same time, changes in women's union representation are argued to be a causal determinant of changes in male–female differences. This holds for both countries but especially Japan, where union membership is one of the "three pillars" of the core employment system, associated with both lifetime employment and seniority-based earnings. The causal determinants of male–female wage differences – particularly their divergence between Germany and Japan – are considered more fully in the next chapter, in the context of relative supply and demand shifts for men and women's employment, as well as human capital determinants of earnings.

Regarding the withdrawal of Japanese women from the labor force in their mid-twenties to mid-thirties, one must also consider maternity leave policies and child care provisions. The more generous these are, the more readily mothers can remain in the labor force during their childbearing and child-rearing years, and thus the less likely they are to become part of the peripheral workforce that serves as a buffer for the core workforce. The substantial differences between German and Japanese policies in this regard appear to be an important contributing factor in accounting for the quite different character of women's employment in these countries. Maternity leave policies and child care provisions in Germany and Japan are considered in an appendix to this chapter, placing the countries in the context of other advanced economies.[4]

Lifetime employment and *nenko* earnings in Japan: persisting institutions

Among the most distinctive elements of Japanese labor relations are lifetime employment and seniority- and merit-based (*nenko*) earnings, which were particularly prevalent at larger firms (*nenko* is a compound word, derived from *nen* for seniority and *ko* for merit (Kumazawa 1996: 35)). These elements make up a mutually reinforcing system for the core of the workforce, full-time employees with "regular" employment status. Of this mutual reinforcement, Nakamura and Nitta write that "seniority-based pay supports lifetime employment by increasing incentives for employees to stay in a company, and lifetime employment makes seniority-based pay acceptable for employees because everybody can climb up the wage ladder in the end" (Nakamura and Nitta 1995: 327).[5] Lifetime employment had its origin in the prewar years as firms faced a shortage of skilled labor. The shortage was particularly problematic in the burgeoning heavy industries (metal, metal products, machinery, and chemicals). In this sense, lifetime employment was originally initiated by employers, who offered regular wage increases for continuing employees in an effort to ensure a more ready and reliable workforce. Employment in these heavy industries was almost exclusively of men, and thus even in its nascent form, lifetime employment applied to them alone (Brinton 1993: 116–19). This contrasts with employment in the textile industry, which along with the food industry dominated manufacturing output in Japan until the 1930s (Macpherson 1987: 18). In the early decades of the century, women made up about 80 percent of employment in the textile industry, which was characterized by very low rates of pay and very high rates of turnover. As of the late 1930s, women's average wages were 34 percent of men's wages for the economy as a whole, having declined dramatically from about 60 percent in the 1880s. Women working in the textile industry were almost exclusively young and single, and were rarely employed for more than a few years, during which their wages were commonly remitted to their parents (Brinton 1993: 112–15, 120).

Lifetime employment and seniority-based earnings applied to few workers during the prewar years. During the war years, the government took an active role in promoting long-term employment and seniority-based wages. The latter were advocated on the grounds that the needs of a head of household over a lifecycle were best met by these means. It was during the war that regular wage increases and the payment of wages on a monthly rather than daily basis became prevalent. During the immediate postwar years, in the face of wide-spread turmoil and a surplus of labor, workers took the lead in pushing for lifetime employment (Lincoln and McBride 1987: 292; Brinton 1993: 121–2). Lifetime employment and seniority-based wages became consolidated after the mid-1950s. Lifetime employment, seniority-based earnings, and enterprise unions – the "three pillars" of the Japanese employment system – are each generally associated with the other (Bank of Japan 1994: 55). The number of unions and union members grew with great rapidity immediately after the war. In 1945, there were about 500 unions and just under 400,000 union members; by 1955, there were over 30,000 unions and over 6 million union members; by 1965, there were over 50,000 unions and over 10 million union members (Nakamura and Nitta 1995: 329).

There are no official data on the number of workers protected by the lifetime employment system, which is based on informal understandings and is by no means absolute. The most common estimate is that about one-third of the work-force receive such protection (Tachibanaki 1987: 669; Schregle 1993: 513). The steady decline in recent years of union representation may reflect a decline in the proportion of workers in the lifetime employment system. As a proportion of wage and salary earners, union representation held steadily from the mid-1950s to the mid-1970s, at roughly 35 percent. From 1975 to 1994, union representation declined steadily, from 35 to 24 percent. The decline in union representation is consistent with the increase in Japanese women's labor force participation as part of the peripheral workforce. At the same time, the number of union members has held remarkably steady since 1975, at somewhat over 12 million, suggesting that the core of the workforce remained the same size in an absolute sense (OECD 1994b: 184; Nakamura and Nitta 1995: 329; OECD 1997: 71).

The future of lifetime employment became a subject of debate as the system came under pressure on several fronts, especially during the severe recession of the 1990s. Of this, Houseman and Osawa write that "Many Japanese analysts believe that recent cyclical volatility, the appreciation of the yen, and the aging of the Japanese work force have strained Japanese industrial relations practices of lifetime employment and of nenko wages and promotions" (Houseman and Osawa 1995: 16). Yet lifetime employment retains its central importance in Japanese labor relations, particularly at larger firms. In his recent study of the lifetime employment system, Schregle describes its persistence as follows:

> The resilience of lifetime employment is strong, both conceptually and in practice. Judging from the pace at which Japanese society has evolved in the past it is safe to predict that whatever changes take place they are likely to be the fruit of careful experimentation, thorough reflection and a very gradual translation into practice at the shop-floor level in Japanese enterprises.
>
> (Schregle 1993: 520)

Accounts very similar to this are given in other evaluations of the continuing viability and persistence of the lifetime employment system in Japan (Bank of Japan 1994: 72, 82; Kawamura 1994; Nakamura and Nitta 1995: 325; Gordon 1998: 209–14). Brown *et al.*, for instance, describe the persistence of the lifetime employment system in a chapter section titled "The Japanese security system under pressure: the challenge of the 1990s." The authors write:

> The deep recession in Japan in the first half of the 1990s put the adjustment mechanisms to a test. As expected, large firms protected "lifetime employment" by slashing overtime, relieving temporary workers, reducing new hires, and making use of early retirements. Many large Japanese firms introduced restructuring plans that were major by Japanese standards, although they appear insignificant by American standards. . . . As would be expected, the groups providing the buffer stock bore the brunt of the recession. Part-timers, foreigners . . . and workers at small companies most frequently lost their jobs. The number of women in the work force fell 0.8 percent during 1993. . . . Nevertheless, *a systematic look at the data do not confirm the major transformation dramatized by the popular press.* Instead, Japanese companies adjusted to the long and painful recession by using the adjustment mechanisms described earlier. In the earlier years of the recession, minor adjustments in hours and buffer stocks were made. As the recession continued past three years, seldom-used adjustments to new hiring, bonuses and wage growth were made.
>
> (Brown *et al.* 1997: 55, emphasis added)

Lifetime employment works hand in hand with seniority-based earnings to insure stable employment for the core portion of workforce. In the classic and still common pattern, regular workers are hired by a firm at a low wage just after graduation from school.[6] A large portion of regular male workers, particularly those hired by larger firms, are provided with understandings of lifetime employment security. Earnings increase steadily after hiring and reach their peak when workers are in their mid-fifties, a pattern that holds into recent years (Nakamura 1995: 157). This is in contrast with Germany, where earnings flatten out for most workers after the age of 30. Looking at earnings in the 1970s by age groups and education levels, this pattern held for workers of all education levels in Germany and Japan (Raschke 1993: 202). In Germany as of the late 1980s, this pattern continued to hold for unskilled workers (though not for university graduates) (Krueger and Pischke 1995: 423). One observes a similar pattern in Germany and Japan by length of job tenure. For male manual workers in manufacturing, earnings increased continually and steeply with length of tenure in Japan, but flattened out after about seven years of tenure in Germany (Seki 1980: 356). Japanese regular employees who lose their jobs and take on a job at a new firm generally do so at a much reduced wage. Since wages increase at about the same rate regardless of age at entry into a firm, the earnings gap between those hired just out of school and of the average mid-point entrant typically does not narrow over time (Kawashima 1987: 602). Brunello describes the exceptionally high cost of losing one's job in Japan as follows:

> An employee who leaves a large Japanese firm (by quitting or by dismissal) usually moves to a smaller firm, where wages are lower, or starts back at the bottom of a steep wage scale in [a] new large firm. Monetary and nonmonetary penalties associated with inter-firm job mobility also include substantial losses in retirement payments, worse career prospects and some degree of social ostracism.
>
> (Brunello 1990: 491)

As with lifetime employment, the system of seniority-based earnings has undergone change. Following the labor shortages of the mid-1960s, the seniority-based system was modified to account more for skill differences. Firms also began offering higher starting wages to men entering in the middle of their working lives. For junior and senior high school graduates, mid-point entrants aged 30 to 44 enter on the same basis as an employee with about nine years' tenure. For women mid-point entrants, however, starting wages are at the same low levels as women hired just out of school (Kawashima 1987: 601–2). The modification of seniority-based wages continued in recent years, particularly at smaller firms and for higher-echelon white-collar workers (Tachibanaki 1982: 451–2; Shimada 1993: 160). Consistent with this, the importance of tenure in earnings for men is estimated to have declined over the 1980s, in firms of all sizes. Length of tenure nonetheless remained an important determinant of earnings for Japanese men (Clark and Ogawa 1992: 340–1). Also suggestive are patterns over time of wage differences by age cohort. For manufacturing firms with ten or more employees, average wage differences between the 20 to 24 age cohort and all other five-year wage cohorts up to 55 to 59 became ever wider from the mid-1970s on (after having just as steadily narrowed from the mid-1950s to the mid-1970s) (Nakamura 1995: 157).[7]

Women are largely excluded from the system of lifetime employment and seniority-based earnings. A number of studies argue that the viability of lifetime employment depends on the exclusion of much of the workforce, particularly of women, and that women's exclusion is a key factor accounting for the peripheral nature of their employment.[8] This basic argument is essentially that made in dual labor market theory, that employment in the secondary sector provides a buffer for employment in the primary sector, the latter of which tends to be rigid with respect to economic fluctuations (Doeringer and Piore 1971: 173).[9] In a passage representative of these studies, Lam writes that

> The smooth operation of the core employment system depends on the existence of a large number of women willing to work as low-cost "peripheral" employees to provide the necessary flexibility. Full employment opportunities for women would not only destabilize the male career hierarchy and the established work practices, but would also upset the flexibility of the employment system.
>
> (Lam 1993: 218)

The growth of part-time employment in recent years, predominately of women, is argued to offset the rigidity and increased costliness of lifetime employment and seniority-based earnings in the face of slower economic growth and an aging workforce (Houseman and Osawa 1995: 16). Very similar points are made in the Bank of Japan's recent report titled "The Japanese Employment System," and thus they do not seem particularly controversial (Bank of Japan 1994: 70).

To a significant extent, the peripheral basis of Japanese women's incorporation into the workforce resulted from the explicit policies of Japanese firms and managers. Kumazawa aptly describes this process for the period beginning in the mid-1950s, which marked the consolidation of the *nenko* employment system, as follows:

> [C]orporations introduced technical innovations that redistributed work so as to concentrate decision-making and planning tasks in fewer hands at the top and increase simple, routine work at the bottom. To accomplish this, managers considered a gender-based division of labor at the point of production an absolute necessity. . . . [I]n the *nenko* system, a path had to be created along which [men] could rise (or escape) from routine work to supervisory positions such as foreman in a factory, or to managerial positions and planning positions in an office. However, *what securely opened this route for male workers was the removal of women workers from this competitive upward track and their permanent restriction to work at the bottom level.*
>
> (Kumazawa 1996: 167, emphasis in original)

This active role of management continued during the oil crises of the 1970s, when Japanese firms undertook what they referred to as "Operation Scale-

Down" (*genryo keiei*) (Nakamura 1995: 224). The main focus of "Operation Scale-Down" was cost reduction, which involved reducing the number of regular employees and making more extensive use of peripheral employees, particularly women working on a part-time basis. Regular employees were rarely fired outright, as firms relied on attrition through retirement, transferring employees to other firms, and making calls for so-called "voluntary" severance or retirement (sometimes through offers of larger severance or retirement allowances but, particularly for higher-paid senior employees, through management pressure) (Nakamura and Nitta 1995: 339–40). The most significant changes occurred at large manufacturing firms, where low-wage part-time women filled formerly high-wage full-time positions. In describing "Operation Scale-Down" and its effect on women, Nakamura writes,

> Cutting back requires firms to economize as much as possible on labor-related expenses. Thus, firms switched from male to female employees and took on more low-wage part-time workers such as housewives. . . . The most important consequence of Operation Scale-Down was the deterioration in employment conditions that it produced.
>
> (Nakamura 1995: 224, 227)

With slower growth after the oil crises, there were fewer high-level positions available, and Kumazawa argues that "managers became even more determined to insure advancement opportunities for men by limiting women's chances to cross the boundary to higher positions" (Kumazawa 1996: 184–7). These observations are telling in light of the widening male–female wage differences and declining women's union representation in Japan since the mid-1970s.

Seniority-based earnings work to women's disadvantage given their less regular employment over business cycles. Wage data is consistent with this. Among the advanced economies, Japan has the widest gap between men and women's wages. Moreover, the wage gap widens as men and women become older, more so than in other advanced economies (Koike 1983b: 114). Looking at 1989 data for Japan by five-year age groups, wages for full-time male workers increased strongly and steadily with age up to the 45 to 49 age group, after which wages declined. For full-time female workers, in striking contrast, wages were flat for age groups 30 to 34 and above, and were flat for part-time female workers for age groups 25 to 29 and above (Brinton 1993: 47). This provides stark evidence of Japanese women's exclusion from the seniority-based earnings system, even for those women working full time.[10] Of this, Lam writes as follows:

> Another crucial phenomenon in Japan is that the wage differences between men and women are rather small when they are young, but the differences increase with age, peaking when they reach middle age. This is a common phenomenon in most countries, but much more accentuated in Japan. . . . [A] high proportion of Japanese women still withdraw from the labour market at

the age of marriage and child-rearing. Such an interrupted career pattern has a negative impact of women's wages and promotion in most countries, but particularly in Japan where the *nenko* system prevails and continuous long-term service is an important criterion in skill formation and promotion in large firms, the discontinuous career pattern of women has a stronger negative impact on women's wages than in other industrial countries.

(Lam 1992: 48–50)

Also relevant to the wage gap is that a disproportionate number of Japanese women work as temporary or part-time employees, who are excluded from the seniority-based system of earnings and receive far fewer benefits than provided to regular workers (Carney and O'Kelly 1990: 134).

The disadvantage to Japanese women of seniority-based earnings is suggested by their patterns of labor-force participation over the course of their lives. Figures 3.4 through 3.7 show women's labor-force participation rates by age groups for Japan, Germany, the US, and Sweden. These rates are shown for the middle of each decade from the 1960s to the 1990s, providing a sense of the manner in which women were integrated into the workforce over these years. From the mid-1960s on, Japanese women's labor-force participation has two pronounced peaks, at ages 20 to 24 and again when women are in their forties. For 1997, the labor-force participation rate for Japanese women aged 20 to 24 is 73 percent; at ages 30 to 34, the participation rate declines to 56 percent; at ages 45 to 49 it swings back up again, strongly, to 72 percent. The *M*-shaped curve in Japan developed as women, particularly older women, entered the workforce in larger numbers.[11] Carney and O'Kelly describe the development of the curve as follows:

Through the 1950s, the female participation rate displayed a "spiked" curve, with women in their late teens and early twenties at the apex. Today the curve is "M-shaped" – the two peaks occurring in the twenty-to-twenty-four and forty-to-forty-nine age groups. The difference is attributable to returned married workers.

(Carney and O'Kelly 1990: 128–9)

In Germany, by contrast, women's labor-force participation rate flattened out by age group from the mid-1960s on. The pattern in the US is quite similar. In both Germany and the US in the mid-1990s, there was a dip in women's labor-force participation rates for women in their thirties, but this was very slight compared to Japan. The pattern of women's labor-force participation rates flattened out most over time in Sweden. The overall level of women's labor-force participation is also remarkably high in Sweden, between 77 and 88 percent in 1997 for women in the 20 to 29 through 55 to 59 age groups. It may not be mere coincidence that these four countries follow the same ranking by other measures of women's employment conditions, such as male–female wage differentials, with Sweden the most egalitarian country, Japan the least, and Germany and the US in the middle range.

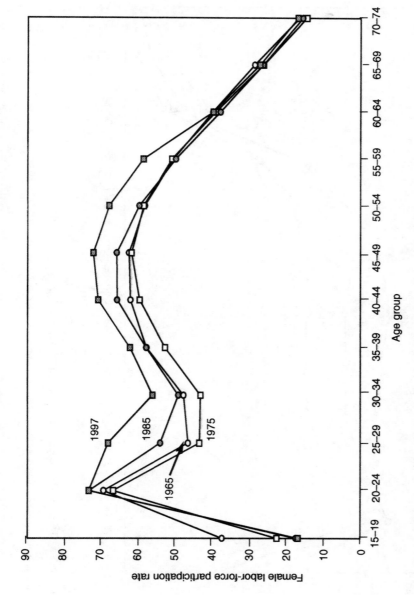

Figure 3.4 Japan: female labor-force participation rate by age group, 1965–97

Source: *ILO Yearbook of Labour Statistics* (1945–89, 1998).

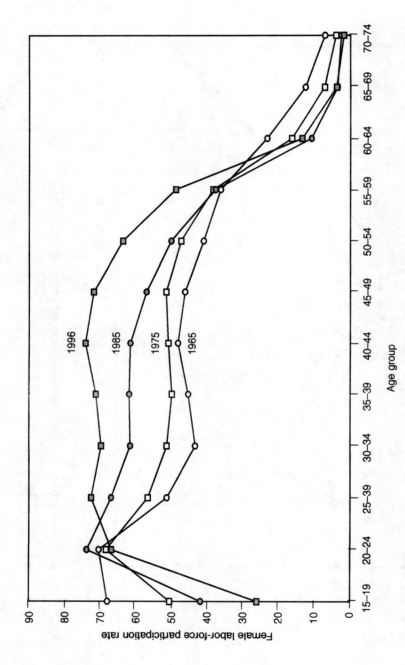

Figure 3.5 Germany: female labor-force participation rate by age group, 1965–96

Source: Bundesministerium für Arbeit und Sozialordnung: *Arbeits- und Sozialstatistik* (1972, 1991, 1998).

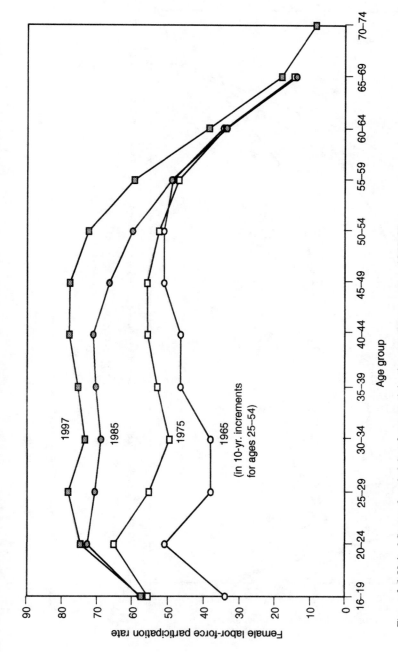

Figure 3.6 United States: female labor-force participation rate by age group, 1965–97

Source: US Bureau of Labor Statistics: *Employment and Earnings* (1965–6, 1975, 1985, 1997).
Note
16–19 age group is 14–19 in 1965.

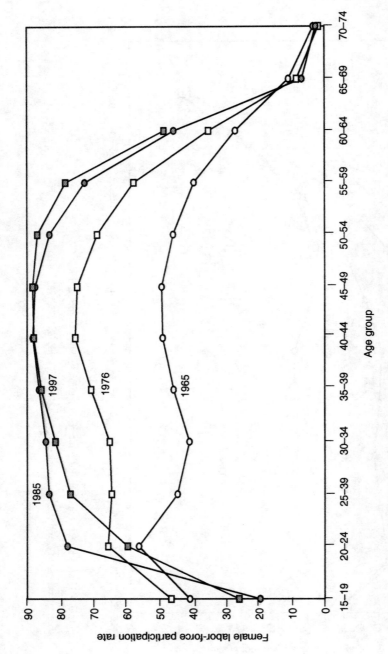

Figure 3.7 Sweden: female labor-force participation rate by age group, 1965–97

Source: *ILO Yearbook of Labour Statistics* (1945–89, 1998).
Note
15–19 age group is 16–19 in 1975 and 1997 and 10–19 in 1985.

These patterns of labor-force participation provide insight into the nature of women's employment. For one thing, the *M*-shaped curve suggests that a great many Japanese women are adversely affected by seniority-based earnings, which requires continuous employment at a firm. The *M*-shaped curve is also related to Japanese women's employment volatility in the face of economic fluctuations. Women with regular employment status are disproportionately young and single, many still living with their parents (Nishikawa and Higuchi 1980–1: 71–2; Brinton 1993: 12). Women returning to the labor force after their mid-thirties typically do so as temporary or part-time employees, for whom employment is exceptionally volatile (Brinton 1992: 100–1). That is, Japanese women's employment fluctuates widely not only over business cycles but also over their lifecycles, and the two patterns are related. Brinton describes the problems of older women workers as follows, considering also the strong emphasis Japanese firms put on in-house training:

> If women are expected to devote a portion of their time as adults solely to raising children, the seniority and training systems of large Japanese companies are fundamentally incompatible with women's lives. Women cannot be hired at a later point in the life cycle after they have received some type of additional training to supplement their early education, because such non-company specific training is perceived as more or less worthless. Nor are companies willing to train women who reenter the labor force after child-drearing, just as they would be unwilling to train mid-career male entrants to the firms. Coming into a firm in one's mid thirties or forties means starting over at the bottom of the wage scale. . . . This is what happened in the postwar period as more and more married women have reentered the labor force after quitting during the early childrearing years. The very traits and behaviors that Japanese employers have chosen to value, largely out of economic exigency, have virtually excluded women *by definition* from the "good" jobs in the economy.
>
> (Brinton 1993: 128–9)

The *M*-shaped curve of Japanese women's labor-force participation is arguably linked with the weakness of maternity leave policies and the scarcity of child care provisions. Also relevant are the early retirement practices of many Japanese firms, particularly for white-collar women. Before a court ruling in 1966, companies could legally force women into mandatory retirement at the customary age of 25 to 30. Though at odds with legal precedent, companies continue to pressure women to retire during these years. One study notes that "Such policies are . . . still widely implemented on an informal basis. Intense pressure is often brought to bear on those who fail to conform, and complainants still resort to the courts" (Carney and O'Kelly 1990: 136).[12] One of the seeming anomalies of these early retirement practices is that many Japanese firms prefer women with junior rather than four-year college degrees on the grounds that the former will be able to work two additional years before leaving the firm (Carney and O'Kelly 1987: 197; Saso 1990: 37).

The lifetime employment system is a fundamental aspect of Japan's "high road" economy, characterized by relatively co-operative labor-management relations and high productivity growth.[13] The relationship between lifetime employment understandings and high productivity growth in Japan is well described by Brown *et al.*, who write as follows:

> [M]any observers attribute these better [productivity growth] outcomes to a key institutional characteristic of the Japanese system: the lifetime employment commitment afforded to many Japanese workers. In this view, a lifetime employment commitment means that productivity and other cost improvements that are generated by EI [employment involvement] do not place the existing work force at risk of a layoff, so that high-performing workers know they will not hurt their peers. Long-term employment security is similarly invoked as a means to enhance skill training, as workers are not then likely to renege on their commitment to their employers; if trained workers are not likely to leave, the company can recoup its training investment. The institution of employment security, in other words, is sufficient to overcome the free rider problems associated with EI and skills training in a market economy and to lift the economy from a low-skill, low-commitment equilibrium to one of high skills and high worker effort.
>
> (Brown *et al.* 1997: 67–8)

There is a good deal of evidence that the Japanese economy combines the high road, characterized by "high skills and high worker effort," with the low road, characterized by "a low-skill, low commitment equilibrium," and that a key aspect of this dualism is gender. For though they make up a large share of the workforce, Japanese women are largely excluded from the lifetime employment and seniority-based earnings systems, consistent with their high employment volatility and low pay relative to Japanese men. Just as important, labor market dualism in Japan exists not only for the economy as a whole but within firms. Labor market dualism appears to have deepened in Japan in the slower growth period after the mid-1970s, during which the combined use of high and low road strategies appears the direct outcome of firms' policies, manifested for instance by "Operation Scale-Down."

Temporary employment as a stepping stone and buffer

In Germany, temporary employees are defined as those with contracts of fixed duration, subject to the constraints of temporary employment law. The German Employment Promotion Act of 1985 extended the allowable period of temporary contracts from six to eighteen months (Dombois 1989: 360). The act represented a significant effort on the part of employers and the conservative coalition government to introduce greater flexibility into the labor market. The act was wide-reaching in scope, addressing the issues of subcontracting, job-sharing, work on a standby basis, and, especially controversial, temporary employment. The act, in effect until 1990, extended the period for which employers could, without special justification, enter into temporary contracts with employers (from six to eighteen months). Temporary contracts of up to twenty-four months were permissible for small new firms. In spite of the controversy surrounding the act, it is questionable whether it had much of an impact on increasing temporary employment, for temporary employment increased substantially before 1985, as measured by the ratio of temporary jobs to job vacancies (from 5.9 percent in 1980 to 15.1 percent in 1984). Moreover, most temporary contracts entered into after the act's passage were of less than six months' duration and were thus permissible without the act (Dombois 1989: 360–1). A study by Buchtemann likewise found that the Employment Promotion Act had little effect on firms' hiring practices, attributing this to the probability that firms had come to accept permanent employment and its associated costs, and that fluctuations in demand could be more cheaply accommodated with overtime work (OECD 1993a: 28).

In Japan, temporary employees are defined as those with contracts between one month and one year in length. Employees with contracts of less than one month's duration are classified as daily workers (OECD 1987: 35). OECD studies compile temporary employment data as percentages of total employment as well as employment in the manufacturing, trade (wholesale and retail), FIRE (finance, insurance, and real estate), and other services sectors. These data also include Japanese employees classified as daily workers (OECD 1991: 50; 1993a: 21, 25; 1996: 8). These data reveal the very similar proportions of temporary employment in Japan and Germany in recent years (Table 3.1). In both German and Japan, roughly one out ten employees worked as temporaries from the mid-1980s to mid-1990s, with somewhat smaller proportions in the manufacturing sector and somewhat higher proportions in the trade sector. The percentage of employees working on a temporary basis in Germany and Japan in 1994 was similar to that in Canada, Denmark, Finland, France, and Sweden (where the percentage ranged between 8.8 (Canada) and 13.5 percent (Sweden)) and higher than in the UK and especially the US (6.5 and 2.2 percent, respectively) (OECD 1996: 8). Though there was no trend increase in Germany and Japan in the proportion of temporary employment from the mid-1980s to the mid-1990s, such did employment increase significantly in both countries prior to the mid-1980s (Dombois 1989: 360–1).[14] For instance, the proportion of Japanese women working on a temporary basis increased from 9.4 percent in 1970 to 15.6 percent in 1990, driving the overall increase in the proportion of temporary employees over these years (Table 3.1).

In contrast with the similar proportions of employees working on a temporary basis in Germany and Japan, there are substantial differences in the proportions of women in temporary employment. As of 1991, 72.3 percent of temporaries in Japan were women, highest among the sixteen OECD countries for which such data are available, compared with only 45.1 percent in Germany (OECD 1993a: 24).[15] As of 1994, 18.3 percent of Japanese women were working on a temporary basis, compared with 11.0 percent of German women (Table 3.1).

Table 3.1 Germany and Japan: temporary workers as a percentage of total dependent employment

Year	Germany			Japan		
	Total	Male	Female	Total	Male	Female
1983	—	—	—	10.3	5.3	19.5
1984	10.0	9.0	11.5	—	—	—
1985	10.0	—	—	—	—	—
1987	11.6	—	—	10.5	—	—
1989	11.0	—	—	10.6	—	—
1991	9.5	—	—	10.4	—	—
1994	10.3 [a]	9.8 [a]	11.0	10.4	5.4	18.3

Year	Japan								
	Total			Male			Female		
	Temp.	Daily	Both	Temp.	Daily	Both	Temp.	Daily	Both
1970	5.0	3.6	8.6	2.8	3.0	5.8	9.4	4.7	14.1
1975	4.9	3.4	8.2	2.4	2.8	5.2	10.0	4.6	14.7
1980	6.4	3.3	9.7	2.8	2.6	5.4	13.4	4.7	18.1
1985	7.4	2.9	10.4	3.1	2.2	5.3	15.3	4.2	19.5
1990	8.1	2.6	10.7	3.6	1.9	5.5	15.6	3.7	19.3
1991	8.0	2.5	10.5	3.6	1.8	5.4	15.0	3.6	18.6
1992	8.0	2.4	10.4	3.6	1.7	5.2	15.0	3.5	18.5
1993	8.1	2.4	10.5	3.7	1.7	5.4	15.1	3.4	18.5
1994	8.1	2.3	10.4	3.7	1.7	5.4	14.9	3.4	18.3
1995	8.2	2.3	10.5	3.9	1.6	5.5	15.1	3.3	18.5

Year	Germany: selected sectors			
	Manufacture	Trade	FIRE	Other services
1983	—	—	—	—
1984	8.1	12.6	8.5	14.4
1985	7.7	12.0	9.0	13.9
1987	8.8	13.9	10.0	15.8
1989	8.2	13.6	10.1	15.4
1991	7.1	10.7	8.7	13.4

Year	Japan: selected sectors			
	Manufacture	Trade	FIRE	Other services
1983	9.2	13.4	3.6	9.9
1984	—	—	—	—
1985	—	—	—	—
1987	9.0	13.9	4.6	10.7
1989	9.0	14.6	4.9	11.1
1991	8.8	14.7	4.9	11.1

Table 3.1 (continued)

| Year | Japan: women's share of employment | | |
	Temp.	Daily	Both
1970	62.4	44.1	54.8
1975	66.1	43.9	57.0
1980	71.1	48.5	63.5
1985	73.8	51.6	67.6
1990	72.8	54.0	68.2
1991	72.1	55.1	68.0
1992	72.4	57.0	68.9
1993	71.8	56.1	68.3
1994	71.7	56.6	68.3
1995	71.6	56.7	68.4

Sources: OECD *Employment Outlook* (1991, 1993, 1996); Japan Statistics Bureau: *Statistical Yearbook* (1995, 1997).
Notes
Trade refers to wholesale and retail trade; FIRE refers to finance, insurance, and real estate; Other services also excludes transport and communication (in addition to trade and FIRE).

a Refers to eastern and western Germany.

Equally significant is the age distribution of temporary employees (Table 3.2). In Germany, the majority of temporaries are in the 15 to 24 age group, whereas the majority of temporaries in Japan are in the 25 to 54 age group. This suggests the more permanent nature of temporary employment in Japan than in Germany, where temporary employment is often a transitional stage in a worker's life, serving as a stepping stone to permanent employment (OECD 1993a: 26; 1996: 18). A comparative study of temporary employment in the United Kingdom and Germany confirms this. The authors argue that British employers sought a disposable labor force providing flexibility in the face of demand fluctuations, referred to as "external numerical flexibility." The authors write,

> West German employers, on the other hand, appeared to be striving for greater "internal functional flexibility." They were willing to make commitments to the workers they hired on temporary contracts, once, that is, they were certain such workers had acquired or were capable of acquiring the range of technical and social skills they needed to form part of a competitive workforce.
>
> (Casey *et al.* 1989: 464)

That is, temporary contracts in Germany commonly served as a probationary recruiting device, not as a means of providing a peripheral workforce.

The more long-term nature of temporary employment status in Japan is described by Hashimoto, who writes, "Casual observation suggests that temporary workers in Japan tend to work for the same employers year after year" (Hashimoto 1993: 139). In Japan, the age-group patterns of temporary employment, combined with womens' disproportionate share of employment

Table 3.2 Germany and Japan: temporary workers by age group percentage distribution in 1991 (percentages in parentheses represent all wage and salary earners)

Age group	Germany	Japan
15–24	58.3 (20.6)	23.4 (16.4)
25–54	39.0 (70.8)	58.0 (71.0)
55–64	2.7 (8.6)	18.6 (12.6)

Source: OECD *Employment Outlook* (1993).

among temporary employees, represent one aspect of the *M*-shaped curve of Japanese women's labor-force participation. In particular, they suggest the peripheral basis on which women returned to the workforce after their child-bearing and childrearing years, the second peak of the *M*-shaped curve. In Japan, temporary employment is one important aspect of the highly dualistic nature of the Japanese employment system, of the way in which Japanese women serve as a buffer workforce. Hashimoto estimates the volatility of regular and temporary employment for men and women in the Japanese manufacturing sector, using annual data for years 1959 to 1988. Hashimoto's measures of volatility are ordinary-least-squares estimates of β in $y = \alpha + \beta z + \varepsilon$, where y and z are the logarithmic growth rates of the relevant employment series and manufacturing output, respectively, and ε is an error term.

Hashimoto's estimates indicate the greater volatility of temporary employment for men and women alike, an estimated 97 percent greater for males and 64 percent greater for females (Table 3.3). Just as important, these estimates reveal the greater volatility of women's than men's employment within the regular and temporary categories. From this, Hashimoto concludes "It is fair to state that the employment fluctuations of female workers and temporary and day workers in Japan provide cushions for the 'lifetime' employment system of male regular workers" (Hashimoto 1993: 141). A more recent study, using quarterly manufacturing data from 1970 to 1994, also finds the much greater cyclic volatility of temporary than regular employment, for men and women alike (Houseman and Osawa 1995: 16–18).[16]

In short, there are three main reasons why temporary employment appears to be an important determinant of Japanese women's high relative employment volatility, particularly in comparison with German women: the high proportion of Japanese temporaries who are women; the high proportion of temporaries in their prime working years (in the 25 to 54 age group, compared with the 15 to 24 age group in Germany); and the high employment volatility of Japanese temporaries. Moreover, the increase in the proportion of Japanese women working on a temporary basis after the mid-1970s is suggestive of the marginal manner in which they were integrated into the workforce.

Table 3.3 Japan: employment volatility for regular and temporary workers in manufacturing, 1958–90 (derived by regressing employment on output, with *t*-statistics in parentheses)

	Regular workers	Temporary and day laborers
Males	0.3121	0.6152
	(4.84)	(1.68)
Females	0.5570	0.9149
	(4.49)	(3.11)

Source: Hashimoto (1993).

Part-time employment from demand and supply sides

In Germany, part-timers are usually defined as those normally working fewer than 36 hours per week (Schoer 1987: 83).[17] In Japan, the definition of part-time employment is more complicated and differs among government surveys. In actual practice, part-time employment status is determined by firms, as is reflected in some survey data (the Bureau of Statistics Employment Status Survey and the Ministry of Labor Survey on the Status of Part-Time Workers) (Hashimoto 1993: 141; Houseman and Osawa 1995: 10). Japanese employers have a strong monetary incentive to classify workers as part-timers, who are not part of the regular system of benefits and seniority-based earnings. Part-time female employees receive only 60 to 70 percent of a regular female employee's wages and far fewer benefits (Kawashima 1987: 604; Houseman 1995: 257). Neither are part-timers protected by the lifetime employment system. Lam describes the classification of Japanese part-timers as follows: "Many employers simply use the term 'part-timer' to distinguish a worker's employment status (as a non-regular employee) from that of the permanent regular employees, whatever their working hours" (Lam 1992: 56). A 1985 survey by the Ministry of Labor estimated that over 25 percent of part-timers in Japan were working full-time hours with an additional 20 percent working just 10 percent less than full-time hours (Saso 1990: 145).[18] As of 1991, 48.1 percent of Japanese part-time workers worked 31 hours or more per week on average, compared with only 4.4 percent of German part-time workers (Houseman 1995: 260). Thus the average part-timer in Japan makes a considerably larger contribution to the economy in terms of hours worked, which is worth bearing in mind regarding the comparison of the numbers of part-time workers between Germany and Japan.

Recent OECD studies compile data on part-time employment as proportions of total, male, and female employment as well as women's share in part-time employment, shown in Table 3.4 for Germany and Japan as well as the G7 countries and Sweden (OECD 1988: 26; 1991: 46; 1994b: 198; 1998: 206). For Japan, data are from the Japan Bureau of Statistics Labor Force Survey, in which part-timers are defined as those working fewer than thirty-five hours per week, and thus do not include those classified as part-timers but

Table 3.4 Part-time employment in the G7 countries and Sweden (percentages)

Year	Part-time employment as a proportion of total employment							
	Canada	France	Germany	Italy	Japan	Sweden	United Kingdom	United States
1973	9.7	5.9	10.1	—	13.9	—	16.0	—
1979	13.8	8.1	11.4	—	15.4	—	16.4	—
1983	16.8	9.6	12.6	—	15.8	—	18.9	—
1987	15.2	—	—	—	16.6	—	—	—
1988	—	—	13.2	—	—	—	—	—
1989	—	—	—	—	17.6	—	21.8	—
1990	17.0	12.2	13.4	8.8	19.1	14.5	20.1	13.8
1991	16.4	12.0	15.5	—	20.0	—	22.2	—
1992	16.7	12.5	14.4	—	20.5	—	22.8	—
1993	19.1	13.7	15.1	—	21.1	—	23.4	—
1994	18.8	14.5	13.5	11.0	21.4	15.8	22.6	13.5
1995	18.6	14.2	14.2	10.5	20.1	15.1	22.3	14.1
1996	18.9	14.3	14.9	10.5	21.8	14.8	22.9	14.0
1997	19.0	14.9	15.8	11.3	23.2	14.2	22.9	13.6
1998	18.7	14.8	16.6	11.8	23.6	13.5	23.0	13.4

Year	Part-time male employment as a proportion of male employment							
	Canada	France	Germany	Italy	Japan	Sweden	United Kingdom	United States
1973	4.7	1.7	1.8	—	6.8	—	2.3	—
1979	6.5	2.4	1.5	—	7.5	—	1.9	—
1983	8.7	2.5	1.7	—	7.1	—	3.3	—
1987	—	—	—	—	—	—	—	—
1988	—	—	2.1	—	—	—	—	—
1989	—	—	—	—	8.0	—	5.0	—
1990	9.1	4.4	2.3	3.9	9.5	5.3	5.3	8.3
1991	8.8	3.4	2.6	—	10.1	—	5.5	—
1992	9.3	3.6	2.9	—	10.6	—	6.2	—
1993	11.0	4.1	2.9	—	11.4	—	6.6	—
1994	10.7	5.5	2.7	4.2	11.7	7.1	6.3	8.0
1995	10.6	5.6	3.4	4.8	10.0	6.8	7.3	8.4
1996	10.7	5.7	3.7	4.7	11.6	6.7	7.7	8.4
1997	10.5	5.9	4.1	5.1	12.9	6.5	8.2	8.3
1998	10.5	5.8	4.6	5.5	12.9	5.6	8.2	8.2

Source: OECD *Employment Outlook* (1988, 1991, 1994, 1998, 1999).
In cases where data differed between volumes, data from the most recent volume are used.
Notes
Refers to persons who usually work fewer than 35 hours per week in Japan and 30 hours per week in other countries.
It should be emphasized that the data for Japan must be interpreted with caution, for reasons noted in Chapter 4; for example, data on part-time employment status as classified by Japanese firms indicate that women's share of part-time employment was about 95% in the mid-1990s (Houseman and Osawa 1995: 13; Brown *et al.* 1997: 52).

Table 3.4 (continued)

Year	Part-time female employment as a proportion of female employment							
	Canada	France	Germany	Italy	Japan	Sweden	United Kingdom	United States
1973	19.4	12.9	24.4	—	25.1	—	39.1	—
1979	25.3	17.0	27.6	—	27.8	—	39.0	—
1983	28.1	20.1	30.0	—	29.2	—	41.3	—
1987	25.3	—	—	—	30.5	—	—	—
1988	—	—	30.6	—	—	—	—	—
1989	—	—	—	—	31.9	—	43.8	—
1990	26.8	21.7	29.8	18.2	33.2	24.5	39.5	20.0
1991	25.5	23.5	34.3	—	34.3	—	43.7	—
1992	25.8	24.5	30.7	—	34.8	—	43.5	—
1993	28.8	26.3	32.0	—	35.2	—	43.9	—
1994	28.6	24.5	27.9	22.3	35.8	24.9	40.4	19.5
1995	28.2	24.3	29.1	21.1	34.7	24.1	40.7	20.3
1996	28.9	24.1	29.9	20.9	36.6	23.5	41.4	20.2
1997	29.4	25.2	31.4	22.2	38.3	22.6	40.9	19.5
1998	28.6	25.0	32.4	22.7	39.0	22.0	41.2	19.1

Year	Women's share of part-time employment							
	Canada	France	Germany	Italy	Japan	Sweden	United Kingdom	United States
1973	68.4	82.3	89.0	—	70.0	—	90.9	—
1979	71.0	82.1	91.6	—	70.1	—	92.8	—
1983	69.8	84.3	91.9	—	72.9	—	89.6	—
1987	71.9	—	—	—	73.3	—	—	—
1988	—	—	90.5	—	—	—	—	—
1989	—	—	—	—	73.0	—	87.0	—
1990	70.1	79.8	89.7	70.8	70.5	81.1	85.1	68.2
1991	70.5	83.7	89.6	—	69.9	—	86.1	—
1992	69.7	83.7	89.3	—	69.3	—	84.9	—
1993	68.3	83.3	88.6	—	67.7	—	84.5	—
1994	68.8	79.9	88.7	76.1	67.6	76.8	85.5	69.0
1995	68.8	79.1	86.3	70.8	70.2	76.8	81.8	68.7
1996	69.1	78.7	85.8	71.5	68.2	76.5	81.4	68.8
1997	69.7	78.8	85.1	71.0	67.0	76.3	80.4	68.4
1998	69.5	79.3	84.1	70.4	67.5	—	80.4	68.0

For Italy, Sweden, and the US, data for years 1973–89 and 1991–3 are excluded, as they appear to use a different definition of part-time employment than other years.
Data for women's share of part-time employment for Sweden in 1998 are also excluded, as the figure provided (97.3) appears to be an error.

working thirty-five or more hours per week.[19] For Germany and the other countries, the part-time employment classification in the OECD data is narrower, defined as those who usually work fewer than thirty hours per week (OECD 1997: 206). Japan relied more on part-time employment than did Germany, with 21.8 percent of employees working on a part-time basis in the former as of 1996, compared with 15.0 percent in the latter. For the countries shown in the table, only in the UK was by this measure consistently higher than in Japan. There was a steady growth in part-time employment for both men and women in Japan and Germany from the early 1970s, a pattern observed across most OECD countries. The proportion of all female employees working part-time was very similar between Germany and Japan until the 1990s, when the measure leveled at 30 percent in the former and increased to about 37 percent in the latter.[20] Again, it was only in the United Kingdom that this measure was consistently higher than in Japan. By these measures, about 90 percent of part-timers in Germany were women, compared with about 70 percent in Japan. The Japan Bureau of Statistics Employment Status Survey, which uses firms' definition of part-time employment, estimates that as of 1992 fully 95 percent of part-timers in Japan were women, considerably higher than the Labor Force Survey estimate (Houseman and Osawa 1995: 12).

The number of part-timers increased rapidly in Japan, from 700,000 in 1975 to 4.67 million in 1991 (Nakamura 1995: 224). The growth of part-time employment also appears dramatic when compared with the growth of full-time employment, especially in Germany. From 1973 to 1983, the number of full-time jobs declined by 4 percent in Germany while the number of part-time jobs increased by 65 percent. Over these same years in Japan, the number of full-time jobs increased by 6 percent while the number of part-time jobs increased by 27 percent (de Neubourg 1985: 565). Similar patterns are observed for more recent years. From 1979 to 1990, part-time employment accounted for over three-quarters of the growth of all employment in Germany. Over these same years in Japan, part-time employment accounted for just under one-half of the growth of all employment (OECD 1994a: 10).

The growth of part-time employment in recent decades is associated with the growing presence of women in the labor force. In particular, the growth in part-time employment is associated with the increased participation of married women and mothers, a pattern similar to that observed in other advanced economies (Vogelheim 1988: 106; Brinton 1993: 135).[21] Given the close association of part-time work with marriage and childrearing, there is no a priori reason to regard part-time employment unfavorably or, in contrast with temporary employment, to suppose that such employment is less secure. Insofar as part-time work enables parents to more readily combine employment with family, it should be considered a boon. This is, in fact, part of IG Metall's (the German union of metalworking industries) argument for the benefits of the thirty-five-hour work week (Vogelheim 1988: 117). Yet Japanese women appear more adversely affected by part-time employment than German women, in spite of the similar proportions of women working on a part-time basis (at least up to the 1990s).

In Germany, part-timers are distinguished by "regular" and "marginal" status. The OECD describes this distinction as follows: "'Regular' part-time workers in western Germany appear to have quite similar employment patterns to full-time workers, while 'marginal' part-timers are less stable, show less confidence in their job stability and are more often found in low-income families" (OECD 1991: 44). The defining characteristic of "regular" part-time employment is whether an employee normally works more than twenty-one hours per week, and in 1988 about 40 percent of German part-timers did so (Kolinsky 1989: 178; OECD 1991: 48). These regular part-timers not only have similar job security as full-timers but receive similar wages and social security benefits, including health and unemployment insurance (Kolinsky 1989: 178, 180–1; Drobnic, Blossfeld, and Rohwer 1999: 144). As of a Supreme Court ruling in the early 1980s, part-time workers were also included in company pension plans (Hesse 1984: 76).

Part-time employment did have adverse effects on German women. Part-time female employees in Germany tend to have lower occupational status than full-time female employees, as well as part-time and full-time male employees. In 1982, for example, 73 percent of part-time female employees were junior workers, the lowest of three status categories of non-manual work, compared with 60 percent of full-time females and 39 percent of part-time males. For manual work, 86 percent of part-time female employees were unskilled and semi-skilled workers, again the lowest of three status categories, compared with 80 percent of full-time females and 73 percent of part-time males (Schoer 1987: 87). Consistent with this, Engelbrech writes that in Germany, "Part-time employment frequently involves a step down the career ladder" (Engelbrech 1991: 114. Cf. Pfau-Effinger 1994: 1362).

The problems of part-time women workers in Germany are not trivial, particularly in terms of occupational status. Yet since 40 percent of part-timers in Germany had regular status, only about 18 percent of all German female employees had what the OECD referred to as marginal part-time status (since about 30 percent of female employees worked part-time) (OECD 1991: 44). In Japan, there are no such offsetting factors. Japanese women with part-time status are argued to provide a safety valve to accommodate the rigidities of the predominantly male lifetime employment system. Edwards describes this as follows:

It should be pointed out that the present system of employing men in full-time jobs and women in more casual, part-time jobs serves the Japanese economy well. With this system, Japanese firms are willing to guarantee many of their male workers job security over the business cycle because the firms have access to a pool of transitory (female) workers who readily enter and exit the labor force and are able to take on part-time employment. . . . True employment equality between men and women would upset the way the Japanese labor market currently adjusts to cyclical variations in aggregate demand.

(Edwards 1988: 249)

As with temporary employment in Japan, part-time employment is one of the means by which Japanese women serve as a buffer workforce. This is revealed in a study by Kawashima, who notes the much greater employment volatility of female part-timers than male and female full-timers over the 1960 to 1982 period. Between 1973 to 1976, for example, part-time female employment declined by about 19 percentage points, compared with about 4 percentage points for full-time female workers and about 2 percentage points for full-time male workers (Kawashima 1987: 606). A more recent study by Houseman and Osawa examines data from the late 1970s to the early 1990s and also finds that part-time employment was highly sensitive to economic fluctuations, for the economy as a whole and for individual sectors (Houseman and Osawa 1995: 16).

There is a fair amount of evidence that part-time employment serves more as an accommodation to childrearing and less as a cost-cutting measure in Germany than in Japan.[22] Throughout the 1980s and early 1990s, for example, there were twice as many involuntary part-time workers in relation to labor force participants in Japan as in Germany, and the majority of these involuntary part-timers were women (about 70 percent in Japan and about 80 percent in Germany) (OECD 1993a: 10, 16–17). In Germany, the number of women seeking part-time work far exceeded the supply of such work. In 1988, for instance, one-quarter of unemployed German women sought part-time employment, yet there were ten times more of these women than part-time job vacancies (Engelbrech 1991: 108). Roughly half of German women returning to the labor force after family leaves sought part-time work (Langkau and Langkau-Herrmann 1980: 38; Hesse 1984: 67). That the demand for part-time employment by German women far exceeds the supply is described by Pfau-Effinger as follows:

> Almost half of all women in full-time employment would prefer part-time employment if this were to be offered by the company they work for (47%). In addition, the lack of adequate part-time jobs leads to a considerable proportion of mothers with children needing care (42%) living involuntarily as housewives rather than being employed.
>
> (Pfau-Effinger 1994: 1363)

Supply-side factors do matter in accounting for the high proportion of Japanese women working on a part-time basis. Among these factors are Japan's income tax and social security systems. Wives earning less than 1.2 million yen a year are not subject to income tax or social security tax, but qualify for basic social security benefits and also receive a dependent's allowance (with figures for fiscal year 1991). The effect of both policies is to discourage Japanese women from participating in full-time employment (Osawa 1995: 128–9. Cf. Kumazawa 1996: 177–8). But neither of these policies changed in a way that could account for the *increase* in Japanese women's part-time employment (as measured both in absolute numbers and by the percentage of Japanese women working on a part-time basis).

Here demand factors appear more important. Lam argues that Japanese firms' motivation for hiring part-time workers changed with the slowdown in economic growth. During the period of more rapid growth prior to the mid-1970s, Lam argues that part-time jobs were created to "encourage more housewives to enter the labour force" in the face of a labor shortage. Since then, "reduction of labour cost and the increasing need for a flexible workforce" were the main motivations for firms hiring part-timers in Japan, particularly women part-timers (Lam 1992: 55–6). Lam's view is consistent with the results of a 1988 survey undertaken by the Japan Ministry of Labor, asking firms if they planned to increase the number of part-time and temporary workers hired, and if so, why. Houseman and Osawa summarize the results of the survey as follows:

> In sum, two principle reasons why Japanese companies say they hire nonregular workers is to lower labor costs and to hire workers on a temporary basis. With respect to the latter, a company may wish to hire part-time and temporary workers who can be more dismissed more easily than regular workers and provide a buffer against fluctuations in demand.
>
> (Houseman and Osawa 1995: 14)

A similar account is provided in the Bank of Japan's "The Japanese Employment System," which also notes the importance of cost and employment flexibility considerations in firms' decisions to hire increasing numbers of part-timers following the oil crises of the 1970s (Bank of Japan 1994: 69–70). These accounts are much like Nakamura's account of "Operation Scale-Down." Taken together, they provide a sense of the deepening dualism of the Japanese employment system and of its causes.

Women and unions

An OECD study sorts countries into three categories by rates of unionization and collective bargaining coverage, with rates expressed in relation to numbers of wage and salary earners. Collective bargaining coverage indicates the proportion of both union and non-union workers covered by agreements between unions and employers, with non-union workers covered by a variety of extension mechanisms (OECD 1994b).

First, countries with high rates of both unionization and collective bargaining coverage include Finland, Norway, and Sweden. For these countries – but also for Austria, noted next – collective bargaining is highly centralized, commonly taking place at the national level (Freeman 1994: 274).

Second, countries in which coverage by collective bargaining considerably exceeds unionization rates include Germany, Austria, France, the Netherlands, and Spain. The case of France is especially striking, with unionization rates of only 10 percent and collective bargaining coverage of 92 percent, as of 1985 (OECD 1994b: 173). With the exception of Austria, collective bargaining in these countries generally takes place at the industry or regional level, placing them in the middle range in terms of centralization (OECD 1997: 71)

Third, countries with below average rates of both unionization and collective bargaining coverage include Japan, Canada, and the US. These countries also feature highly decentralized collective bargaining, with agreements typically made with individual firms or plants rather than more aggregate levels (even though unions are organized by trade and industry in Canada and the US).

For Japan in 1989, the unionization rate was 25 percent and the collective bargaining coverage rate was 23 percent.[23] For Germany in 1992, the unionization rate was 32 percent and the collective bargaining coverage rate was much higher, at 90 percent (OECD 1994b: 173). From 1980 to 1994, the unionization rate declined in both countries, from 36 to 29 percent in Germany and from 31 to 24 percent in Japan. The pattern of declining unionization rates over these years was common to thirteen of nineteen OECD countries, including Germany and Japan. Unionization rates increased in Canada, Finland, Norway, Spain, and Sweden, even though they had long been quite high in the three Scandinavian countries, and held even in Denmark (OECD 1997: 71).

One of the distinctive characteristics of the Japanese employment system is the enterprise union, in contrast with the trade and industrial unions of the other advanced economies. Enterprise unions include both blue and white collar employees, excepting only management, with a comparatively narrow earnings gap between these groups of workers (Kawashima 1987: 600; Brinton 1993: 110).[24] Trade unions did develop early in the century in Japan. Their decline resulted from a labor struggle, of which Taira writes that "After a series of clashes with labor over the shape of new relations, major enterprises succeeded in subduing or expunging trade unions by the early 1930s" (Taira 1989: 186). The establishment of enterprise unions was, in turn, largely a product of the postwar years, of co-evolution with lifetime employment and seniority-based earnings (Kumazawa 1996; Gordon 1998). As with the decline of trade unions, the establishment of enterprise unions in Japan resulted from intense struggles between labor and management. In his recent history of postwar Japanese industrial relations, Price describes this as follows: "The terrain of Japan's labor history is littered with the skeletons of independent unions. Pale shadows of them – enterprise unions – are often all that remain" (Price 1997: 264). The establishment of enterprise unions and contemporary Japanese industrial relations more generally was not the ineluctable outcome of Japanese cultural predisposition or national character. Recent histories by Makoto Kumazawa (1996) and Andrew Gordon (1998) make these arguments with eloquence, describing the contested evolution of both Japanese labor-management relations and Japanese systems of production.

German unions are organized by industry, with collective bargaining agreements undertaken by these unions at the regional (*Bundesländer*) level. Collective bargaining coverage is formally extended to non-union workers by labor legislation specifying that bargaining agreements are binding only if more than 50 percent of employees within the industry and region are covered (OECD 1994b: 178). It is worth emphasizing the centralization of wage setting emphasized here is quite a different thing from the co-ordination of wage setting. It is the latter that is relevant to the debates on wage-setting institutions and unemployment, and by which both Germany and Japan rank high (Soskice 1990; OECD 1997: 71). The point is discussed in Chapter 1. It is on the basis of the level of centralization at which wages are formally set that Germany and Japan are generally given middle and low rankings, respectively in relation to other OECD countries. To provide a sense of the difference between Germany and Japan in this regard, it is worth considering the vast difference in the average size of unions. In Germany in 1991, the membership of the sixteen industrial unions comprising the DGB (*Deutscher Gewerkshaftsbund* or Federation of German Trade Unions, the largest federation of unions in Germany) was 11,800,412, an average of 737,576 members per union (Statistisches Bundesamt 1991: 733). IG Metall was the largest of these unions, with over 3.5 million members. In Japan in 1991, there were 71,785 unions with a total membership of 12,369,592, an average of only 173 members per union (Nakamura and Nitta 1995: 329).

Research by Blau and Kahn suggests that a key determinant of male–female wage differences across countries is the centralization of wage-setting institutions, with greater centralization associated with greater overall earnings equality which in turn creates a tendency for greater earnings equality between men and women. The authors write:

> Skill prices can be affected by relative supplies, by technology (e.g., high-tech industries place a premium on highly trained workers), by the composition of demand, or, as emphasized in this paper, by the wage-setting institutions of each country. Specifically, centralized wage-setting institutions, which tend to reduce interfirm and interindustry wage variation and are often associated with conscious policies to raise the relative pay of low-wage workers (regardless of gender), may indirectly reduce the gender pay gap.
>
> (Blau and Kahn 1995: 107)

Germany and Japan fit this pattern in terms of both male–female wage differences and the level of centralization at which wages are set. In terms of male–female wage differences among the OECD countries, Germany ranks roughly in the middle and Japan at the very bottom, as measured by ratios of female-to-male hourly earnings for non-agricultural employees (Figure 3.2). In Japan, wage increases for unionized workers are attained though the annual "Spring Offensive" (or *Shunto*), organized by a federation of company unions. Though it represents a centralized element in an otherwise decentralized system, the "Spring Offensive" addresses percent increases in base pay set at the enterprise level and thus has no effect on overall wage inequality. While Blau and Kahn's analysis does not include Japan, other studies indicate that inter-industry wage inequality in Japan is highest among the OECD countries (Tachibanaki 1987: 662–3).

Regarding inter-firm wage inequality, an important consideration in Japan is the size of firms. Compared with wages in firms of 500 or more employees as of 1990, wages were 21 percent lower in firms with 100 to 499 employees, 40 percent lower in firms with thirty to ninety-nine employees, and 45 percent lower in firms with five to twenty-five employees (Nakamura 1995: 156). Earning inequality between the largest and smaller firms steadily increased between the mid-1970s and 1990, after having steadily narrowed after the mid-1950s (Nakamura 1995: 156; Price 1997: 222; Kume 1998: 74). This closely parallels the movement of male–female wage inequality in Japanese both manufacturing and non-agricultural employment. The reason seems clear enough, for Japanese women are more heavily concentrated in smaller firms than are Japanese men. This is indicated, for instance, by Figure 2.3, showing that the female percentage of employment for all manufacturing firms is consistently several percentage points higher than for manufacturing firms with thirty or more employees. The concentration of Japanese women in smaller firms and Japanese men in larger firms holds for the economy as a whole. As of 1979, the percent distribution of workers by firm size (by number of employees) in Japan was as shown in Table 3.5.

Regarding the relationship between unions and male–female wage differentials, Figures 3.1, 3.2, and 3.3 show the parallel movements in Germany and Japan between female union propensity and male–female hourly wage differences since the mid-1970s for both manufacturing and non-agricultural employees. There is one notable exception to this pattern. For small Japanese manufacturing firms, with between five and twenty-nine employees, there is no discernible trend in male–female wage differences (Figure 3.1). But unions are concentrated in larger Japanese firms, part of the pattern of dualism by firm size that characterizes Japanese industrial relations. This pattern is therefore consistent with (indeed provides indirect support for) the view that the decline in female union propensity in Japan is one of the causes of the decline in the female-to-male hourly earnings ratio.

Blau and Kahn's work provides a compelling explanation of the large difference between Germany and Japan in male–female wage differences. The experience of Germany and Japan also suggests that more centralized labor institutions can be better advocates of policies facilitating women's more equal treatment in the workplace. This observation holds not only between the two countries but within Germany as well, where national union federations play an important role in improving female employment conditions and where works councils at the plant level tend to treat women workers less favorably. It appears that more centralized institutions are more inclined or better able to act

Table 3.5 Japan: percentage distribution of male and female workers by firm size, 1979 (in number of employees)

Size of firm	1–29	30–99	100–499	500–999	1,000+
Men	36.1	16.9	17.3	5.2	24.4
Women	39.0	19.0	18.1	4.4	19.5

Source: Brinton 1993: 50.

in the interests of women workers, perhaps because they are less directly affected by practices benefiting women workers at the shopfloor level. A related point is made by Blau and Kahn, who write that "the effect of gender-specific policies to raise female wages may be greater under centralized systems where such policies can be more speedily and effectively implemented" (Blau and Kahn 1995: 111).

In Germany, a considerable amount of trade union effort was devoted to improving conditions for working women. Unions pushed for passage of the 1973 legislation that secured government support for family day care, the new marriage and divorce laws of 1975 that enabled women to work without requiring their husbands' permission, and legislation that extended child care leaves. Unions also advocated increasing the number of places available in nursery schools and kindergartens (Cook 1984: 66–8). In recent years, IG Metall and other unions associated with the DGB have made special efforts to recruit women workers. In 1990, IG Medien (the union of paper and printing industries and the arts) established an affirmative action program in an effort equitably to provide women workers with continuing job training (Mahnkopf 1992: 76).

Unions generally opposed the extension of part-time work, arguing that it would lead to divisions in the workforce and to more intensified work. This opposition to part-time work was part of unions' arguments in support of shortening the work week to thirty-five hours, which they also argued would allow a more equitable distribution of homework and employment between husbands and wives (Cook 1984: 68–9). Vogelheim describes these elements of the push behind the thirty-five-hour work week as follows:

> This movement for reduced working time is not only a strategy to tackle unemployment by opening up more positions as the average work time is reduced. It is also a strategy pushed for by the women of IG Metall as part of their concern for improving the working conditions of women. They hope that a reduction in the work week, via a reduction in the work day to seven hours, will reduce some of the pressure on families and encourage a better and more equitable distribution of domestic labor and family responsibilities between women and men. Union members have clearly expressed their ideas on these matters and have put them on the table in union negotiations with employers.
>
> (Vogelheim 1988: 117)

Unions also played an important role in the passage of legislation in 1979 by which unemployed workers who previously worked part-time were no longer required to accept available full-time jobs or lose their unemployment benefits. The new legislation allowed an unemployed worker to refuse a full-time job provided young children or family members needed care at home. The legislation also extended sickness benefits to part-timers who worked at least ten hours per week or forty-five hours per month (Cook *et al.* 1992: 212).

The Women's Division of the DGB played a central role not only in pressing for more progressive legislation for working women, but also in coordinating the efforts of a broad range of German women's organizations. The key figure in this linkage was Maria Webber who in the mid-1960s became head of the DGB's Women's Division. Following her leadership, the DGB abandoned its ambiguous stance on working mothers, changing its official position to one of active support for combining employment and childrearing. Webber simultaneously headed the German Council of Women, an umbrella organization of women's groups (Cook 1984: 66–7). The monthly publications of the Council as well as the trade unions served as important means of informing women's organizations and union members of developments on family and labor law (Cook *et al.* 1992: 40).

The DGB declared 1972 the Year of the Working Woman, prompting a major drive to enroll women workers in unions. Since that time, the percentage of female union members and female union propensities have increased steadily, for the manufacturing sector as well as the economy as a whole. From the mid-1970s to 1980, the number of male union members declined while the number of female union members increased enough to more than offset the loss of male members.[25] White-collar occupations were particularly important in accounting for the growth of women's membership in the DGB (Cook 1984: 70). It was also during the 1972 Year of the Working Woman that unions attacked the light-wage categories that account for much of male–female wage differences within German industries and firms (Cook *et al.* 1992: 38). The inflow of women into the labor force occurred simultaneously with their increased representation in unions, suggestive of the more solid manner with which they were integrated in comparison with women in Japan.

The German system of labor-management relations is dualistic in that unions deal with industry-wide issues such as wages and working hours, while works councils deal with issues specific to a firm, including layoff procedures. This dualism was argued to act to women's disadvantage, since upper-level union officials tended take women's concerns more seriously than local-level officials and works councilors. In *The Most Difficult Revolution: Women and Trade Unions*, the authors argue that "Officers at the top of many unions, particularly those with large female memberships, tend to be more inclined than local leaders are to keep women's interests in mind" (Cook *et al.* 1992: 85). Works councils are legally required to use "social considerations" as one criteria in determining which workers are to be laid off or fired, and this has been used to single out married women whose husbands were employed (Cook 1984: 78). Cook describes the problems occurring at local levels as follows:

> The fact is that many of the problems of German working women are embedded in the dual bargaining system, where decisions made by works councils can outflank both regional agreements and national legislation, particularly on such matters as layoffs and wage drift. For many councillors share employers' beliefs that protective laws affecting women's

employment add enough to costs and personnel officers' workloads to create a bias against women's employment in positions above the lowest wage levels. Hence the appeals for more women in bargaining commissions, as well as in works councils.

(Cook 1984: 80)[26]

That Japanese women were incorporated on a much more peripheral basis than German women is reflected in a number of factors, including declining female representation in unions at the manufacturing sector and aggregate levels. An important aspect of lifetime employment and seniority-based earnings is that they are associated with union membership, for which regular employee status is a precondition. Female union propensity was high in Japan compared with Germany, and it was not until recent years that the measure in Germany exceeded that in Japan (Figure 3.3). Yet the benefits to Japanese women of union membership should also be viewed in the context of their life courses. Women working full-time and having regular employee status are generally young, having yet to encounter the early retirement practices of Japanese firms as well as Japan's relatively short maternity leaves and scarce child care provisions. Older women workers typically return to the workforce as part-time or temporary employees, which precludes union membership and inclusion in the lifetime employment system.[27]

Unions' support of working women has been more ambiguous in Japan than in Germany. This is unsurprising, given the enormous gap that exists in Japan between disproportionately male core employees and disproportionately female peripheral marginal employees in terms of pay, benefits, promotion, and job security. The enterprise basis of unions and their association with lifetime employment are of central importance in this regard. Throughout the postwar years, it has been the policy of unions to limit membership to a number assuring uninterrupted employment for its members. Taira writes of "an almost total absence of effort on the part of established unions to organize the unorganized" (Taira 1989: 191). More than that, unions have been vehement in their support of seniority-based earnings, which severely penalize working women (Tachibanaki 1982: 451). As in Germany, unions have supported legislation favorable to women workers regarding maternity leave, equal pay provisions, and early retirement for women workers (Hanami 1984: 226; Simpson 1985: 223). In contrast with Germany, however, the support of unions has not led to improvement of women's employment conditions relative to men's.

After the first oil crisis in 1973, there was a significant centralization in the structure of the federation of Japanese unions. Private sector unions established the Trade Union Conference for Policy Promotion (TUCPP), referred to as an "important turning point for the labor movement" (Nakamura and Nitta 1995: 350). One of the items on the TUCPP's agenda was the "promotion of women's welfare and status" (ibid.: 351). The four Japanese trade union federations established in the 1950s were eventually consolidated into one federation, the Japanese Trade Union Confederation (JTUC), with a membership of 8 million, three-quarters of all union members. The JTUC developed a number of channels to advocate its positions, including consultation with political parties, employer organizations, and the Ministries of Labor and International Trade and Industry. It is striking that during the same years that union federations advocated improving women's conditions, women's representation in unions declined and male–female wage differences widened. Simpson suggests the contradictory interests of Japanese enterprise unions and women workers as follows:

> It is . . . clear that unions have by no means been unequivocal in their support of women workers. In some cases, unions have made contracts with employers limiting women's work tenure whereas in other cases they have supported women in opposing early retirement. The "lifetime" employment of well-organized workers in large corporations is secured because they are pitted against the unorganized sector of the work force. Women workers as a whole are particularly affected because a large proportion of them work on a part-time or temporary basis.
>
> (Simpson 1985: 223)

There are vast differences in employment conditions in Japan between unionized employees in the core and non-unionized employees in the periphery, a reflection of the deeply dualistic nature of Japanese employment relations. At least at the enterprise level, unions appear in a zero-sum situation, in which maintaining secure employment for long-standing members is at odds with recruiting new members.

Conclusion

This chapter considers labor market institutions of central importance in determining women's employment conditions. In line with other literature on this issue, it is argued that lifetime employment in Japan, predominantly applying to men, creates an inflexibility in hiring and firing, an inflexibility accommodated by women's movement into and out of employment and the labor market. This, in turn, has consequences for male–female wage differences, given the system of seniority-based earnings for which continuous employment is a prerequisite. Japanese women's employment and labor force participation fluctuates widely not only over business cycles but also over their lifecycles, resulting from the early retirement practices of many Japanese firms (as well as comparative shortness of maternity leaves and scarcity of child care provisions). Japanese women leave the labor force in large numbers in their twenties and return again in their thirties and forties, typically as temporary and part-time employees for whom job security and pay are low. Among the OECD countries, Japan has the highest proportion of temporary employees that are women. This is in contrast with Germany, where the majority of temporaries are men. More than that, most temporaries in are in the 15 to 24 years age group in Germany and in the 25 to 54 years age group in Japan, suggestive of the more truly temporary nature of such employment in Germany. Similar proportions of employed women work part-time in the two countries. Yet about 40 percent of German part-timers have regular employment status, providing them with very similar job security and pay to regular full-time employees.

Western observers of Japanese employment relations sometimes focus overmuch on core employment, characterized by its so-called three pillars: lifetime employment, seniority-based earnings, and membership in an enterprise union. From this point of view, Japan is held to rely exceptionally heavily on internal flexibility and labor markets, to take the high road of labor-management relations. There is truth in this view, in a broad comparative sense, but it is only partial. For Japan relies simultaneously on both internal and external labor markets, on both high and low roads, for the economy as a whole and for individual firms. This situation has proved sustainable to date, enabling Japanese firms to reap the productivity advantages of a committed workforce and the cost and flexibility advantages of a dispensable workforce. These dichotomies represent a decided dualism in Japan, a dualism that appears to have deepened over time. From its establishment, men have been disproportionately represented within the core and women disproportionately within the periphery of the Japanese employment system. The deepening of this dualism since the mid-1970s is argued to be reflected in the widening of male–female wage differences and the decline in women's representation in unions. In Germany, in contrast, these measures moved in roughly the opposite direction. The divergence in these measures occurred as women's labor-force participation grew in a nearly identical manner in Germany and Japan.

There is a fair amount of evidence that the deepening of the dual structure and the worsening of women's relative employment conditions in Japan were partly the outcome of deliberate policies undertaken by Japanese firms, called "Operation Scale-Down." One important piece of evidence is a survey by the Japanese Ministry of Labour regarding the reasons firms hired part-time and temporary workers, who are disproportionately women. Most important to these firms are the cost and flexibility advantages provided by such workers (Houseman and Osawa 1995: 14). Also important in Japan were unions' policy of limiting membership in an effort to provide secure employment for their members. In Germany too, movements in the measures of women's employment conditions appear to be at least partly a reflection of deliberate policies, as the DGB and unions staged successful campaigns to recruit women workers and took other measures to improve women's lot.

These differences in policy are usefully viewed in the context of the unique institutional legacy of Japan. Both firms and unions in Japan undertook considerable efforts to maintain the predominantly male core employment system of lifetime employment and seniority-based earnings. In the face of slower economic growth, an increasingly competitive world economy, and an aging workforce, the inflexibility and costliness of the core employment system were accommodated, in large measure, by Japanese women serving strongly as a low-paid buffer workforce.[28]

Appendix: policies supporting the employment of mothers

Maternity leave policies

Maternity leave and child care provisions provide an important means of sustaining mothers' connection to the labor force. A key piece of legislation regarding maternity leave in Germany was the Protection of Mothers Act of 1974. Under the Act, working women were protected from dismissal during pregnancy and until four months after childbirth. Women on leave also received a child care benefit, the cost of which was shared by semi-public social insurance companies and the employer (Schiersmann 1991: 63). For the six weeks prior to and eight weeks after childbirth, this benefit was equal to the mother's prior earnings. For the remainder of the mother's leave, only the base portion of the benefit provided by social insurance companies continued. Thus the child care benefit is equal to the mother's earnings only for a fourteen-week period, an arrangement that continues to the present (Gornick, Meyers, and Ross 1997: 57).

The Federal Child Care Benefit Act of 1986 extended leave and child care benefits to fathers, though as of 1987, 98.5 percent of benefits were claimed by mothers. The Act also extended the protection against dismissal period to twelve months, which increased to eighteen months in 1990. A benefit of 600 marks per month is provided by social insurance for the first six months of leave, and benefits are paid on a means-tested basis afterwards. The benefit of 600 marks is roughly equivalent to 25 percent of the median monthly earnings for a blue-collar female worker (Schiersmann 1991: 63). After unification of the two Germanys, the federal government legislated parental leaves of up to three years, with the benefit provided for two years and local states asked to provide for the third.[29] Parents on leave can work up to nineteen hours per week, though only for the employer from whom they are on leave, and employers are not required to provide part-time work. In 1987, 95 percent of women claiming benefits took leaves without working part-time (Schiersmann 1991: 63–4, 78. Cf. Gustafsson *et al.* 1996: 228–9 and OECD 1995: 175–8 for accounts similar to Schiersmann's).[30]

Maternity leaves provided by government policies are complemented by the policies of many larger firms, with their efforts in regard to women's employment conditions focused largely on such measures (Mahnkopf 1992: 75). Company-provided leaves are negotiated between work councils and management and often provide for a longer period of protected leave than do state policies. Schiersmann describes company-provided leaves as follows:

> The central theme of these company agreements or programs is a more or less binding assurance of reemployment after the employment relationship has been interrupted in order to take on child care and/or the possibility of continuing the employment relationship in part-time form at the end of the legal child care leave. . . . The length of the leave is limited, according to each company's specifications, to between three and seven years after the

birth of the child. . . . Generally the commitment to reemployment refers to a job that is equivalent to the earlier one or that utilizes the vocational knowledge and ability of the person concerned.

(Schiersmann 1991: 70–1)

That a parent on leave can return to their same job is not specifically provided for by legislation, but rather depends on the conditions of the employment contract. Nonetheless, the general practice has been that workers on leave return to employment on the same conditions on which they left (Schiersmann 1991: 67).

There is an important debate as to whether these policies provide for maternity leave that is too long, in the sense that it lessens women's earnings and attachment to the labor force, particularly over the long run. Both sides of the debate are described by Gornick, Meyers, and Ross as follows:

> In contrast to child care, which enables mothers to spend more time at work, maternity leaves enable working mothers to spend more time at home – even though they remain officially "employed". Some scholars hypothesize that policies that enable long leave periods may limit certain career-enhancing opportunities that require a degree of continuity at work (e.g. opportunities for training and promotion). This constraint may have a negative long-term effect on mothers' earnings and, in turn, their labor supply. However, to the extent that job guarantees and wage replacement lessen the probability that mothers will exit paid work or change jobs following each childbirth, maternity provisions would strengthen mothers' long-term labor-market attachment.
>
> (Gornick, Meyers, and Ross 1997: 48)

The evidence on whether long maternity leaves have a negative impact on women's labor force attachment and earnings is mixed, and relatively few studies have been done to date. Yet there is evidence that taking maternity leave has an adverse impact on German women's employment conditions, particularly regarding their long-run earnings. While seniority is not as an important a determinant of earnings in Germany as in Japan, it is important nonetheless. One study indicates that the longer women in Germany remain out of the workforce, the more adversely their income is affected. Using 1984 data, the study estimated that each year of a woman's withdrawal from the workforce is associated with a permanent wage reduction of 1 percent for women workers aged 34 and over, and of 3 percent for younger women workers (Rekko *et al.* 1993: 114–15).[31]

A very high proportion of parents eligible for leaves took them, with an "initial take-up rate" of 96 percent as of 1991 (OECD 1995: 186). The average length of leave in recent years is three years for women up to 35 years of age (Schiersmann 1991: 54). About one-half of women taking maternity leaves return to work after the leave's end (Meulders *et al.* 1993: 161; OECD 1995: 188).

The issues of maternity leave policies and child care provisions are particularly pressing in the case of Japan, as suggested by the *M*-shaped curve of Japanese womens' labor-force participation in the context of the seniority-based earnings system. Maternity leaves are shorter in Japan than Germany. Until 1985, women were provided with maternity leave under the Labor Standards Law of 1947. This provided for twelve weeks of maternity leave, six weeks before and six weeks after childbirth, with pay at the firm's discretion. A 1978 survey by the Japanese Ministry of Labor found that 39 percent of firms surveyed provided some pay to women on leave and that 15 percent of firms allowed longer leaves (Hanami 1984: 232). Mothers on leave were provided with 60 percent of their past daily earnings through social insurance. In addition to the twelve-week leave period, mothers could not be fired within thirty days after the end of the leave period (Nakanishi 1983: 614). The 1985 Equal Employment Opportunity law extended maternity leave periods to ten weeks prior to and eight weeks after childbirth (Edwards 1988: 248). The Law Concerning Childcare Leave was implemented in 1992. It allows leaves of up to one year to care for newborns and also requires that firms provide workers with their old job or a similar job upon their return. A benefit of 25 percent of earnings is paid over the entire period. Either the mother or father is eligible for leave and benefits, in common with most other OECD countries as of the mid-1990s (OECD 1995: 175–9). In the first year after the law went into effect, 48 percent of eligible women took leaves as provided for by the law (Ishibashi 1995: 4). As in Germany, maternity leave and benefits are also provided by companies in Japan. According a 1993 survey by the Japanese Ministry of Labor, 9 percent of firms provided leaves longer than the legal minimum and about 28 percent of firms provided a leave benefit (OECD 1995: 199–200).

At present, then, the differences in parental leave between Germany and Japan are considerable, up to three years in the former and one year in the latter. These differences do not by themselves provide an adequate sense of the constraints imposed on Japanese working mothers in comparison with their German counterparts. In Japan, career-oriented jobs, with regular employment status and seniority-based earnings, require continuous employment in a firm. Thus Japanese women who are unable to return to work within the period provided by leaves essentially forgo their chances at such jobs (Edwards 1988: 247). The problems of combining children and career in Japan are strikingly indicated by a consideration of the family circumstances of female managers ranked "section chief" or higher. According to a survey commissioned by the Japanese Ministry of Labour, 59 percent of these women are single and only 36 percent of those married had children. In total, only 26 percent of these women had children (Kumazawa 1996: 197–8). Japanese maternity leave policies should also be evaluated in light of the customary retirement of women upon marriage or between the ages of 25 and 30. As a consequence of these practices, women often leave the labor force before they have children and are thus unable to take advantage of the maternity leaves provided. This is in contrast with Germany, where a large majority of women employees took career breaks as a result of their having children.[32]

Child care provisions

The more generous the system of child care provision, the more readily women can benefit from maternity leave policies. Child care provisions are more generous overall in Germany than Japan, though availability differs considerably by the age of children. An OECD study compiled data on the availability of pre-primary education and registered child care in Japan and Germany (OECD 1990b: 130). For pre-primary education, enrollment rates are higher in Germany than Japan (Table 3.6). The data on registered child care availability are not directly comparable for Japan and Germany in the OECD study. For children up to age 5 in Japan, there were places in registered child care for about 20 percent of children in recent years. For children up to age 3 in Germany, there were places for only about 10 percent of children (OECD 1990b: 131–2). One cross-country study shows that only two percent of children up to age 2 were in publicly funded child care in recent years in Germany. However, 78 percent of children from ages 3 to school age were in publicly funded child care (Gornick, Meyers, and Ross 1997: 56). It is worth emphasizing that parental leaves are currently of up to three years' length in Germany, and thus child care is widely available for the period after which leaves end, but only until the child reaches school age. As the OECD study notes for Germany, "only 4 per cent of school-age children with working mothers have a place in a school-related daycare center" (OECD 1990b: 132). Consistent with this, in their ranking system of "policies that support employment for mothers," Gornick, Meyers, and Ross rank Germany last among six countries for mothers with school-age children. Germany gets a middle ranking among fourteen countries (which did not include Japan) for three other categories: mothers with children under 6, children under 3, and children aged 3 to school age (Gornick, Meyers, and Ross 1997: 60).

Children in Germany between ages 3 and 6 can attend kindergartens, for which there are facilities for 80 percent of children in this age range (Schiersmann 1991: 56). But most kindergartens are open only during the morning hours, making it difficult for mothers with young children to work full-time. School hours for older children are also short by international standards (Hesse 1984: 78; Joshi and Davies 1992: 566). Moreover, children in school are generally sent home for lunch. Germany was one of only two countries of fourteen studied for which this was so (the other being Luxembourg) (Gornick, Meyers, and Ross 1997: 59).

Table 3.6 Germany and Japan: enrollment rates in pre-primary education, mid-1980s

	Germany	Japan
Age 2	12.6	—
Age 3	38.7	14.8
Age 4	72.3	53.7
Age 5	85.5	64.5

Source: OECD *Economic Outlook* (1990).

Considering the pattern of child care availability and the structure of schooling, it is unsurprising that models of female labor supply for Germany provide evidence that having children has a strongly negative effect on women's labor-force participation. This is in contrast with Sweden and France, for example, where systems of subsidized child care and (at least for France) the length of the school day are argued significantly to offset such negative effects (Gustafsson 1992: 78–9; Joshi and Davies 1992: 566, 569). Consistent with this, as of 1988 the employment rate of German mothers was lower than in France and especially Sweden, across three age classifications for the youngest child. By these measures, Germany was in the middle range of European Community countries, while Sweden ranked the highest (Joshi and Davies 1992: 563).[33] These patterns correspond too with rankings of policies that support employment for mothers, by which Sweden and France rank very high (Gornick, Meyers, and Ross 1997: 60). These differences contrast with the labor-force participation rate of women one year prior to the birth of the first child, which was higher in Germany than in Sweden (Gustafsson *et al.* 1996: 223).

In Japan, the Working Women's Welfare Law of 1972 encouraged employers to provide child care facilities and child care leave, with the Ministry of Labor offering subsidies to co-operating firms (Nakanishi 1983: 614). In spite of this, child care facilities remain scarce. In a survey of Japanese working women by the Prime Minister's Office, 65 percent of respondents indicated a belief that the lack of child care acts as a barrier to continuous employment (*Fuji Economic Review* 1990: 12). Carney and O'Kelly write,

> It cannot be over-emphasized that the double burden of Japanese working women is rendered particularly severe because of the difficulty of finding reasonably priced and convenient child care, the absence of the husband from the domestic sphere, and the general cultural assumption that he will be only marginally, if at all, involved in domestic work and child-rearing.
>
> (Carney and O'Kelly 1987: 206)

The problems of the double burden of Japanese working women (combining employment with household work) are made worse by the long work week in Japan as well as the pattern of after-hours socializing for men (ibid.: 203).

That said, there is one mitigating factor that can facilitate Japanese women's labor-force participation even in the absence of adequate child care: the extended family structure that persists in many Japanese households. The percentage of people aged 65 and over living with their children was 65 percent in 1985 (down from 75 percent in 1974 and 80 percent in 1953) (OECD 1994d: 105).[34] In their analysis of female labor supply in Japan, Ogawa and Ermisch write that women residing in three-generation households are "much more likely to work full-time and less likely to work part-time or to be full-time housewives. It appears, therefore, that the presence of parents or parents-in-law in their household reduces home time demands on Japanese women" (Ogawa and Ermisch 1996: 698). Without the extended family household, the scarcity of child care provisions might make Japanese women's employment even more tenuous. However, if women need to provide care for the elderly with whom they live, this can have the opposite effect on their labor-force participation in terms of the probability of working full-time versus working part-time or not at all.

The difficulty for Japanese women of combining child care with employment is argued by Ishibashi to be a contributing factor in Japan's low birth rate, 1.46 births per woman of childbearing age in 1993, well below the 2.08 births required to maintain population levels. Ishibashi also argues that the low birth rate prompted the Japanese Government to make child care more readily available to working women. Beginning in 1995, the government undertook a ten-year plan to expand child care facilities. The plan includes expanding the capacity of government-subsidized nurseries (for children up to age 2) from the 450,000 openings extant in 1995 to 600,000; to increase the number of public day-care centers to 7,000, a threefold increase; and to increase the number of public after-school centers for young grade school children to 9,000, a twofold increase (Ishibashi 1995: 4).

These recent developments appear to present a promising opportunity for improving the employment conditions of Japanese working women, for adequate parental leaves and child care accommodations provide a concrete means by which to counter the effects of the lifetime employment system and seniority-based earnings. At the same time, increasing Japanese women's attachment to the core employment system in this manner will put additional pressure on lifetime employment and seniority-based earnings, eliminating what a Bank of Japan report argues to be a key factor in maintaining the viability of the Japanese employment system (Bank of Japan 1994: 70). If, for example, the greater availability of child care enables women to retain regular full-time employment status over the course of their lives, it is not clear by what means the rigidities of the system would be buffered and whether firms could bear the costs of providing seniority-based earnings for both men and women.

4   Foreign trade, employment, and earnings

Introduction: skills bias and gender bias

A good deal of attention has been paid to the "skills bias" of labor demand, the extent to which the demand for skilled workers outpaced the demand for unskilled workers. Such a skills bias is widely held to be a key determinant of the increasing earnings inequality observed in a number of advanced economies in recent years, and is thought to reflect the effects of skills-biased technical change or trade expansion with developing economies (Burtless 1995: 800–1). Much less attention has been paid to the "gender bias" of labor demand, even though women's manufacturing employment is concentrated in industries identified by most studies as "trade losers," particularly regarding trade with developing countries (Wood 1991a: 22). The first part of this chapter uses factor content analysis to estimate the effects of world, OECD, and non-OECD trade expansion on men and women's manufacturing employment in Germany and Japan. This analysis provides evidence of both countries losing employment from non-OECD trade, but with a gender bias away from women's manufacturing employment in Japan and no gender bias to speak of in Germany. For Japan, this conclusion is similar to that of earlier country studies of the gender bias of trade expansion (Schumacher 1984: 342–3; Lee and Schmitt 1996: 14). As Wood has hypothesized, OECD trade for both countries is estimated to be gender neutral, affecting men and women's employment in a roughly proportionate manner, with Germany gaining and Japan losing employment from such trade (Wood 1991b: 168).

The second part of this chapter considers patterns of male–female wage differences – narrowing in Germany and widening in Japan since the mid-1970s – in the context of the gender bias from trade expansion, and overall demand and supply shifts for men and women's manufacturing employment. In a sense, the gender bias from non-OECD trade expansion seems to match with changes in the gender earnings gap in Germany and Japan, the latter moving similarly for both manufacturing and non-agricultural employees. For Japan, that is, the gender bias from trade away from women's manufacturing employment seems to match with the widening gender earnings gap; for Germany, the lack of a gender bias from trade seems at least consistent with the narrowing gender earnings gap. But trade constitutes only one component of employment demand. What is relevant for the gender earnings gap is overall demand for men and women's manufacturing employment. At odds with the gender bias from trade expansion, evidence is provided that demand shifted away from women's employment in Germany, for both the manufacturing sector as a whole and for manufacturing industries with high female percentages of employment. No such demand shifts occurred in Japan. That is, for both Germany and Japan domestic factors not directly related to trade were more important in determining overall shifts in women's manufacturing employment. Of these domestic factors, it is argued that women in the advanced economies are concentrated in manufacturing industries for which the income elasticity of demand is relatively low, creating an internal dynamic away from women's manufacturing employment even in the absence of trade. It is suggested that this dynamic is offset in Japan by persisting demand for manufactured goods produced in the traditional labor-intensive manner, particularly textiles, apparel, footwear, and foodstuffs: goods produced disproportionately by women.

As with overall demand shifts for men and women's manufacturing employment, labor supply factors do not appear helpful in accounting for changes in male–female wage differences in Germany and Japan. There were nearly identical increases in the female percentage of labor-force participants in Germany and Japan since the mid-1970s, and the female percentage of college graduates was also broadly similar. A consideration of other human capital determinants of earnings also fails to provide a satisfactory explanation of the widening gender earnings gap in Japan. It is argued that more purely institutional factors play an important role in accounting for the changes in male–female wage differentials in Japan, specifically the closely parallel movement of earnings inequality between large and small firms, women's share of temporary and part-time employment, and women's representation in unions.

Union membership has a special significance in Japan. Along with lifetime employment and seniority-based earnings, union membership makes up one of the "three pillars" of the Japanese core employment system, each pillar generally associated with the others. The decline in female union representation along with the widening gender earnings gap since the mid-1970s suggests that Japanese women's increasing integration into the paid workforce was on the expanding periphery of a highly dualistic employment system, a system marked largely along gender lines.

Part 1: foreign trade and men's and women's employment

Trade winners and losers

We are in the midst of a second wave of economic globalization, the first beginning in the latter half of the nineteenth century, peaking with the First

World War, and falling off thereafter. As measured by the growth of world foreign direct investment and foreign trade in relation to world GDP, the current wave of globalization took off around the early 1970s (Milberg 1997). With the liberalization and expansion of international markets came increasing concern with their consequences. A wide-ranging debate developed in the advanced economies on the employment and earnings effects of expanding foreign trade. Of particular concern was trade with developing countries, which brought workers in the advanced economies into increasingly direct competition with low-wage workers around the world.

A sense of the growing importance of foreign trade is provided by measures of import penetration, defined as imports as a percentage of domestic consumption. Import penetration of manufactures for Germany, Japan, and the G7 average (unweighted) are shown for world and non-OECD trade in Figures 4.1 and 4.2. The non-OECD region provides a working definition of the developing countries, and the OECD region a working definition of the advanced countries. As with most trade studies, the focus of this chapter is on the manufacturing sector, as it is manufactured goods that are most readily tradeable and that have generated the most policy concern (Wood 1991a: 21). For world trade, levels of import penetration are considerably higher in Germany than Japan, indicating the former's greater reliance on imports. The measure grew steadily in Germany and Japan from 1970 to 1990, from 13.4 to 25.0 percent in the former and from 4.0 to 6.8 percent in the latter.[1] The pattern for Germany is very similar to the G7 average. For non-OECD trade, import penetration of manufactures in both Germany and Japan is similar to the G7 average in terms of both level and increase. From 1970 to 1990, the measure increased from 1.4 to 2.4 percent in Germany and from 1.1 to 2.3 percent in Japan. Import penetration for non-OECD trade increased at very nearly the same rate as import penetration from world trade in Germany, and at a somewhat faster rate in Japan. It is noteworthy, though, that given the attention that such trade has received, levels of import penetration for non-OECD trade remain fairly low.

There is considerable controversy over whether foreign trade expansion is an important cause of overall job loss in the advanced economies, but little controversy that some industries are affected more than others. Adrian Wood summarizes studies identifying industries in the advanced economies most strongly affected by trade with the developing economies. He writes,

> All the studies have identified the same sets of winning and losing sectors. The losers include food processing, wood products, textiles and clothing, and leather goods and footwear. These losses have been largely offset, however, by increased employment in the machinery and chemicals industries.
>
> (Wood 1991a: 22)

In both Germany and Japan, women are concentrated in industries identified as trade losers. For Germany, the top three industries by female percentage of employment are first, wearing apparel; second, leather products and footwear;

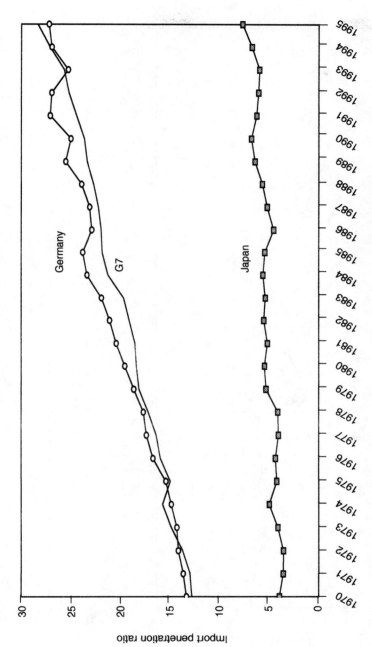

Figure 4.1 Germany, Japan, and the G7: import penetration for world trade of manufactures, 1970–95 (world imports as a percentage of domestic consumption)

Sources: OECD *STAN Database for Industrial Analysis* (1998); OECD *Bilateral Trade Database* (1998).

Note

For Germany, trade data include East Germany after 1990.

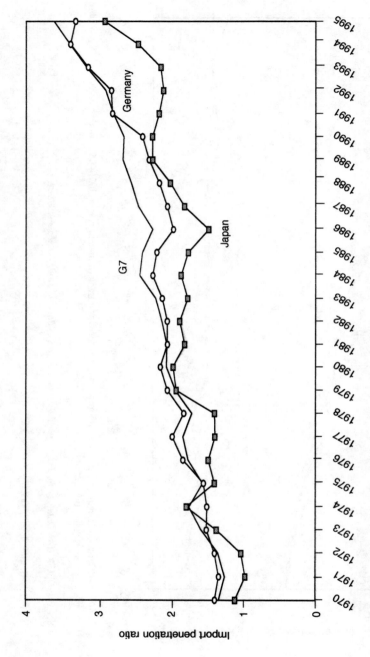

Figure 4.2 Germany, Japan, and the G7: import penetration for non-OECD trade of manufactures, 1970–95 (non-OECD imports as a percentage of domestic consumption)

Sources: OECD *STAN Database for Industrial Analysis* (1998); OECD *Bilateral Trade Database* (1998).

Note

For Germany, trade data include East Germany after 1990.

and third, textiles. Food, beverages and tobacco ranks a close fifth, just behind professional goods. That is, four of the top five industries by female percentage of employment are identified by Wood as trade losers (based on annual averages of the female percentage of employment from 1970 to 1991 for the sixteen manufacturing industries classification noted in Table 2.8).[2] The picture for Japan is very similar, where the top four industries by relative female share of employment are first, wearing apparel; second, textiles; third, food, beverages and tobacco; and fourth, leather products and footwear, all characterized by Wood as trade losers. Regarding industries Wood identifies as trade winners, the female percentage of employment in Germany is below the manufacturing sector average in the machinery and equipment industry, though not in the chemical products industry; in Japan the female percentage of employment is below average in both the machinery and equipment and chemical products industries. In short, women in both Germany and Japan are over-represented in trade-loser industries and under-represented in trade-winner industries. So it seems worth asking whether women's manufacturing employment is disproportionately affected by manufacturing trade expansion, whether there is a gender bias from trade expansion away from women's employment.

As suggested by the above rankings, one of the striking aspects of women's share of employment among manufacturing industries is the cross-country similarity. Women are distributed among manufacturing industries in a remarkably similar manner, not only between Germany and Japan, but across the other G7 countries as well. This is revealed by the very high correlation coefficients between countries by the female percentage of employment among manufacturing industries (Table 2.11), based on the OECD's twenty-two-industry classification (Table 2.12). The average of correlation coefficients between pairs of G7 countries as well as Australia, Denmark, and the Netherlands is 0.90.[3] This indicates that sizeable differences among these countries in the gender bias of trade cannot be the result of different patterns of gender segregation among industries.

Trade theory can also motivate the question whether expanding foreign trade might cause women in the advanced capitalist countries to experience disproportionate employment losses. The Heckscher-Ohlin principle, at its most basic, holds that a country's comparative trade advantage depends on the factor of production with which it is better endowed. Germany and Japan, being among the world's most advanced economies, are better endowed with capital than labor, particularly compared with developing economies, and thus are argued to have a comparative advantage in capital-intensive goods and a comparative disadvantage in labor-intensive goods (OECD 1994a: 94). There is evidence that this is so, for labor-intensive industries in both Germany and Japan are less trade competitive with non-OECD than OECD countries, based on industry-level correlations between labor coefficients and measures of trade performance.[4]

In both Germany and Japan, female percentages of employment are higher in labor-intensive manufacturing industries.[5] Since Germany and Japan appear to have comparative disadvantages in labor-intensive goods relative to developing countries, the Heckscher-Ohlin principle suggests there might be relative demand shifts away from labor-intensive industries within these countries in the face of expanding foreign trade with developing countries. Such relative demand shifts create a tendency for relative employment shifts away from labor-intensive industries. In the absence of sufficiently offsetting factors, expanding foreign trade would in this way cause women's employment to decline relative to men's.

It is controversial, though, whether comparative trade advantages affect the numbers of employed. Trade theorists typically emphasize relative price shifts rather than relative demand shifts in addressing the effect of foreign trade on earnings inequality, as is noted by Belman and Lee. They write that

> standard trade models assume balanced trade and full employment overall, which is why their predictions center on changes in commodity and factor prices (which have to be flexible in order for markets to "clear" and thus maintain full employment with balanced trade).
>
> (Belman and Lee 1996: 71)

To this the authors counter as follows:

> In reality, prices and wages are not so flexible, and imbalanced trade and unemployment frequently coexist. Under these circumstances, trade can have a variety of effects not contemplated in conventional models. For example, the impact of trade can be felt more on employment than on wages. Trade deficits, especially if concentrated in high-wage sectors such as manufacturing, can have an especially depressing effect on both employment and the average wages of those employed.
>
> (Belman and Lee 1996: 71)

Belman and Lee's view, that trade may affect employment more directly than wages, motivates the use of factor content analysis.

Empirical analysis of foreign trade effects

Factor content analysis is widely used to estimate the effects of foreign trade expansion on employment, and uses input–output data to capture direct and indirect effects. It is referred to as "factor content" analysis since it provides an estimate of the amount of a factor of production – labor in this case – embodied in a given volume of output. This analysis provides evidence that foreign trade expansion of manufactures had a more negative effect on women's than men's manufacturing employment in Japan, and nearly equal effect in Germany, with most of the gender bias in Japan resulted from trade with non-OECD countries. That is, foreign trade created a gender bias away from women's manufacturing employment in Japan, but no bias to speak of in Germany.

In standard fashion, the input-output model is described as follows:

$$L = \hat{E}((I - A)^{-1} T) \tag{1}$$

where L is a vector (by industry throughout) of direct and indirect employment in worker years (the amount of employment used to produce T), $\hat{E}$ is a diagonal matrix of labor coefficients (employment per unit of output), I is an identity matrix, A is a matrix of technical coefficients (input per unit of output), and T is a vector of demand from trade expansion. Data used to construct $\hat{E}$ and A are from 1990. Though the A matrix includes both manufacturing and non-manufacturing industries, the direct and indirect employment effects from the latter are omitted.[6]

Following Sachs and Shatz (1994: 26–8):

$$T = [X^{95} - (X^{95} (x^{78}/x^{95}))] - [M^{95} - (M^{95} (m^{78}/m^{95}))] \tag{2}$$

where superscripts reflect the data year, X is a vector of exports, M is a vector of imports, and where x and m are vectors of export and import propensity respectively: that is, exports and imports in an industry divided by the domestic production of that industry. Put in words, T is the difference between actual export and import levels in 1995 and what these levels would have been in 1995 if the exports and imports had borne the same relationship to domestic production as in 1978. Taking expressions (1) and (2) together, T provides a measure of the effect of trade expansion on final demand in each industry, and so when $(I - A)^{-1}$ is post-multiplied by T, this provides a measure of the output change associated with trade expansion. This output change is subsequently converted to employment change via labor coefficients $\hat{E}$.

Studies by both Sachs and Shatz (1994) and Lee and Schmitt (1996) also consider the period beginning in 1978, in large part because of data problems for earlier years (Sachs and Shatz 1994: 3). This study does so for the sake of comparability, but also because of missing data for Germany for earlier years.[7] The endpoints were calculated as three-year averages. Thus "78" refers to the average for 1978 to 1980 and "95" refers to the average for 1993 to 1995. These averages are used to account for the volatility of export and import propensities, small ratios that can fluctuate widely solely as a result of not so large fluctuations in domestic production. For Germany, trade data (though not production and employment data) include the former East Germany after 1990, and so the analysis runs up to the average for 1988 to 1990.

The female labor embodied a volume of trade-induced demand is given by the following:

$$L^f = \hat{F}L \tag{3}$$

where L^f is vector of change in female employment associated with the vector of demand from trade expansion (T), and $\hat{F}$ is the diagonal matrix of female coefficients of employment (number of female employees divided by the number of total employees) based on 1990 data, to match with data for $\hat{E}$ and A.

The change in male employment is defined as:

$$L^m = (I - \hat{F})L \tag{4}$$

where L^m = vector of change in male employment associated with T. That is, the standard assumption is made that employment changes for men and women in an industry are proportionate to the actual distribution of men and women within an industry.

Since our interest is also in trade with developing countries, the vector of demand from trade expansion with non-OECD countries is defined as follows:

$$T_n = [X_n^{95} - (X_n^{95}(x_n^{78}/x_n^{95}))] - [M_n^{95} - (M_n^{95}(m_n^{78}/m_n^{95}))] \tag{5}$$

where the subscript n refers to non-OECD trade and all else is as defined in the previous equations. The employment changes for non-OECD trade may then be written as follows:

$$L_n = \hat{E}[(I - A)^{-1}T_n] \tag{6}$$

$$L^f_n = \hat{F}L_n \tag{7}$$

$$L^m_n = [I - \hat{F}]L_n \tag{8}$$

The effects of OECD trade expansion are then the difference between the results for world and non-OECD trade. The breakdown by OECD and non-OECD trade provides a test of Wood's hypothesis that "North–North trade in manufactures, unlike North–South trade, appears to be gender-neutral" (Wood 1991b: 170). Consistent with Wood's discussion of trade winners and losers, the issue is one of gender segregation by industry. Wood describes this as follows:

> It is widely believed that female workers have been affected much more than male workers by the rapid expansion of developing country manufactured exports to developed countries over the past three decades. Women constitute a high proportion of the labour force in some conspicuous parts of developing-country export-oriented manufacturing (clothing and electronic products, and export processing zones). In developed economies, women are over-represented in the sectors on which manufactured imports from developing countries have been concentrated, and under-represented in the manufacturing sectors which export to developing countries. Similarly, in developed countries women are over-represented among trade-displaced workers.
>
> (Wood 1991b: 168)

This study makes use of the most recent versions of the OECD's *STAN Structural Analysis* databases, the *Input–Output Database* (1995) for input–output data, the *Bilateral Trade Database* (1998) for trade data, and the *STAN Database for Industrial Analysis* (1998) for output, total employment, and price deflator data (the last derived from data on value added in real and nominal terms). These datasets have the advantage of being largely standardized by industry classification, following what the OECD calls an "Adjusted ISIC Revision 2 Classification," for which there are twenty-two distinct manufacturing industries. Regarding the definition of the OECD and non-OECD regions in the *Bilateral Trade Database*, the data documentation states: "The relatively new OECD member countries (Czech Republic, Hungary, South Korea, Mexico and Poland) are currently included in the Non-OECD" region.

Estimated employment effects in worker years are shown in Table 4.1. For Germany, the gains from OECD trade roughly offset losses from non-OECD trade, such that 15,000 worker years are estimated to be lost as a result of world trade. Still, the estimated loss for Germany from non-OECD trade of nearly 430,000 worker years is striking, given the low levels of import penetration of such trade. For Japan, there are estimated losses from both OECD and non-OECD trade, totaling nearly 850,000 worker years for world trade, with non-OECD trade accounting for about 575,000 of the total. The results for Japan seem surprising at first, given the prevalent perception of Japan's international trade competitiveness. It turns out that the results for Japan in terms of overall employment loss are very sensitive to the year in which one begins the analysis (though not to the year in which one ends, at least for the 1990s). Considering the span of years from 1970 to 1991, for instance, Japan is estimated to gain about 8,000 worker-years of employment from world trade, with losses of about 145,000 worker-years from non-OECD trade roughly offset by gains from OECD trade (Kucera 1998). The difference results from Japan's considerably less favorable trade performance in the latter period.[8] In terms of the gender bias of trade expansion, though, the main concern of this chapter, the results for Japan are robust with respect to these different periods.

Table 4.2 shows employment effects from manufacturing trade expansion expressed as percentages of total, male, and female manufacturing employment in 1978.[9] Both numerator and denominator refer only to manufacturing employment. A gender bias is then defined as the difference between the estimated percent change of female and male employment, female minus male, with a negative measure indicating a relative shift away from women's employment. Panel I of the table shows measures that correspond directly to Table 4.1, referred to as "unadjusted."

For Germany, the measure of gender bias from world trade is only –0.49, with OECD and non-OECD trade contributing nearly equally (though the gender bias from OECD trade results from lesser employment gains for women, while that from non-OECD trade results from greater employment losses). For Japan, the measure of gender bias from world trade is –3.88, with

Table 4.1 Germany and Japan: employment effects from trade of manufactures in worker
years

	Unadjusted Total	*Male*	*Female*
Germany (1978–90):			
World trade	−14,996	−2,140	−12,856
OECD trade	412,340	303,973	108,367
Non-OECD trade	−427,336	−306,113	−121,223
Japan (1978–95):			
World trade	−848,953	−436,795	−412,158
OECD trade	−273,556	−151,108	−122,448
Non-OECD trade	−575,397	−285,686	−289,710

Sources: OECD *STAN Database for Industrial Analysis* (1998); OECD *Bilateral Trade Database*
(1998); OECD *Input–Output Database* (1995); UNIDO *Industrial Statistics Database* (1999); Japan
Ministry of Labour: *Yearbook of Labour Statistics* (1990).

somewhat over three-quarters of this accounted for by non-OECD trade. This
is the key result of the analysis: that there is little gender bias of trade
expansion for Germany and a sizeable gender bias for Japan, the bulk of the
latter driven by non-OECD trade. For Germany and Japan, this provides
support for Wood's hypothesis regarding the gender neutrality of North–North
(that is, OECD) trade. For the other G7 countries as well as Australia,
Denmark, and the Netherlands, OECD trade is gender-neutral for France, the
United Kingdom, and the US, with biases very near zero; the measure is
positive and ranges between 1.42 and 4.67 percentage points for the other
countries excepting Canada, for which the measure is −4.03. This prevailing
pattern of gender neutrality or of positive gender biases from OECD trade is in
decided contrast with non-OECD trade, for which there are negative gender
bias for all countries but Italy, with negative measures of greater than 2.5
percentage points in absolute value for Australia, Canada, Denmark, the
Netherlands, and the US, as well as Japan (Kucera and Milberg 2000).

Several adjustments are made to the above analysis, in part to address
common criticisms of factor content analysis. The key results regarding the
gender bias of trade are robust with respect to all these adjustments. First, an
adjustment is made to abstract from changes in the female percentage of manufacturing employment between 1978 and 1990 (the latter the year of $\hat{F}$), as
follows:

$$L^f = \hat{F}[(I-A)^{-1}T](i^{78}/i^{90})$$ (9)

where i^{78} and i^{90} refer to the female percentage of manufacturing employment.
The rationale is that these changes influence the results on gender bias, even
though they may be primarily the result of domestic demand and supply
factors. Since the female percentage of employment in Japan rose between

Table 4.2 Germany and Japan: employment effects from trade of manufactures as percent changes (in relation to average annual employment in 1978–80)

I: Unadjusted

	Total	Male	Female	Gender bias (female minus male)
Germany (1978–90):				
World trade	−0.17	−0.03	−0.53	−0.49
OECD trade	4.62	4.69	4.43	−0.26
Non-OECD trade	−4.79	−4.72	−4.96	−0.24
Japan (1978–95):				
World trade	−6.12	−4.79	−8.67	−3.88
OECD trade	−1.97	−1.66	−2.57	−0.92
Non-OECD trade	−4.14	−3.13	−6.09	−2.96

II: Abstracting from changes in the female percentage of manufacturing employment

	Total	Male	Female	Gender bias (female minus male)
Germany (1978–90):				
World trade	−0.17	−0.03	−0.53	−0.50
OECD trade	4.62	4.67	4.49	−0.18
Non-OECD trade	−4.79	−4.70	−5.02	−0.32
Japan (1978–95):				
World trade	−6.12	−5.04	−8.18	−3.13
OECD trade	−1.97	−1.73	−2.43	−0.70
Non-OECD trade	−4.14	−3.31	−5.75	−2.44

III: Using average technical and labor coefficients

	Total	Male	Female	Gender bias (female minus male)
Germany (1978–90):				
World trade	−0.22	0.02	−0.85	−0.86
OECD trade	7.64	7.83	7.14	−0.70
Non-OECD trade	−7.86	−7.82	−7.98	−0.17
Japan (1978–95):				
World trade	−7.98	−6.29	−11.21	−4.93
OECD trade	−2.56	−2.15	−3.35	−1.20
Non-OECD trade	−5.41	−4.14	−7.86	−3.73

Sources: OECD *STAN Database for Industrial Analysis* (1998); OECD *Bilateral Trade Database* (1998); OECD *Input–Output Database* (1995); UNIDO *Industrial Statistics Database* (1999); Japan Ministry of Labour: *Yearbook of Labour Statistics* (1990).

1978 and 1990, the female employment effects are adjusted downward. The opposite holds for Germany. But the effect of these adjustments are slight, as shown in the second part of Table 4.2.

One criticism of factor content analysis is that is does not account for technical change, particularly that of domestic origin (Leamer 1994). This is of concern given the construction of the trade demand vector T, which is driven both by recent trade gaps (M^{95}, X^{95}) and by changes in import and export propensities from 1978 to 1995 (m^{78}/m^{95}, x^{78}/x^{95}). The concern is addressed by using average technical (A) and labor coefficients ($\hat{E}$) over the 1978 to 1995 period (to 1990 for Germany).[10] Results are shown in panel III of Table 4.2. For OECD and non-OECD trade in both Germany and Japan, the estimates of employment change jump up considerably. This results from there being more labor embodied in a given volume of goods in the earlier part of the period in question (using average technical coefficients alone reveals very little difference from the unadjusted results). Given the construction of T, the best estimate of employment changes resulting from trade expansion would seem to lie between the unadjusted estimates and those using average labor and technical coefficients. But this modification had little substantive effect on the gender bias of trade expansion, since the percent changes of estimated employment gains and losses increase more or less proportionately for men and women.

One last adjustment is considered. There are four industries for which exports and imports are exceptionally volatile: shipbuilding and repairing, aircraft, other transport (which includes railway cars), and petroleum and coal products. This was determined simply by looking at growth rates of exports and imports as well as export and import propensities. For the first three industries, trade volatility seems to be largely a result of the sheer size of these commodities, resulting in lumpiness of orders and shipments. For petroleum and coal products, trade volatility seems to be a price effect. Factor content analysis was redone excluding these industries. This too had little effect on estimates of the gender bias of trade expansion.[11]

In much the same way as the literature addressing the skills bias of trade, the premise for studying the gender bias of trade is the uneven distribution of women's employment along industry lines, with women concentrated in labor-intensive industries identified as "trade losers." So it is worth having a looking at industry-level results, to see which industries drive results for the manufacturing sector as a whole. These results are shown for Germany and Japan in Tables 4.3 (pages 136–7) and 4.4 (pages 138–9) respectively. Headings for industries identified by Adrian Wood as "trade losers" are shown in in italicized letters; headings for industries identified as "trade winners" are shown in bold letters. Wood focuses on North–South trade, represented by figures in columns 6 and 7. For Germany, sixteen of nineteen industries, so-called winners and losers alike, are estimated to lose employment from non-OECD trade. Industries that do show estimated employment gains from non-OECD trade show only very small gains, as measured by employment in worker-years. In decided contrast, only one German manufacturing industry is estimated to lose employment from OECD trade, the office and computing machinery industry. As with Germany, most

Japanese industries are estimated to lose employment from non-OECD trade. Only two industries in Japan show sizeable gains in worker-years of employment from non-OECD trade, the non-electrical machinery and professional goods industries. For Japan's trade with the OECD regions, sixteen of twenty-two industries are estimated to lose employment from trade. It is worth emphasizing that Germany is estimated to have lost a higher percentage of employment from non-OECD trade than Japan, –4.79 percent of 1978 employment compared with –4.14 percent for Japan. The key difference between the two countries lies with OECD trade, with Germany's trade successes spread across manufacturing industries.

Strikingly, the result of a gender bias from trade for Japan disappears with the exclusion of just one industry: textiles, apparel, leather and leather goods, which includes leather footwear. (This is a set of industries really, but they are lumped together as one in the OECD adjusted ISIC classification used in the factor content analysis.) The industry is among those identified by Wood as "trade losers." Excluding this industry, the measures of gender bias in Japan are actually positive, though quite small, for OECD and non-OECD trade (0.05 and 0.11 respectively). For Germany as with Japan, the main difference is for non-OECD trade, where a gender bias of –0.24 percentage points becomes 0.90 percentage points with the exclusion of the textiles, apparel, leather and leather goods industry. For non-OECD trade expansion from 1978 to the mid-1990s, a very similar result holds for most other G7 countries as well as for Denmark and the Netherlands, with Australia and Italy the only exceptions among the ten countries considered. The measures of gender bias from non-OECD trade for the ten countries with and without the textiles, apparel, leather and leather goods industry are shown in Figure 4.3. The reasons for this result are clear enough, for the industry is both highly labor intensive and highly female intensive, the female percentage of employment being

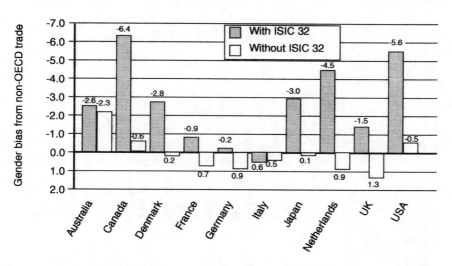

Figure 4.3 Gender bias from non-OECD trade with and without textiles, apparel, leather and leather goods (ISIC 32), 1978–95

Table 4.3 Germany: employment effects from trade of manufactures at the industry level, 1978–90

ISIC code and industry	Percent female 1990	Actual 1978–80 employment	Percent change in actual employment 1978–90	Employment effects from trade of manufactures			
				OECD trade		Non-OECD trade	
				Worker years	Percent change from 1978–80	Worker years	Percent change from 1978–80
31	*Food, beverages and tobacco*	42.2	924,000	−11.04	12,700	1.37	−3,562	−0.39
32	*Textiles, apparel, leather and leather goods*	60.5	806,000	−31.68	18,440	2.29	−60,280	−7.48
33	*Wood products and furniture*	20.8	453,667	−12.49	14,888	3.28	−7,783	−1.72
34	*Paper, paper products and printing*	27.9	421,000	2.85	28,723	6.82	−7,673	−1.82
351+352–3522	**Industrial chemicals**	27.3	625,127	2.40	46,820	7.49	−26,510	−4.24
3522	**Drugs and medicines**	—	—	—	—	—	—	—
353+354	**Petroleum and coal products**	13.0	38,206	−18.37	687	1.80	475	1.24
355+356	**Rubber and plastic products**	28.6	331,000	24.67	19,472	5.88	−17,580	−5.31
36	*Non-metallic mineral products*	21.9	377,667	−17.30	10,376	2.75	−5,527	−1.46
371	*Iron and steel*	8.5	621,809	−22.59	24,020	3.86	−62,630	−10.07
372	*Non-ferrous metals*	15.2	172,858	10.09	9,845	5.70	−13,360	−7.73
381	*Fabricated metal products*	22.0	810,240	−2.43	41,669	5.14	−49,780	−6.14
382–3825	**Non-electrical machinery**	15.7	837,490	3.91	59,472	7.10	−51,060	−6.10
3825	**Office and computing machinery**	30.1	76,333	31.88	−10,310	−13.51	−10,540	−13.81
383–3832	*Electrical apparatus, other*	37.7	1,111,333	9.36	22,200	2.00	−74,220	−6.68
3832	*Radio, TV and communication equipment*	—	—	—	—	—	—	—
3841	*Shipbuilding and repairing*	6.0	59,667	−40.78	853	1.43	488	0.82
3842+44+49	*Other transportation equipment*	—	—	—	—	—	—	—
3843	*Motor vehicles*	15.2	878,027	11.27	54,150	6.17	−31,430	−3.58
3845	*Aircraft*	14.1	49,667	32.89	3,109	6.26	1,162	2.34

385	Professional goods and precision instruments	40.2	245,938	12.15	37,286	15.16	2,724	1.11
39	Jewelry, musical instruments, toys and sporting goods, misc.	50.4	89,000	−15.36	17,940	20.16	−10,250	−11.52
3	Total	27.1	8,929,027	−2.82	412,340	4.62	−427,336	−4.79

Sources: OECD *STAN Database for Industrial Analysis* (1998); OECD *Bilateral Trade Database* (1998); OECD *Input–Output Database* (1995); UNIDO *Industrial Statistics Database* (1999).

Notes

ISIC 351+352-3522 also includes ISIC 3522 and ISIC 383-3832 also includes ISIC 3832. ISIC 3842+44+49 is omitted, as input-output data for it is spread among industries in such that a correction is not feasible. Industries in italicized letters are classified by Adrian Wood as "trade losers." Industries in bold letters are classified by Wood as "trade winners."

Table 4.4 Japan: employment effects from trade of manufactures at the industry level, 1978–95

ISIC code and industry	Percent female 1990	Actual 1978–80 employment	Percent change in actual employment 1978–95	OECD trade		Non-OECD trade	
				Worker years	Percent change from 1978–80	Worker years	Percent change from 1978–80
31 Food, beverages and tobacco	54.5	1,383,667	28.52	−20,220	−1.46	−32,910	−2.38
32 Textiles, apparel, leather and leather goods	68.7	2,066,297	−10.45	−88,100	−4.26	−280,000	−13.55
33 Wood products and furniture	30.8	887,375	−33.17	−24,450	−2.76	−41,490	−4.68
34 Paper, paper products and printing	31.4	1,016,040	16.83	−4,050	−0.40	−16,370	−1.61
351+352–3522 Industrial chemicals	26.0	407,909	6.69	3,669	0.90	−8,362	−2.05
3522 Drugs and medicines	26.0	117,357	18.15	697	0.59	860	0.73
353–354 Petroleum and coal products	13.3	56,774	−14.11	−358	−0.63	572	1.01
355–356 Rubber and plastic products	38.6	596,744	43.15	−10,440	−1.75	−32,780	−5.49
36 Non-metallic mineral products	25.0	683,333	−11.12	−11,230	−1.64	−6,700	−0.98
371 Iron and steel	10.9	433,469	2.57	−16,780	−3.87	−32,530	−7.50
372 Non-ferrous metals	20.3	144,864	15.56	−6,725	−4.64	−4,315	−2.98
381 Fabricated metal products	26.9	1,138,013	8.79	−31,000	−2.72	−81,300	−7.14
382–3825 Non-electrical machinery	20.5	1,324,623	11.26	48,440	3.66	23,280	1.76
3825 Office and computing machinery	41.9	196,082	86.51	55,669	28.39	−9,829	−5.01
383–3832 Electrical apparatus, other	41.9	798,142	40.40	11,380	1.43	−32,960	−4.13
3832 Radio, TV and	41.9	867,484	48.06	−118,160	−13.62	−16,340	−1.88
3841 Shipbuilding and repairing	18.5	198,711	−44.92	−8,781	−4.42	2,925	1.47
3842+44+49 Other transportation equipment	18.5	54,183	−1.64	−26,158	−48.28	−1,902	−3.51
3843 Motor vehicles	18.5	857,091	27.34	−36,640	−4.27	−16,780	−1.96
3845 Aircraft	18.5	32,157	14.74	16,925	52.63	145	0.45

385	Professional goods and precision instruments	37.9	305,717	-22.13	-3,290	-1.08	15,150	4.96
39	Jewelry, musical instruments, toys and sporting goods, misc.	49.6	315,840	-10.18	-3,954	-1.25	-3,761	-1.19
3	Total	36.3	13,881,873	10.94	-273,556	-1.97	-575,397	-4.14

Sources: OECD *STAN Database for Industrial Analysis* (1998); OECD *Bilateral Trade Database* (1968); OECD *Input–Output Database* (1995); Japan Ministry of Labour; *Yearbook of Labour Statistics* (1990) (using data for firms with five or more employees).

Notes

Industries in italicized letters are classified by Adrian Wood as "trade losers." Industries in bold letters are classified by Wood as "trade winners."

considerably higher than for any other manufacturing industry (Table 2.12). A lack of trade competitiveness in this industry thus translates into considerable losses of women's manufacturing employment. The case of the US is worth noting, for the gender bias from non-OECD trade away from women's manufacturing employment is very large, at –5.60 percentage points. In spite of this, male–female wage differences in the US narrowed rapidly over this period (Figure 3.2).

Part 2: foreign trade and diverging gender wage gaps in Germany and Japan

Foreign trade in the context of overall demand and supply shifts for labor

An emphasis on relative demand shifts for skilled and unskilled labor underlies the two most prevalent explanations of recent increases in overall earnings inequality, skills-biased technical change (e.g. Bhagwati and Kosters 1994) and North-South trade expansion (e.g. Wood 1994).[12] Relative shifts in the supply of college-educated workers are emphasized by other studies (e.g. Katz, Loveman, and Blanchflower 1995: 48). Less attention has been paid to the gender bias of labor demand resulting from these forces, and less yet to analogous effects on male–female wage differences, even though earlier studies found that in a number of advanced economies women are more negatively affected by foreign trade than men (Schumacher 1984: 342–3; Lee and Schmitt 1996: 14). Just as changes in overall earnings inequality can be viewed in the context of skills-biased labor demand, so can changes in male–female wage differences be viewed in the context of gender-biased labor demand. The logic is the same, the motivation as compelling.

For both manufacturing and non-agricultural employees, female-to-male hourly earnings ratios increased in Germany after the mid-1970s and, until the 1990s, declined in Japan. For German manufacturing (plus mining and utilities), the measure increased fairly steadily over the postwar years, though the rate of increase slowed after the mid-1970s. For Japanese manufacturing, the measure increased quite rapidly after 1958 and then did a turnabout in 1973 and declined fairly steadily thereafter, though jumping up in 1991 (Figure 3.1). It is worth emphasizing that one finds the same patterns of divergence with ratios based on the unweighted average of female-to-male hourly earnings ratios for sixteen individual manufacturing industries, which abstracts from changes in the number of employees per industry. That is, the diverging patterns of female-to-male hourly earnings are by and large the result of changes within industries, not of compositional shifts of German women into higher-paying industries and of Japanese women into lower-paying industries.[13] There are very similar patterns of divergence at the more aggregate level, for female-to-male hourly earnings ratios for non-agricultural workers (Figure 3.2). (Cf. Hill 1996: 153–7 and Kumazawa 1996: 160 for similar ratios for the economy as a whole.) The causes of divergence appear wide-ranging, pervasive.

At first sight, there appears to be a fairly neat match for Germany and Japan between gender bias from trade expansion of manufactures and changes in male–female wage differences. In Japan, the gender bias away from women's employment appears to match the widening male–female wage gap. In Germany, the lack of gender bias appears at least consistent with the narrowing male–female wage gap. But the gender bias from trade expansion must be viewed in the context of overall gender bias in the demand for labor. The issue can be put more generally, leaving aside gender considerations: how important are trade-induced employment changes in relation to actual, observed employment changes? The answer is sensitive to the method used as well as the countries and span of years considered. But based on the methods employed here and the years considered, the answer seems clear. For both Germany and Japan, trade performance is not a good indicator of actual employment changes. More generally, this is the prevalent view of most economists who have studied the issue, Wood being the most notable exception (Freeman 1995: 30; Wood 1994).

As was noted earlier, world trade expansion for Germany from 1978 to 1990 is estimated to have had little effect on total employment, with an estimated employment loss of 15,000 worker years (Table 4.1). Actual employment loss in German manufacturing was considerably greater, declining by 252,039 employees over these years (a percentage change of –2.82, with endpoints calculated as three-year averages). For Japan, the contrast is even more striking. World trade expansion from 1978 to 1995 is estimated to have resulted in an employment loss of nearly 850,000 worker years, but actual employment increased by 1,518,458 (a percentage change of 10.94).

Germany's more favorable trade performance is also indicated by changes over these years in net exports of world trade of manufactures relative to GDP. The measure increased by 2.99 percentage points in Germany and declined by 0.74 percentage points in Japan.[14] This result is of course entirely independent of factor content calculations and their limitations. Regarding changes in actual manufacturing employment, the contrast between Germany and Japan is also indicated by Figure 4.4, which shows manufacturing employment as a percentage of civilian employment for both countries as well as for the G7 average. Though the measure remained higher in Germany than Japan throughout the 1960 to 1995 period, it declined persistently in Germany after 1970 – much like the G7 as a whole – and held steady in Japan from the mid-1970s to 1992.[15]

Neither is the correlation strong between trade-induced and actual employment changes at the industry level. The measure of trade-induced employment changes is $((Q_i + TQ_i)/Q)-(Q_i/Q)$, where Q_i is defined as employment in an industry in 1978–80, TQ_i as trade-induced employment change in an industry from 1978–80 to 1993–95, and Q as total manufacturing employment in 1978–80. (The rationale of taking the simple difference and not the percentage difference is that it is the absolute change that determines the impact of trade on employment.) The measure of change in actual employment

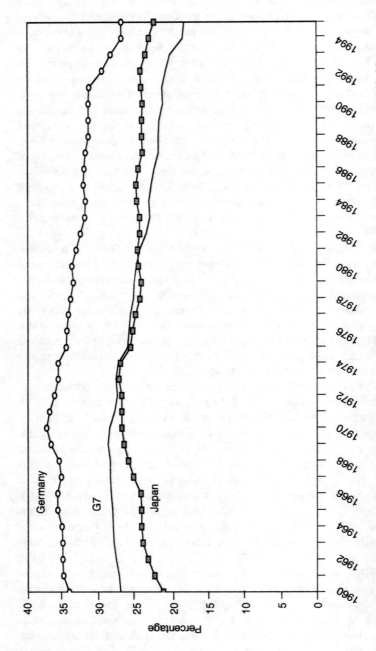

Figure 4.4 Germany, Japan, and the G7: manufacturing employment as a percentage of civilian employment, 1960–95

Source: OECD *Historical Statistics, 1960–95.*
Note
For Germany, data include East Germany after 1990.

is constructed in more or less parallel fashion as the difference between 1978–80 and 1993–95 of employment in each industry as a share of total manufacturing employment. For Germany, the correlation between these measures based on world trade is 0.32 (0.175 significance), with the correlation driven more by OECD than non-OECD trade; for Japan, the correlation between these measures based on world trade is 0.38 (0.094 significance), with the correlation driven in contrast more by non-OECD than OECD trade.

These results suggest that the finding of a gender bias from trade for Japan and no such bias for Germany tell little about overall demand shifts for men and women's employment. Chapter 2 considered the female percentage of manufacturing employment for Germany and Japan over the postwar years (Figure 2.3). From the mid-1970s until the 1990s, there was divergence in the measure for Germany and Japan, declining in the former and increasing in the latter. Figure 4.5 shows the ratio of the female percentage of manufacturing employment to the female percentage of the labor force, normalizing the former relative to aggregate female labor supply. Given the very similar pattern of increase in Germany and Japan in female labor supply (Figure 2.1), a similar pattern of divergence holds. The year 1970 marks a turning point for Germany, after which the ratio declines strongly, holding steady meanwhile in Japan (most clear-cut for data including all firms for Japan, not just those with thirty or more employees).[16] The pattern of divergence between Germany and Japan is of course just the opposite one would expect if the gender bias from trade expansion were the dominant determinant of overall demand shifts for men and women's manufacturing employment. That is, women's manufacturing employment in Japan increased in the face of a trade-induced gender bias away from women's employment; women's manufacturing employment in Germany declined in spite of there being no trade-induced gender bias.

The question remains as to what causes the diverging pattern of German and Japanese women's share of manufacturing employment. This is usefully viewed at the industry level, which suggests the importance of domestic demand factors not directly related to trade (though perhaps indirectly so). Correlation coefficients were constructed between, on the one hand, the female percentage of manufacturing employment and, on the other hand, employment growth, investment growth, and labor productivity growth (Table 4.5). These measures are constructed for sixteen manufacturing industries as annual averages for years from 1970 to 1991, roughly the period of strongest divergence between Germany and Japan in terms of women's share of manufacturing employment. For Germany, the correlation coefficient between the female percentage of employment and employment growth is –0.75, a striking result significant at the 1 percent level.[17] For Japan, the coefficient is practically zero. The evidence suggests that both compositional shifts in investment and labor productivity had a more negative effect on German than Japanese women's share of manufacturing employment. While investment growth was relatively low in female-intensive industries in both Germany and Japan, the correlation was stronger in Germany and statistically significant; labor productivity growth was

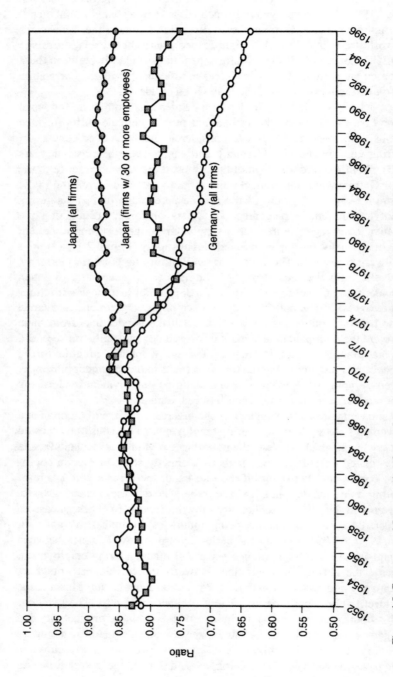

Figure 4.5 Germany and Japan: ratio of manufacturing to labor-force female percentage, 1952–96

Sources: *Arbeits-und Sozialstatistik. Hauptergebnisse; Statistiches Iahrbuch für die Bundesrepublik Deutschland*; Japan Ministry of Labour: *Yearbook of Labour Statistics*; ILO *Yearbook of Labour Statistics*.

Table 4.5 Germany and Japan: correlation coefficients and probabilities (in parentheses) between relative female percentage of employment and the growth of relative employment, investment, and labor productivity (based on annual averages from 1970–91 for sixteen manufacturing industries)

	Employment growth (log)	*Investment growth (log)*	*Labor productivity growth (log)*
Germany			
Female percentage of employment	−0.75 (0.001)	−0.64 (0.008)	0.41 (0.111)
Japan			
Female percentage of employment	0.03 (0.899)	−0.18 (0.501)	−0.28 (0.294)

Sources: OECD *STAN Database for Industrial Analysis* (1995); Bundesministerium für Arbeit und Sozialordnung: *Arbeits- und Sozialstatistik. Hauptergebnisse*; Japan Ministry of Labour: *Yearbook of Labour Statistics*.
Note
For each year, variables are indexed relative to the manufacturing total, with growth rates for employment, investment, and labor productivity based on these variables expressed in relative terms.

relatively high in female-intensive manufacturing industries in Germany but not in Japan. In the context of high employment loss and low investment growth, it seems clear that the high labor productivity growth in female-intensive manufacturing industries in Germany is less the result of labor-displacing technical change than of the decline of less-productive marginal producers.

What domestic factors might account for these differences between Germany and Japan? With the growing wealth of a country and its inhabitants, it should be no surprise that basic commodities such as textiles, apparel, footwear, and foodstuffs make up a declining share of domestic consumption and thus a declining share of domestic employment, for reasons having nothing to do with trade (Engel's law). That is, women are concentrated in the production of manufactured goods for which the income elasticity of demand tends to be low relative to other manufactured goods. In Japan, though, in spite of the rapid Westernization of consumption in the postwar years, there remains a strong demand for goods produced in the traditional, labor-intensive manner (cottons, silk, kimonos, *geta*). Regarding Japan's economic development, for instance, Kuznets writes that "the persistence of demand for traditional goods – whether agricultural, manufactured, or services – has been a source of strength in the economic growth of Japan, minimizing the adoption of far more costly Western consumer goods" (Kuznets 1968: 404). This seems likely to account for the increase in employment in the food, beverages, and tobacco industry and the relatively small decline in employment in the textiles, apparel, leather and leather goods industry in Japan from 1978 to 1995 (Table 4.4). This contrasts with Germany, in which employment declined sharply in these industries from 1978 to 1990. In the textiles, apparel, leather and leather goods industry, for instance, employment plummeted by 32 percent (Table 4.3).

It is worth mentioning that changes in the composition of investment and patterns of labor productivity growth among manufacturing industries may result not only from domestic but also from international economic forces. Compositional shifts in investment may be driven by patterns of foreign investment from or into Germany and Japan; technical change may be driven by "defensive innovation," an attempt by firms to maintain international trade competitiveness (Wood 1995: 67). These effects may be of considerable importance but they, especially the latter, are very difficult to isolate and thus to weigh.[18]

The divergence in male–female wage differences in Germany and Japan also occurred in the face of remarkable similarities in female labor supply, as indicated by the female percentage of the labor force (Figure 2.1). From 1973 to 1991, the years of greatest similarity, the measure increased from 37 to 41 percent in Germany and from 38 to 41 percent in Japan. Germany and Japan are also broadly similar in terms of the percentage of women among the college-educated, shown in Table 4.6 (pages 148–9), with breakdowns by junior college graduates, university graduates, and all college graduates (combining junior college and university graduates), as well as female junior college graduates as a percentage of all female college graduates. Most similar between the countries is the female percentage of all college graduates. The measure increased more steadily in Japan than Germany, such that by the early 1990s about 48 percent of all college graduates in Japan were women, compared with 44 percent of all college graduates in Germany. The female percentage of junior college graduates was a good deal higher in Japan than Germany, and the female percentage of university graduates a good deal lower; and, after the mid-1970s, there was a higher proportion of female junior college graduates relative to all female college graduates in Japan than in Germany. This suggests that women are not quite as well educated relative to men in Japan as in Germany, possibly relevant to the wider gender wage gap in Japan. But in terms of the divergence of this gap between Germany and Japan from the mid-1970s and 1990s, narrowing in the former and widening in the latter, what is most relevant is that in Japan the female percentage of all college graduates and of university graduates both increased fairly steadily. Shifts in neither labor supply nor demand fit with actual patterns of male–female wage differences.

Given that women make up large shares of the labor force in Japan and Germany, the world's second and third largest economies, this evidence provides a significant counter-example to the supply and demand shift approaches so prevalent in discussions of earnings inequality. Continuing the argument of the previous chapter, the effects of supply and demand shifts appear overwhelmed by institutional factors. This emphasis on labor market institutions is in the spirit of Freeman and Katz's work on the causes of changes in overall earnings inequality in the advanced economies. Regarding the widely-varying patterns of earnings inequality changes among countries, Freeman and Katz write, "Supply and demand factors . . . cannot by themselves explain all of the differing changes in inequality among advanced countries.

Why? Because supply and demand moved in roughly similar ways in these countries" (Freeman and Katz 1994: 43). The authors argue that the large increases in overall earnings inequality in the US and United Kingdom in the 1980s resulted from the declining strength of unions, a decline not offset by the presence of other centralized wage-setting institutions, such as a high minimum wage or the extension of collective bargaining agreements to non-unionized workers (Freeman and Katz 1994: 53). This view is supported by the empirical analysis of Nicole Fortin and Thomas Lemieux, who provide evidence that much of the increase in wage inequality in the US in the 1980s is attributable to institutional factors, with deunionization of particular importance for men's wage inequality and the decline in the real value of the minimum wage of particular importance for women's wage inequality (Fortin and Lemieux 1997). Similarly, this chapter emphasizes women's representation in unions as a determinant of the diverging patterns of male–female wage differences in Germany and Japan. Women's declining representation in unions in Japan is argued to reflect the more marginal basis on which Japanese women were integrated into the labor force since the mid-1970s, with an increasing proportion of Japanese women on the periphery of a deeply dualistic employment system.

Human capital and institutional determinants of the gender wage gaps

Before briefly considering institutional determinants, it is useful to address human capital determinants of earnings. The human capital approach suggests that the underlying determinant of differences in male–female hourly earnings is not gender in and of itself, but that women are less skilled than men, that an hour of women's work contributes less to production than an hour of men's work. Yet for Japanese men and women, human capital determinants appear of less importance than one might expect.

Probably the most definitive work in this regard is by Tachibanaki, who uses analysis-of-variance (ANOVA) estimation procedures to decompose the effects of six factors on overall wage differences for the years 1958 to 1978: gender, job tenure, firm size, age, occupation, and education. After controlling for all these factors, Tachibanaki concludes that "sex appeared to be the most important factor in the determination of wage differentials, and its role increased over time" (up to 1978, that is) (Tachibanaki 1982: 448). Tachibanaki reports that gender accounted for an estimated 44.7 percent of wage differences in 1978. The remaining factors in order of importance were job tenure, accounting for an estimated 20.1 percent of wage differences, firm size at 15.6 percent, age at 13.3 percent, occupation at 5.0 percent, and education at 1.4 percent (Tachibanaki 1982: 451). That gender was two-and-a-half times more important than job tenure in a seniority-based earnings system such as Japan's seems remarkable. It is also striking that education counts for so very little, perhaps an indication of Japanese firms' heavy reliance on in-house training. In more recent work, Tachibanaki updated this analysis. For 1985, the most recent

Table 4.6 College graduates in Germany and Japan

Year	Female percentage of all college graduates (levels 5–7)		Female percentage of junior college graduates (level 5)	
	Germany	Japan	Germany	Japan
1970	—	39.8	—	81.7
1971	32.2	37.8	—	81.1
1972	34.0	37.0	—	81.1
1973	—	37.6	—	—
1974	—	38.7	—	—
1975	39.7	—	43.5	—
1976	—	42.1	—	84.4
1977	44.3	43.2	51.6	86.1
1978	44.7	43.7	52.2	86.9
1979	44.2	43.7	51.5	86.3
1980	45.1	43.3	64.2	87.0
1981	45.4	43.3	63.1	87.7
1982	46.1	44.1	62.5	88.0
1983	46.6	44.1	62.4	88.0
1984	46.5	—	63.7	—
1985	46.2	44.2	63.3	87.9
1986	—	—	—	—
1987	43.4	—	57.9	—
1988	—	47.7	—	88.7
1989	42.7	—	54.0	—
1990	—	—	—	—
1991	—	47.8	—	88.7
1992	44.4	—	55.8	—
1993	—	—	—	—
1994	—	—	—	—
1995	45.3	—	55.1	—

Source: *UNESCO Statistical Yearbook* (various years from 1974 to 1998).
Note
Junior college graduates are referred to as Level 5 or A in the *UNESCO Statistical Yearbook*.
Level A is defined in the 1974 Yearbook (p. 398) as follows:

> Diplomas and certificates not equivalent to a first university degree. These correspond to higher studies of reduced duration (generally less than three years). They include, for instance, certificates awarded to certain types of technicians, nursing diplomas, land-surveying diplomas, associate degrees, certificates of competence in law, etc.

University college graduates are referred to as Levels B and C or 6 and 7 and indicate first or postgraduate university degrees. For Germany, data for 1992 and 1995 are for unified Germany.

year reported, Tachibanaki notes that gender accounted for an estimated 37.4 percent of overall wage differences compared with job tenure next at 31.7 percent, age at 21.7 percent, firm size at 5.3 percent, occupation at 2.5 percent, and education at 1.4 percent (Tachibanaki 1996: 41). Though its importance declined relative to both age and job tenure, gender remained the single most important determinant of overall wage differences.[19]

It is worth asking, though, the extent to which job tenure is an indicator of skill, of a worker's contribution to production, as opposed to the extent to which

Table 4.6 (continued)

Year	Female percentage of university graduates (levels 6–7)		Female junior college graduates as a percentage of all female college graduates	
	Germany	Japan	Germany	Japan
1970	—	19.6	—	66.7
1971	—	19.0	—	65.0
1972	—	18.9	—	63.8
1973	—	—	—	—
1974	—	—	—	—
1975	34.9	—	61.2	—
1976	—	22.2	—	64.2
1977	36.1	23.4	61.2	62.8
1978	36.1	23.8	62.4	62.7
1979	35.6	24.1	63.2	62.3
1980	34.1	24.2	52.3	61.1
1981	35.2	23.7	51.0	62.1
1982	36.7	23.9	49.7	62.9
1983	37.1	24.0	50.2	62.8
1984	36.8	—	49.6	—
1985	36.8	24.2	48.6	62.3
1986	—	—	—	—
1987	36.0	—	45.2	—
1988	—	25.9	—	64.6
1989	37.1	—	41.8	—
1990	—	—	—	—
1991	—	27.4	—	61.8
1992	38.6	—	42.3	—
1993	—	—	—	—
1994	—	—	—	—
1995	40.7	—	39.0	—

is simply an indicator of Japanese women's exclusion from the core employment system. There appears to be truth in both views. Japan is commonly characterized as having high road labor-management relations, of which a central notion is the association of job security with high productivity growth. Combined with Japanese firms' reliance on continuous in-house training for core workers, this suggests that longer job tenure does indeed translate into greater productivity. At the same time, it also is reasonable to believe that differences in job tenure and pay reflect women's exclusion, by and large, from the core system of lifetime employment and seniority-based earnings. Suppose for instance that job tenure tells nothing of actual productivity and that Japanese women are just as productive as Japanese men. Even in such circumstances, Japanese women's employment volatility over business cycles and their lifecycles works against their attaining the continuous employment on which seniority-based earnings are based. A gender earnings gap would emerge even in the face of equal productivity between men and women.

Suppose the opposite were true, that job tenure is a pure measure of a worker's productivity. The question still remains as to why women's job tenure is less than men's. This book compiles much evidence that the role of Japanese women as a buffer workforce is systemic, that Japanese women's employment provides an offsetting flexibility that accommodates the rigidities of the predominately male system of lifetime employment and seniority-based earnings. Even if Japanese women strongly desired to work continuously over business cycles and their lifecycles, there are strong institutional impediments to their doing so.[20] A number of studies argue that the viability of the predominantly male core employment system in Japan depends on the exclusion of much of the workforce, particularly of women (e.g. Tachibanaki 1987: 669; Ono 1990: 87–8; Hashimoto 1993: 141). That is, the marginal nature of women's employment is a fundamental characteristic of the Japanese system of labor-management relations as well as economic competitiveness. This is described by Lam as follows:

> [O]ffering women true equal opportunities would imply redistribution of the promotion changes between men and women. This would disrupt the job security and long-service promotion expectations of the male employees which are part of the long-standing implicit understanding between management and the male employees. This customary expectation has been the major force generating high commitment, high output effort and willingness to co-operate in furthering the aims of the company. The benefits that management derives from these long-standing practices are considerable, and it is not at all clear that Japanese companies are willing to give them up.
>
> (Lam 1993: 218)

Lam's words echo a main argument of this book, that the Japanese economy is characterized by both high and low roads of labor-management relations, for which gender is a key marker, enabling Japan to reap both the productivity advantages of the high road and the cost and flexibility advantages of the low road.

Regarding institutional determinants of the diverging patterns of male–female wage differences in Germany and Japan, evidence is provided by patterns of women's representation in unions. Women's union representation is measured by their union propensity, the female percentage of unionized employees divided by the female percentage of all employees. For German manufacturing and non-agricultural employees, the measure increased steadily after the early 1970s. For Japanese manufacturing and non-agricultural employees, the measure declined steadily after the early 1970s, until the 1990s (Figure 3.3). For the sake of comparison, the female percentage of union members for manufacturing and all employees, not divided by the female percentage of all employees, is shown in Figure 4.6. International comparative studies indicate that around the world, union workers tend to be better paid than non-union workers (Freeman 1994: 273, 280).[21] But union membership has

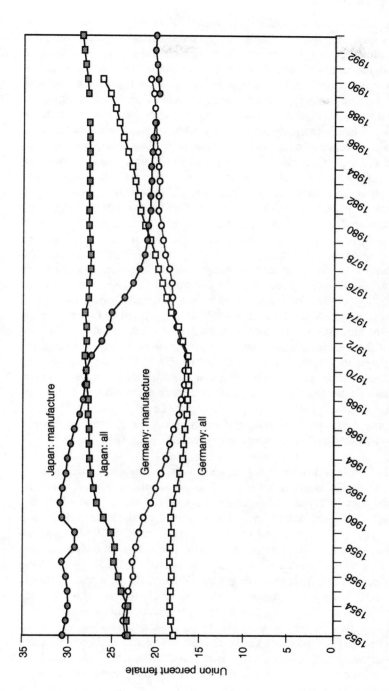

Figure 4.6 Germany and Japan: female percentage of union members for manufacturing and all employees, 1952–93

Sources: Bundesministerium für Arbeit und Sozialordnung: *Arbeits- und Sozialstatistik. Hauptergebnisse;* Statistisches Bundesamt: *Statistisches Jahrbuch für die Bundesrepublik Deutschland;* Japan Ministry of Labour: *Yearbook of Labour Statistics.*

special significance in Japan, where along with lifetime employment guarantees and seniority-based earnings it is one of the "three pillars" of the core of the Japanese employment system, each of the pillars generally associated with the others. Given the informal nature of the lifetime employment system, unionization data is probably the best available indicator of a Japanese worker's inclusion in the core, a proxy standing for more than union membership alone. The decline in women's representation in unions in Japan thus provides evidence that Japanese women's integration into the workforce was on an increasingly marginal basis, evidence of deepening labor market dualism along gender lines.

Blau and Kahn provide evidence that greater inter-firm and inter-industry earnings inequality are generally associated with greater male–female earnings differences (Blau and Kahn 1995). From the 1970s, though, inter-industry wage inequality moved in the opposite direction to male–female earnings inequality in both Germany and Japan (and in the US, Blau and Kahn note, which they refer to as "swimming upstream"). That is, inter-industry earnings inequality declined overall in Japan from 1970 to the early 1990s. Roughly the opposite pattern is observed in Germany, where inter-industry earnings inequality increased overall from 1970 to the early 1990s (Galbraith, Darity, and Lu 1998: fig. 1). The evidence on inter-firm inequality for Japan is more clear-cut. Inequality between large and small firms declined in Japan from the mid-1950s to the mid-1970s and increased thereafter, parallel with the movement of the female-to-male wage ratios for manufacturing and non-agricultural employment (Nakamura 1995: 156; Price 1997: 222; Kume 1998: 74). As Price writes, "There is some debate about the scale of the gaps [between large and small firms] but all sources confirm the general trend toward convergence in the 1960–73 period and growing gaps later" (Price 1997: 222). Japanese women are disproportionately concentrated in small firms, one aspect of the labor market dualism in Japan along gender lines (Brinton 1993: 50; Figure 2.3).

During the 1990s recession in Japan, there was a turnabout in the trend of widening male–female wage differences. For both manufacturing and non-agricultural employees in Japan, male–female wage differences narrowed overall after 1990, prior to which was the period of sustained widening extending back to the mid-1970s. The narrowing of the gender wage gap in the 1990s occurred in the face of an overall decline in the female percentage of manufacturing employees, after a fairly sustained increase in the measure extending back to the mid-1970s (Figure 2.3). This narrowing was not the result of a compositional shift of Japanese women into higher paying industries, for (as with the prior widening of male–female wage differences) the same pattern held for the unweighted average of female-to-male hourly earnings ratios for sixteen manufacturing industries.[22] Consistent with the emphasis on institutional determinants of male–female wage differences, there was also in the 1990s a parallel turnabout in Japanese women's representation in unions. After a long period of sustained decline, women's union propensity for both manufacturing and non-agricultural employees increased slightly overall after 1990 (Figure 3.3).

Also suggestive in this regard are patterns of women's temporary and part-time employment in Japan. Women's share of temporary employment declined in the 1990s (from 72.8 in 1990 to 71.6 percent in 1995), after a period of steady increase from the 1970s (Table 3.1); similarly, women's share of part-time employment declined overall in the 1990s (from 73.0 in 1989 to 67.5 percent in 1998), also after having increased steadily from the 1970s (Table 3.4). Data for temporary and part-time employment refer to the whole economy, but the closely parallel movement between manufacturing and non-agricultural employees for women's union propensity and the female-to-male hourly earnings ratio is shown in Figures 3.1, 3.2 and 3.3. (Temporary and part-time employees are included in the Japanese earnings data, except for daily employees – those with contracts of less than one month's duration – who worked less than eighteen days in each of the two calendar months prior to the survey.) As union membership is typically restricted to workers with full-time, regular employment status, the movements in these three measures – women's union propensity and women's share of temporary and part-time employment – seem of a piece, not just for the 1990s but dating back to the 1970s. As was argued in the previous chapter, the very different nature of women's temporary and part-time employment in Germany and Japan plays a complementary role with union representation in shaping women's employment conditions, including earnings.[23] Japanese women's temporary and part-time employment is both low paid and particularly vulnerable to job loss in downswings. If and when the Japanese economy experiences a sustained recovery, women's share of temporary and part-time employment seems likely to increase. Though it depends on how a range of other factors comes into play, this may well bring about some widening of the gender wage gap in Japan.

Conclusion

The pattern of women's segregation across manufacturing industries is remarkably similar in Germany and Japan, with women's employment in both countries concentrated in industries characterized as "trade losers," particularly regarding trade with developing, non-OECD countries. Only in Japan, though, was there a gender bias from trade expansion away from women's manufacturing employment, primarily the result of Japan's poor trade performance with non-OECD countries in the textiles, apparel, leather, and leather goods industry. But relative demand shifts from trade for men and women's manufacturing employment tell little of actual employment patterns. In spite of the similar effects of trade on men and women's manufacturing employment in Germany, female-intensive industries experienced disproportionate employment losses, and there was a steady decline from 1970 in the ratio of the female percentage of manufacturing employment to the female percentage of the labor force. This contrasts with the picture in Japan, for which female-intensive industries did not experience disproportionate employment losses and the ratio of the female percentage of manufacturing employment to the female percentage of the labor force held steady from the 1970s up to the 1990s. This provides evidence that there was a relative overall shift in labor demand away from women's manufacturing employment in Germany, but no such shift in Japan.

Since the early 1970s, women's labor supply was much alike between Germany and Japan. The female percentage of labor-force participants increased in a nearly identical manner in both countries, and the rise in Japan in the female percentage of college graduates suggests that the skill levels of Japanese women increased. In the face of these supply and demand shifts, women's hourly earnings relative to men's increased in Germany and – until the 1990s – declined in Japan, for non-agricultural and manufacturing employees alike. This divergence was not the result of compositional shifts of German women into higher-paying and Japanese women into lower-paying manufacturing industries, for the same pattern held within industries.

On the face of it, it is reasonable to think that large relative supply and demand shifts for men and women employees would have a predictable effect on men's and women's relative earnings. This logic underlies the more widely-held explanations of changes in overall earnings inequality, which emphasize the skills bias of labor demand. Yet there are plainly limits to such abstract conceptions of earnings. More purely historical and institutional factors come into play, factors that can completely offset the effects of supply and demand shifts.

5   German reunification

Introduction: the question of convergence

After forty years of separation, the reunification of the former East and West Germany (German Democratic Republic and Federal Republic of Germany, respectively) rapidly brought together two fundamentally different economic systems. Key events and dates in the unification process were the fall of the Berlin Wall in November 1989, the adoption of the West German mark as the common currency in July 1990, and formal political unification in October 1990. The economies of the former East and West differed both in the systemic sense – largely planned versus largely market-driven – and in terms of levels of development. In short, the West attained much higher productivity levels over the course of the postwar years.

With policies of economic reunification aimed more at rapid privatization than at broader industrial policy considerations, the general macroeconomic outcome was predictable. Reunification brought to the East dramatic declines in output and employment and dramatic increases in unemployment. By 1991, output had fallen by half (Hunt 1997: 3). Total employment fell from 9.2 to 6.1 million from 1989 to 1993. Manufacturing sector employment fell by a much greater proportion, from 3.2 to 1.2 million during this same period (Quack and Maier 1994: 1266). The number of registered unemployed in the East increased from 7,400 in January 1990 to well over a million by 1992 (Engelbrech 1991: 108–9). The number of unemployed remained above one million throughout the 1990s, and unemployment rates for the 1992 to 1997 years averaged 14.4 percent for the East compared with 7.7 percent for the West (Table 5.1). More recently, the German economy showed signs of recovery from the post-reunification recession, but this was limited to the West. In the last three quarters of 1999, for instance, the numbers of unemployed declined steadily in the West but increased just as steadily in the East, a worrisome divergence after a decade of unification (*International Herald Tribune*, November 10 1999).

Large as they are, the figures on employment decline and unemployment increase in the East would be considerably larger were it not for several forms of disguised unemployment and other exceptional factors, of particular importance in the years just after reunification. An early retirement program was in

Table 5.1 Unemployment in western and eastern Germany (end of April or May, with
number of unemployed in 1,000s)

	Number of unemployed						Western	Eastern
	Western			Eastern				
	Total	Male	Female	Total	Male	Female	% fem.	% fem.
1992	1,705	919	786	1,149	423	726	46.1	63.2
1993	2,197	1,233	964	1,118	412	706	43.9	63.2
1994	2,590	1,489	1,101	1,216	441	776	42.5	63.8
1995	2,564	1,475	1,090	1,040	387	653	42.5	62.8
1996	2,769	1,614	1,156	1,198	524	674	41.7	56.3
1997	3,031	1,760	1,271	1,315	588	728	41.9	55.3

| | Unemployment rates | | | | | | Eastern unemployment rates/ | | |
| | Western | | | Eastern | | | Western unemployment rates | | |
	Total	Male	Female	Total	Male	Female	Total	Male	Female
1992	5.3	4.9	6.0	13.9	9.9	18.3	2.61	2.03	3.05
1993	6.8	6.5	7.3	13.8	9.8	18.2	2.02	1.50	2.50
1994	8.1	7.9	8.3	14.9	10.3	19.9	1.85	1.30	2.41
1995	8.0	7.9	8.2	12.8	9.0	16.9	1.59	1.14	2.06
1996	8.7	8.7	8.7	14.8	12.2	17.6	1.70	1.40	2.03
1997	9.4	9.5	9.4	16.1	13.6	19.0	1.71	1.43	2.02
Avg: 1992–7	7.7	7.6	8.0	14.4	10.8	18.3	1.86	1.43	2.30

Sources: Bundesministerium für Arbeit und Sozialordnung: *Arbeits- und Sozialstatistik. Hauptergebnisse*; Statistisches Bundesamt: *Statistisches Jahrbuch für die Bundesrepublik Deutschland.*
Note
Unemployment rates in this table are constructed to include the self-employed, as per the standard definition of the unemployment rate. They are consistently lower than official German unemployment rates.
This has little effect on ratios of eastern to western unemployment rates, which are very similar using
annual average official unemployment rates.

effect from October 1990 to December 1992, through which 866,600 persons
retired early (for women at age 55 and for men at age 57 initially and then at
55). As of 1993, 382,000 persons were in government job training programs and
an additional 250,000 held public works jobs (Hunt 1997: 3–4). There were also
large numbers of so-called "short-time workers" in the years just after reunification. Short-time workers were paid about two-thirds of their former earnings
by the government and an additional one-fifth of their former earnings by firms.
In one sample from 1991, short-time workers put in an average of 10.3 fewer
hours per week than regular full-time workers (Krueger and Pischke 1995: 427).
Short-time workers numbered 370,000 in 1992, down to 50,000 by 1997
(*Statistisches Jahrbuch*). As of 1992, there were also about 425,000 workers
commuting from the East to jobs in the West (Quack and Maier 1994: 1272).
Perhaps most striking, between 1989 and 1992 there was a net emigration from
East to West of an estimated 955,000 persons (Eberstadt 1994: 151). Taking
these factors together, several million directly experienced economic dislocation
as a result of reunification, this relative to a working age population (ages 15 to
64) of 10.7 million in 1991 (*Arbeits- und Sozialstatistik*).

Just as contrasting as the economic systems of the former East and West Germany were patterns of women's labor-force participation as well as social policies supporting women's labor-force participation. In 1989, 85 percent of East German women between the ages of 15 and 60 were employed, compared with 55 percent of West German women (Quack and Maier 1994: 1260). Women's labor-force participation rates in the East remained high throughout the 1990s, though declining for most age groups and particularly for younger women. These patterns for the East in 1991, 1994, and 1996 and the West in the 1996 are shown in Figure 5.1.

Even with increases in women's labor-force participation in recent decades, West Germany continued to adhere by and large to the model of the male breadwinner household. The difference between East and West in this regard is also suggested by comparisons of child care availability and women's part-time employment. In 1989, 24.5 percent of West German women in the labor force worked part-time – fewer than 35 hours per week – and child care provisions were of limited availability (Adler 1997: 42; Quack and Maier 1994: 1264). In contrast with women in the West, only 9.7 percent of East German women in the labor force worked part-time by this definition in 1989, and these generally at only somewhat reduced hours (Adler 1997: 42; Trappe and Rosenfeld 1999: 13).[1] In the East, full-time employment for women was the norm. East German women's labor-force participation was facilitated by the near universal availability of publicly funded child care (Quack and Maier 1994: 1264).

With reunification came the expectation of institutional convergence, but convergence on what terms, to what level? Regarding women's labor-force participation, the treaty of German unity addressed this issue explicitly, stating that "given the different legal and institutional starting points in mothers' and fathers' labour-market participation, legislation will have to be shaped in such a way as to make family and career compatible" (Beck 1998). But the transition has not unfolded so smoothly. For one thing, the availability of publicly funded child care in the East declined rapidly after reunification (Ferree 1993: 105, Adler 1997: 43, Hunt 1997: 5). The very high levels of East German women's unemployment – particularly compared with men and women in the West and men in the East – is suggestive of the strong downward pressures on their labor-force participation. For East and West in the 1990s, the upper panel of Table 5.1 shows the number of unemployed by sex and by the female percentage of unemployed; the upper panel of Table 5.2 shows like breakdowns for labor-force participants aged 15 to 64. In the West, the female percentage of the unemployed was similar to the female percentage of labor-force participants, both around 42 percent in the mid-1990s. In the East, the female percentage of the unemployed exceeded the female percentage of labor-force participants by a large margin, 16.0 percentage points in 1994. In the East, that is, the unemployment burden fell disproportionately on women.

As telling is a comparison of men and women's unemployment rates in East and West. The lower panel of Table 5.1 shows unemployment rates by sex and

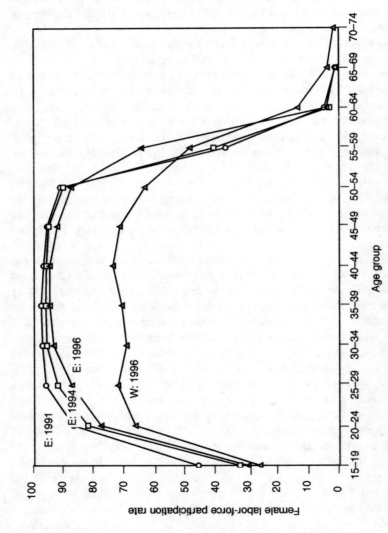

Figure 5.1 Western and eastern Germany: female labor-force participation rate by age group, 1991–96

Source: Bundesministerium für Arbeit und Sozialordnung: *Arbeits- und Sozialstatistik* (1998).

Table 5.2 Labor-force participation in western and eastern Germany (end of April or May, from ages 15 to 64, with number of labor-force participants in 1,000s)

	Number of labor-force participants				Western	Eastern
	Western		Eastern			
	Male	Female	Male	Female	% fem.	% fem.
1991	18,392	12,660	4,546	4,168	40.8	47.8
1992	18,597	12,975	4,261	3,973	41.1	48.3
1993	18,711	13,093	4,192	3,876	41.2	48.0
1994	18,598	13,192	4,249	3,890	41.5	47.8
1995	18,451	13,164	4,283	3,866	41.6	47.4
1996	18,341	13,205	4,276	3,817	41.9	47.2

	Labor-force participation rates			
	Western		Eastern	
	Male	Female	Male	Female
1991	82.2	58.4	86.1	77.3
1992	82.2	59.5	80.9	74.9
1993	81.9	59.6	78.7	73.4
1994	81.8	60.0	79.2	73.9
1995	81.3	59.9	79.7	74.0
1996	80.5	59.7	79.4	73.3

Sources: Bundesministerium für Arbeit und Sozialordnung: *Arbeits- und Sozialstatistik. Hauptergebnisse.*

the ratio of these rates by sex, East relative to West. For the 1992 to 1997 period, total (men and women's) unemployment was 86 percent higher in the East. But this difference was driven much more by women's than men's unemployment. For men, unemployment rates were 43 percent higher on average in the East than West, whereas for women unemployment rates were on average 130 percent higher. The difference between men and women in the East was particularly marked from 1992 to 1994, with unemployment rates twice as high for women. Women also made up somewhat more than three-quarters of the East's long-term unemployed in 1995 (those unemployed for longer than a year) (Adler 1997: 43). That is, women in the East were not only disproportionately affected by unemployment; once unemployed, they also had a more difficult time finding their way back into employment.

This chapter describes key characteristics of women's employment in East Germany before reunification. In some respects, women's employment in East Germany was exceptional relative not only to West Germany but to all countries, including the former Eastern Bloc countries. Most notable in this regard were women's remarkably high levels of labor-force participation, facilitated by the near universal availability of publicly funded child care as well as other supportive social policies. However, East Germany did not differ greatly from West Germany in terms of the gender earnings gap and gender segregation by industry and occupation, even though women's educational attainment relative to men's was considerably higher in the East than the West.

The chapter goes on to address why women in the East were so disproportionately affected by unemployment after reunification. The deeply embedded pattern of gender segregation in the East plays a central role in this regard, for the low wage jobs in which women were disproportionately employed were particularly hard hit by layoffs: that is, by declining labor demand (Hunt 1997). The effects of supply side factors on East German women's unemployment and labor-force participation are less clear. In particular, the effects of the sharp decline in the availability of publicly funded child care appear somewhat roundabout, perhaps not greatly affecting East German women's labor force-participation, but seeming to be among the factors contributing to the truly dramatic declines in birth rates in the East following reunification. The chapter then returns to the question of the convergence of women's labor-force participation – its probability and consequences – between the former East and West Germany.

Women's employment in East Germany and persisting inequalities

Women's labor-force participation in the East began increasing in the 1950s, the result of economic necessity in the face of postwar economic hardship (particularly harsh in the East) and of severe labor shortages (Rueschemeyer 1993: 78; Trappe 1996: 362).[2] The increase in women's labor-force participation was facilitated by the increasing availability of child care. The provision of publicly funded child care for East and West Germany over the postwar years is shown in Table 5.3. In the East, the measures increased rapidly for all age groups of children. By the mid-1970s, both the overall levels and age group contours of women and men's labor-force participation in the East were very similar. By the late 1980s, women's labor-force participation rates for the age group 25 to 44 were in fact somewhat higher than men's (Quack and Maier 1994: 1260–1; Trappe 1996: 363).

In the West, publicly funded child care for children under 3 and over 6 was scarce. As of the mid-1990s, only about 2 to 3 percent of children under age 3 were in public child care, and only a slightly higher percentage of children aged 6 to 10 were in after-school public child care (Table 5.3; Rueschemeyer 1993: 78). Child care for 3 to 6 year olds (*kindergarten*) had increased to very high levels by the 1980s. However, most of these child care facilities were only open for half days. In the East, child care facilities were generally open for full days, and they also provided hot meals (Maier 1993: 272–3). In terms of child care provision, East Germany was exceptional not only relative to West Germany and other OECD countries, but also relative to other Eastern Bloc countries. For children to age 3 as of 1989, for instance, publicly funded child care was available for only 16 percent of children in Czechoslovakia, 13 percent in Bulgaria, 9 percent in Hungary, 6 percent in Romania, and 5 percent in Poland (Trappe 1996: 374). As one study summarizes, "The provision of childcare for working mothers was more extensive in East Germany than in any other country in the world" (Antal and Krebsbach-Gnath 1993: 59).

Table 5.3 Provision of publicly funded child care in East and West Germany (by available places as a percentage of the number of children in corresponding age groups or school grades)

	West Germany			East Germany		
	0–3 years	3–6 years	After-school grades 1–4	0–3 years	3–6 years	After-school grades 1–4
1950	—	—	—	8.0	34.5	—
1955	—	—	—	—	—	13.0
1960	—	32.8	2.2	14.3	46.1	25.9
1965	—	32.7	2.1	18.7	52.8	44.0
1970	—	38.4	1.8	29.1	64.8	48.6
1975	—	65.4	2.1	50.8	84.5	69.8
1983	—	80.0	4.0	68.1	91.1	81.3
1989	—	79.0	4.4	80.2	95.1	81.2
1996	2	78	5			

Sources: Quack and Maier (1994) for data from 1950 to 1989, Deven *et al.* (1998) for 1996 data.

The differences between East and West Germany in women's labor-force participation and publicly funded child care also reflected differences in attitudes towards childrearing. Sabine Walper describes this difference between East and West Germany as follows:

> Extensive and early extrafamilial child care has been critically discussed in the West, where private childcare by the family was the politically and ideologically preferred option. Thus, it is not only the lack of child-care facilities that keeps West German mothers from the labor market, but also their higher skepticism about extrafamilial child care. Full-time day care, especially during infancy, is considered detrimental to children's development by almost two-thirds of West German adults, whereas two-thirds in East Germany think it is not. Beneficial effects of full-time kindergarten are acknowledged by about 20 percent of West German adults but over 60 percent of East German adults.
>
> (Walper 1995: 8)

Publicly funded child care was just one of the factors supporting the high levels of women's labor-force participation in the East. Also important were generously paid maternity leaves, forty days per year paid leave to care for sick children under 15, a paid day off per month for housework, and the possibility of reduced working hours for mothers with children under 16 (Rueschemeyer 1993: 79; Trappe and Rosenfeld 1999: 10). In addition, universities helped students combine childrearing with their studies, and parents were given strong preference in obtaining housing (Ferree 1993: 94; Walper 1995: 5). These policies not only facilitated women's labor-force participation. They also contributed to early family formation, the high percentage of women with children, and the equality of educational attainment between men and women.[3]

Regarding the last, 94 percent of East German female employees had completed either vocational training or a college or university degree as of 1990, compared with 69 percent of West German female employees (Quack and Maier 1994: 1260–1). By the 1980s, East German women accounted for about 55 percent of college or university graduates compared with about 45 percent of West German women (Antal and Krebsbach-Gnath 1993: 55, Table 4.6).

In spite of the very high levels of women's labor-force participation and educational attainment, there remained in East Germany considerable gender inequality in two important respects: earnings differences and segregation by occupation and industry. Together, these play a central role in explaining why job loss and unemployment in the East following reunification fell so disproportionately on women.

Of those in East Germany working full time as of the late 1980s, women made about 75 percent as much as men on average, compared with about 65 to 70 percent in West Germany (Rudolph, Appelbaum, and Maier 1990: 37; Quack and Maier 1994: 1265).[4] For full-time workers in 1988, the share of East German women in different monthly earnings categories is shown in Figure 5.2, revealing that women were strongly over-represented in low earnings categories. The large gender earnings gap in East Germany seems all the more notable given the equality of education attainment between men and women and the similarity between men and women's labor-force participation in terms of both levels and continuity over life course.

Recent studies employ individual-level datasets in an effort to isolate determinants of the differences in earnings between men and women in East and West Germany. Krueger and Pischke's study uses the *Survey on Income of Blue- and White-Collar Households in the GDR* for East Germany and the *Socioeconomic Panel* dataset for West Germany (Krueger and Pischke 1995). For 1988, the authors examine determinants of monthly earnings for full-time non-agricultural non-self-employed workers aged 18 to 65. Looking at men and women's earnings in separate regression models, the authors find similar positive returns to education (measured by years of schooling) for women in East and West Germany, and similar positive returns to education for men in East and West Germany, with returns to education somewhat higher for women than men in both countries (ibid.: 424–5). In regression models including both men and women, the authors find that sizeable gender earnings differences remain after accounting for differences in labor-force experience and education (measured by either years of schooling or level of educational certification): 23 percent for East Germany and 25 percent for West Germany (ibid.: 420). That is, women earned about one-quarter less than men in both East and West Germany, even after accounting for differences in education and experience.

Using a different dataset, Sorensen and Trappe find very similar results regarding gender earnings differences in East Germany (Sorensen and Trappe 1995). The dataset is from the *East German Life History Study*, based on interviews in October 1990 with persons from the former East Germany by four birth cohorts, 1929 to 1931, 1939 to 1941, 1951 to 1953, and 1959 to 1961. The

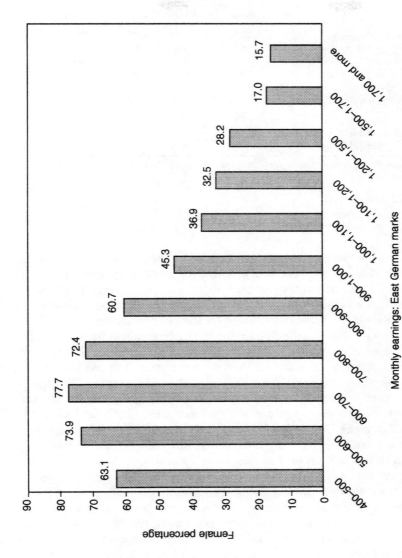

Figure 5.2 East Germany: female percentage of full-time employees by earnings category, 1988

Source: Brander (1990).

Table 5.4 Female percentage of employment by sector in West and East Germany, 1988

	[1]	[2]	[3]	[4]
	Female percentage		*Sector % female relative to total % female*	
	West	*East*	*West*	*East*
Agriculture and forestry	44.8	37.7	1.15	0.77
Manufacturing and craft production[a]	26.7	40.0	0.69	0.82
Construction	10.3	17.0	0.27	0.35
Transport and communication	23.6	35.2	0.61	0.72
Wholesale and retail trade	56.2	72.0	1.45	1.47
Other services (including FIRE)[b]	51.1	70.0	1.32	1.43
Total	38.8	48.9		
Correlation between Columns [1] and [2] (or [3] and [4]):		0.91		

Source: Rudolph, Appelbaum, and Maier (1990), from *Statistical Yearbook* of GDR and *Statistical Yearbook* of FRG.
Notes
Does not include apprentices.

a For East Germany, industry and craft production.
b Finance, insurance, and real estate.

authors examine monthly earnings for all full-time and part-time workers at the end of 1989. The authors report actual, unadjusted monthly earnings for women from 23 to 26 percent less than for men for the three most recent birth cohorts and 47 percent less than for men for the earliest birth cohort. After accounting for the influence of education (measured by level of educational certification), gender earnings differences decline for the earliest birth cohort but not at all for the three most recent birth cohorts. Even after controlling for the influence of full-time employment, full-time labor-force experience, and the industry in which workers are employed, similar levels of gender earnings differences persist. For the two most recent birth cohorts, for instance, women's adjusted earnings are an estimated 24 percent less than men's, essentially the same as for unadjusted earnings. Controlling for occupation matters more than the combined effects of education, full-time employment, full-time labor-force experience, and industry, but women's adjusted earnings after accounting for all these determinants are still between 19 to 21 percent less than men's for the three most recent birth cohorts and 31 percent less for the earliest birth cohort (ibid: 403).[5]

Taking the results of both studies together, a similar gender earnings gap remains in East and West Germany after accounting for the determinants of earnings for which data are available.[6] One can disagree about the extent to which these residual earnings gaps result from unobserved differences in human capital between men and women or from gender discrimination. Most important to note though: there is no evidence of any less gender discrimination in earnings in East than in West Germany.

There was also a high degree of gender segregation by occupation and industry in East Germany, broadly similar to West Germany. Table 5.4 shows the female percentage of employment for six broad sectors of the economy for East and West Germany in 1988. Dividing these sectoral female percentages by the total female percentage of employment enables a more direct comparison between the countries, shown in the right-hand side of the table. In both countries, women were under-represented in manufacturing and craft production, construction, and transport and communication, what might be regarded (with the exception of communication) as more typically male sectors. But the degree of under-representation was somewhat less in these sectors in East Germany. Women were over-represented in a very similar manner in both countries in wholesale and retail trade and other services, more typically female sectors. Women were over-represented in agriculture and forestry in West Germany and under-represented in East Germany, but on balance the patterns of gender segregation were broadly similar at this level of aggregation.

At the more detailed industry and occupational level, gender segregation also appears similar between East and West. In part, this results from the prewar system of vocational education inherited by both East and West, a system based on apprenticeships that generally defined later occupations. This is described by Rudolph, Appelbaum, and Maier for East Germany as follows:

> The statistics on apprentice contracts and on areas of specialization of college and university students reflect the coexistence of traditional structures with new developments in East Germany. Following old patterns, public planners earmarked apprenticeship slots for women completing secondary school mainly in sectors with traditionally high female participation rates. Thus women are highly overrepresented in textiles and clothing, leather, retail trade, and in low-level scientific "crafts" (laboratory technicians, for example), as well as in sales and other services. More than half the women apprentices are to be found in ten occupations. Six of these ten are in almost exclusively "female" areas, and here women constitute 95 percent of the apprentices.
>
> (Rudolph, Appelbaum, and Maier 1990: 34–5)

The ten occupational apprenticeships in which women are over-represented are out of an available 289 (Dölling 1991: 9). Consistent with the gender segregation of apprenticeships, East German women made up 92 percent of employees in social services, 83 percent in health services, 77 percent in education, and 69 percent in postal and telephone services (Antal and Krebsbach-Gnath 1993: 53). Similar to both West Germany and Japan, women made up about two-thirds of employees in the textile and apparel industries, which were particularly vulnerable to trade losses and economic decline more generally (Ferree 1993: 92–3; Tables 4.3 and 4.4).

East German women did make significant headway into some occupations that had been traditionally male. By the late 1980s, for instance, over half the doctors and lawyers in East Germany were women, and 30 percent of all managers in East Germany were women (though these tended to be lower status and lower-paid management positions), compared with 14 percent of managers in West Germany (Dölling 1991: 9; Antal and Krebsbach-Gnath 1993: 50–2).[7] Because industry and occupational data are not directly comparable, it is difficult to say definitively whether there was more or less gender segregation in East than West Germany. Some suggest there was more (Quack and Maier 1994: 1262; Walper 1995: 7) and others less (Trappe and Rosenfeld 1999: 17). Most important, all accounts concur that there was a great deal of gender segregation in East Germany. This deeply entrenched segregation plays a central role in accounting for the considerable differences in the way men and women were affected by job loss and unemployment in East Germany following reunification.

After the Wall: women's high unemployment and demographic shocks

Many of the social policies supporting women in the East were eliminated or greatly weakened after reunification.[8] These developments are summarized by one study as follows: "One of the most disturbing aspects of the transition to a reunited Germany has been the rapidity with which the legislated achievements of East Germany have been dissolved" (Antal and Krebsbach-Gnath 1993: 63). Federal subsidies for child care were ended in mid-1991. State and local governments continued to subsidize child care, but in the East they were largely bankrupt (Ferree 1993: 105). Many child care facilities in the East were affiliated with workplaces, and as these workplaces closed so did these child care facilities (Adler 1997: 43). As a result, the availability of publicly funded child care declined rapidly, especially for children under 3 and between the ages of 6 and 10 (Adler 1997: 43; Hunt 1997: 5). The availability of after-school child care for those in grades one to four (ages 6 to 10), for example, declined from 94 percent coverage in 1989 to 32 percent coverage by mid-1992 (based on data for four of the six regions of the East) (Hunt 1997: 5). With support remaining primarily for children from ages 3 to 6 (kindergarten), the availability of publicly funded child care rapidly converged to patterns in the West. In short, there were not only severe labor demand shocks resulting from reunification but also severe labor supply shocks.

Recent studies by Jennifer Hunt address whether the labor demand or labor supply side (particularly regarding declining child care availability) was more important in accounting for the disproportionate job loss experienced by women in the East following reunification (Hunt 1997, 1999). Her studies look at the 1990 to 1994 and 1990 to 1996 periods using the *Socioeconomic Panel* dataset for East Germany, with results largely the same for both periods. From 1990 to 1994, the employment rate for men aged 18 to 60 fell from 94 to 78 percent compared with a decline of 84 to 63 percent for women, five percentage points greater than for men (Hunt 1997: 1). Based on her analysis, Hunt argues that the main cause of the gender difference in job loss is not gender in and of itself. Rather the probability of job loss is much higher for low wage earners, and women made up a disproportionate share of low wage earners. She writes, "The message is clear: men and women with similar wages had similar rates of employment exit – women have had a much larger decline in employment largely due to having had lower wages in 1990" (ibid.: 15). In this sense, the greater job loss for women in the East following reunification is partly a legacy of gender segregation prior to reunification. Figure 5.2 provides a useful picture in this regard, suggestive of how disproportionate job losses for low wage earners translate into disproportionate job losses for women. One of the consequences of the disproportionate job losses for low wage women workers was a 10 percentage point narrowing of the gender wage gap in the East between 1990 and 1994, with an estimated 42 percent of this narrowing resulted from disproportionate job losses for low wage women workers (ibid.: 20).

Hunt tests whether the declining availability of child care was an important determinant of women's disproportionate job loss, and her findings suggest that it was not. Having children aged 1 to 4 is not estimated to affect women's probability of job loss. Having children less than a year old is estimated to double women's probability of job loss, but the overall effect on women's job loss is argued to be negligible given that there were few children of this age (Hunt 1997: 19, 22). Hunt's analysis also suggests that the effect of wages on employment is through layoffs, not through low-wage workers' choosing to leave employment. In sum, Hunt argues that the disproportionate job loss for women workers in East Germany was driven by changes in labor demand, not labor supply. What then caused the disproportionate job losses for low-wage workers in the East? Here the available evidence is largely anecdotal. Hunt suggests the disproportionate job losses may have resulted from unions' policies of raising the relative wages of low-wage workers. Consistent with this view, wages increases between 1988 and 1991 for low-wage workers were somewhat higher than the average for all workers (Krueger and Pischke 1995: 431).

However, other factors also appear to play a role in accounting for the disproportionate job losses and disproportionately high unemployment of women workers. Some of these factors relate to the comparative fortunes of industries, determined not just by abstract market forces in the aftermath of reunification but also by government and union policies of supporting industries in which men were concentrated. Maier describes this as follows:

> [W]omen had been over-represented in those sectors which reduced employment and production most sharply, primarily textiles, electronics, food processing, precision mechanics, and optics. In core industries like steel, ship-building, automobiles and mechanical engineering the restructuring process was slowed down by state and trade-union intervention, whereas in female dominated industries exposure to the market had an immediate effect.

> (Maier 1993: 274)

In addition to the "core" industries noted by Maier, another predominately male industry that fared well after reunification was construction (though by the late 1990s, the industry experienced a great deal of job loss) (Andrews 1997; *International Herald Tribune*, November 10 1999). An analogous process appears to have occurred at the occupational level within industries. That is, women were concentrated in administrative and clerical positions, which are argued to have been more vulnerable to cutbacks after reunification (Maier 1993: 274).

There are also several pieces of evidence indicating that unemployed women had a more difficult time than unemployed men in finding their way back into employment. As of mid-1990, for instance, women were 53 percent of the unemployed in Berlin but only 29 percent of those receiving referrals for new employment (Ferree 1993: 104). Of the 425,000 workers commuting from East to West in 1992, only 20 percent were women, with the greater family responsibilities of East German women argued to constrain their possibilities in this regard (Quack and Maier 1994: 1272). Women also made up 77 percent of the long-term unemployed in the East in 1995, compared with 63 percent of the total unemployed (Adler 1997: 43; Table 5.1).

As noted, Hunt's analysis suggests that the probability of job loss is twice as high for East German women with children less than a year old. There were too few children of this age, however, for this factor greatly to affect women's overall job loss. It is worth considering in this light the dramatic drop in fertility and marriage rates in the East following reunification. From 1989 to 1994, the number of births per thousand persons dropped from 12.0 to 5.1 and the number of marriages per thousand persons dropped from 7.9 to 3.4 (Adler 1997: 41). The decline in the East German birth rate occurred at the same time as a decline in the number of abortions, and thus the former resulted from pregnancy avoidance (Eberstadt 1994: 140). Eberstadt conveys the historical uniqueness of the declining birth rate in the East as follows: "Such an abrupt and precipitous drop in fertility is unprecedented for an industrialized society during peacetime. . . . Eastern Germany's adults appear to have come as close to a temporary suspension of childbearing as any such population in the human experience" (ibid.: 138–9).[9]

The timing of the declines in birth and marriage rates is suggestive. Births dropped particularly sharply at two points: in August 1990, nine months after the fall of the Berlin Wall, and in July 1991, nine months after formal political unification. Marriage rates dropped sharply in July 1990, when the common currency was adopted (Eberstadt 1994: 139, 144). Also suggestive in this regard is a study by Witte and Wagner, which evaluates the predicted probability of East German women giving birth depending on whether they responded "yes" or "no" regarding whether they were "optimistic about the future," "concerned about general economic developments," and "concerned about personal economic situation." The study covers the 1990 to 1992 period and distinguishes between first births and all births. For the first two questions, there was little difference in the probability of giving birth between those women who responded "yes" and those who responded "no." But women who responded "yes" to being "concerned about personal economic situation" were much less likely to give birth, particularly a first birth, than those who responded "no" (Witte and Wagner 1995: 391). As part of the tumultuous economic and social change following reunification, the effect of the rapidly declining availability of publicly funded child care appears somewhat round-about, possibly one of the factors affecting women's decisions to have children and marry but not having, according to Hunt's evidence, a decisive effect on women's job loss. This view of the implications of declining child care avail-ability is expressed by as follows by Trappe:

> [T]he severe decline in the availability of affordable child care is not expected to lead automatically to younger women's exclusion from the labor market. Other "solutions," as indicated by the vast decrease in fertility or a renewed importance of child care provided by other family members, are possible as well.
>
> (Trappe 1996: 373)

According to one study, "Official scenarios already calculate that the labor market participation rate in the former GDR will 'adjust' to the much lower West German level" (Rudolph, Appelbaum, and Maier 1990: 39). Labor-force participation rates for women in the East aged 15 to 64 declined by 4.0 percentage points from 1991 to 1996 (Table 5.2). This decline was concen-trated in the three youngest age groups. The measure declined by 16.3 percentage points for the 15 to 19 group, 9.1 percentage points for the 20 to 24 group, and 8.5 percentage points for the 25 to 29 group. One must question whether these disproportionate declines for young women are partly attrib-utable to declining child care availability, at least for the two older groups. Such a view is not necessarily at odds with Hunt's evidence regarding the greater importance of demand than supply factors in terms of job loss, for the disproportionate decline in young women's labor-force participation may have resulted from fewer women entering the labor force than would have been the case had child care availability not declined. There was also a 27.6 percent increase from 1991 to 1996 in the labor-force participation rate of women in the 55 to 59 age group, reflecting a convergence to the customary retirement age for women in the West (Hunt 1997: 3). Even with the decline in women's overall labor-force participation rates, women's overall labor force partici-pation rate in 1996 remained 13.6 percentage points higher in the East than the West, and the female percentage of labor-force participants 5.3 percentage points higher (Table 5.2).

In order for the female percentage of labor-force participants in the East to decline to 41.9 percent, the level in the West in 1996, the number of female labor-force participants in the East would have to decline to 3,079,000 from the 1996 figure of 3,817,000, meaning that 738,000 women would have to leave the labor force. Since the labor-force participation rate of men in East and West was nearly identical in 1996, the effect of equalizing women's labor-force participation rates yields very similar numbers (Table 5.2).[10] The number of East German woman needing to leave the labor force for women's labor-force participation rates to converge is somewhat higher than the number of unemployed women in the East in 1996, at 674,000. Following through with this convergence scenario, if one assumes that the East German women to leave the labor force are those already unemployed, and thus that women's unemployment rates in the East were zero, then the hypothetical total unemployment rate in the East, combining men and women, would have been 7.0 percent in 1996, 1.7 points lower than the actual rate in the West.

Several studies suggest that such notions of convergence are at odds with the wishes of East German women. These studies are based on surveys of women's attitudes towards employment in East and West Germany, and find that a higher percentage of East than West German women considered work more important than leisure (37 to 26 percent) and that a lower percentage of East than West German women considered being a homemaker their ideal job (3 to 25 percent) and preferred part-time to full-time employment (45 to 69 percent) (summarized in Adler and Brayfield 1997: 250–1). Another study uses multivariate regression analysis to address the underlying determinants of the differences in work attitudes between East and West Germany. Looking at data for 1991, the study concludes that differences in work attitudes between East and West result largely from the greater economic necessity of employment in the East rather than from more deep-seated differences. The authors write:

> We are unconvinced by the popular claim that women in (former) socialist countries place greater emphasis on the intrinsic value of a job for self-actualization than do women in the West. . . . [G]ender-role attitude differences in the East and West are somewhat superficial and the basis of present differences is job insecurity and penury.
>
> (Braun, Scott, and Alwin 1994: 44)

Other studies of women's employment attitudes in East Germany, though not directly comparative with West Germany, take economic necessity into account in their survey questions. A 1991 survey asked a sample of East German women employees whether they would want to remain employed even if their husbands earned enough to provide for the entire family. Fully 70 percent responded they would definitely want to remain employed, 20 percent responded that they would probably want to remain employed, and only 10 percent responded that would not want to remain employed. Of married East German women employees in this survey who were married and had two children under 6 years old, only 13 percent responded that would not want to remain employed (Quack and Maier 1994: 1271). A 1990 survey also asked East German women employees whether they would want to remain employed if their husbands could provide for the whole family. The result was fairly similar, with 76 percent of respondents indicating that they would want to remain employed and 24 percent indicating that they would not (Brander 1990: 44).

Women's very high rates of unemployment and the rapidly declining availability of child care in the East create strong downward pressures on East German women's labor-force participation. The pace and extent of convergence between women's labor-force participation rates in the East and West depends, then, on the intersection of these downward pressures and the convergence between East and West of women's attitudes towards employment, with the latter determined to an uncertain extent by the economic necessity of women's employment.

Conclusion

Since reunification, the difference in unemployment rates between the former East and West Germany have been very large, over twice as high in the East in the years just after reunification. This difference has been driven very disproportionately by the unemployment rates of East German women, which – at nearly 20 percent – were also twice as high as East German men's unemployment rates in the years just after reunification. The effects of labor supply conditions on East German women, particularly the rapidly declining availability of child care, are not entirely clear-cut. It is suggestive in this regard that much of the 4.0 percentage point decline in East German women's overall labor-force participation rate from 1991 to 1996 is driven by the declining labor-force participation of young women, from ages 15 to 29. Having a child less than age 1 is estimated to double the risk of job loss for East German women, but there were too few children of this age for this factor greatly to effect women's overall job loss (Hunt 1997: 19, 22). At the same time, the declining availability of child care may also have contributed to the historic declines in birth rates in East Germany following reunification.

The main cause of the disproportionate unemployment and job loss of East German women appears to result from the demand side, from women's over-representation in low wage jobs which were particularly hard hit by layoffs following reunification (Hunt 1997: 15). That is, gender segregation plays a central role in explaining why East German women were so disproportionately affected by job loss. The theme of gender segregation and its implications runs throughout this book. One clear implication of gender segregation is that it can have adverse effects on women's employment in the face of economic transformation. For one thing, women's employment in the manufacturing sector is disproportionately concentrated in industries for which the income elasticity of demand is low, particularly textiles, apparel, footwear, and foodstuffs (Table 2.11). As incomes rise with economic growth, this Engel's law effect creates a persistent internal dynamic away from women's manufacturing employment. For a number of OECD countries, it was also seen that manufacturing trade expansion with non-OECD countries created a gender bias away from women's manufacturing employment. This gender bias resulted from women's disproportionate concentration in the textiles, apparel, leather, and leather goods industries, labor-intensive industries that were trade losers from the viewpoint of OECD countries. Looking that the G7 countries and Australia, Denmark, and the Netherlands, the gender bias of manufacturing trade expansion away from women's manufacturing employment basically disappears once one subtracts from the effect of the textiles, apparel, leather, and leather goods industries (Australia and Italy are the exceptions, as these countries had solid trade performance in these industries, far better than the other eight countries considered) (Figure 4.3). Taken together, these results suggest that the implications of gender segregation are usefully viewed in a dynamic sense, in the context of economic growth and trade expansion as well as the more abrupt transformations taking place in the transition economies of Eastern Europe.

Appendix
Data notes to Chapters 2 and 4

All data are annual unless otherwise noted. Unless otherwise noted, all data for Germany refer specifically to the former West Germany or, in most recent years, to the regions of the former West Germany.

Chapter 2

Aggregate-level data

Japan   Labor-force and employment data are from the Japanese Ministry of Labour's *Yearbook of Labour Statistics* (YLS), based on household labor-force surveys. Data are annual averages.

Germany   Labor-force and employment data are from the Bundesministerium für Arbeit und Sozialordnung's *Arbeits- und Sozialstatistik: Hauptergebnisse (AS)*, based on a combination of household and establishment surveys. The surveys are combined in the data source itself. (In the 1991 volume of *Arbeits- und Sozialstatistik*, the data are described as follows: "aufgrund der Ergebnisse der Volks- und Arbeitsstättenzählung" (p. 26); in the 1975 volume, the data are described similarly as follows: "auf Grund der Ergebnisse der Volks- u. Berufszählung" (p. 26).) Labor-force data is derived from the sum of all workers and unemployed workers. Non-agricultural employee data is derived from the difference between all employees and agricultural employees. All pre-1958 data are from the 1962 *AS*. For data on all workers, all employees, and agricultural employees, data for 1958 to 1959 are from the 1965 *AS*; data for 1960 from the 1975 *AS*; data for 1961 to 1969 from the 1980 *AS*; data for 1970 to 1987 are from the 1991 *AS*; data for 1988 to 1991 are from the 1996 *AS*; and data for 1992 to 1996 are from the 1997 *AS*. Unemployment data from 1958 to 1966 are from the 1972 *AS*; unemployment data from 1967 to 1990 are from the 1991 *AS*; and unemployment data for 1991 to 1996 are from the 1997 *AS*. Data are annual averages and do not include Berlin until 1960.

Sectoral-level data

Japan   Employment data are from the *YLS*, based on establishment surveys which cover only firms with thirty or more employees. Data are for employees only and do not include self-employed and unpaid family workers. Employment data include "production and related employees" and "non-production employees" (the latter are referred to as "salaried employees" after 1967). While Japanese data include temporary and part-time employees, they do not include daily employees who worked less than eighteen days in each of the two calendar months prior to the survey. Those included in the survey are defined in the data documentation as follows (from the 1972 *YLS*. The same definition holds for manufacturing-industry data):

> Employees i) employed indefinitely or under a contract for a period longer than one month [i.e., regular and temporary employees]; ii) employed for 18 and more days in each of the last two calendar months, of those employed on a daily basis or under contract for a period less than one month [i.e., casual and daily workers]; iii) such officials as directors who attend regularly and receive monthly payments; vi) family members of a self-employed, who work with him regularly and receive monthly payments.

Service-sector data for Japan from establishment surveys are not published prior to 1971. Data are for the end of December.

Germany   As with aggregate-level data, sectoral-level data are from the *AS*, based on a combination of household and establishment surveys. Data are for employees only and do not include self-employed and unpaid family workers. Employment data include "*arbeiter*," "*angestellte*," and "*beamte*," or, respectively, wage employees, salaried employees, and civil servants. See "Aggregate-level data" for volumes from which data is drawn. Data are annual averages and do not include Berlin until 1960. Regarding data for regressions with and without foreign workers: from the Statistisches Bundesamt's *Statistisches Jahrbuch für die Bundesrepublik Deutschland (SJ)*, a dataset from 1975 to 1993 was available at the seven-sector level that distinguished between foreign and all workers. These data are for the end of June of each year, whereas the data used in the above sectoral analyses are based on annual averages.

Manufacturing industry data

Japan   Employment data are from the *YLS*, based on establishment surveys. As with sectoral-level results, data are for employees only and do not include self-employed and unpaid family workers. Employment data include "production and related employees" and "non-production employees" (the latter are referred to as "salaried employees" after 1967). While Japanese data include temporary and part-time employees, they do not include daily employees who worked less than eighteen days in each of the two calendar months prior to the survey. Japanese establishment survey data covers only firms with thirty or more employees. An ordnance classification was introduced into the *YLS* tables from 1955 to 1957 and mentioned with miscellaneous after 1985 and thus ordnance was added to miscellaneous from 1955 to 1957 (consistent with International Standard Industrial Classification (ISIC) codes, "miscellaneous" is labeled "Jewelry, musical instruments, toys & sporting goods, misc." in tables showing industry headings and the following industry classifications refer to those in *YLS*, which are easily matched with ISIC codes). In 1958, primary metal products was divided in the *YLS* tables into 1) iron and steel and 2) non-ferrous metal products. These were kept together as primary metal products. Tobacco products and food and kindred products were combined in the *YLS* tables in 1969, and were thus combined for earlier years. A plastics classification was added in 1985 in the *YLS* tables. This was added to miscellaneous from 1985 on as the drop in employment in miscellaneous in 1985 suggests is the correct procedure. In order to attain consistency with German data, furniture and fixtures was folded into lumber and wood products and petroleum and coal products and rubber products were folded into chemical and allied products. Data are for the end of December. The Okinawa region is included in the data after 1973.

Germany   Data from 1952 to 1961 are from *SJ*. Data from 1962 to 1996 are from *AS*. Data are for employees only and do not include self-employed and unpaid family workers. Data include "*arbeiter*," and "*angestellte*," or wage and salaried employees. "*Beamte*," or civil servants, are included in data up to 1961 (from *SJ*) but not thereafter (from *AS*). Three different industry classification systems were used for years 1952 to 1961, 1962 to 1972, and 1975 to 1996. The industry mapping codes to make these three different classification systems consistent are shown in Table A1. Changes from 1961 to 1962 and from 1972 to 1975 are omitted from data series, so that regressions consider only changes within survey types. Office and computing machinery is included with electrical machinery and apparatus. For data from 1952 up to and including to 1976, all data points are for the end of September with the following exceptions: 1952 data is actually for the end of December 1951 and 1953 data is for the end of March 1954 (since male–female breakdowns were not available in data for years 1952 and 1953). From 1977 to 1996, data is for the end of June. Data for 1952 to 1954 are from the 1956 *SJ*; data for 1955 to 1961 are from the *SJ* dated two years after the date of the data itself; data from 1962 to 1970 are from *AS* tables for which the date of the volume is not given; data for 1972 is from the 1974 *AS*; and data for 1975 to 1996 are from the *AS* dated one year after the date of the data itself. Data were not published for years 1963, 1965, 1967, 1969, 1971, 1973 and 1974. Data up to 1961 do not

Table A1 Industry mapping codes for German manufacturing industries

1975–96 data (AS)	1962–72 data (AS)	1952–61 data (SJ)
Chemicals and allied products (9 to 13)	(22, 40, 42, 58, 59)	(20, 25)
Non-metallic mineral products (14 to 16)	(25, 51, 52)	(7 to 10)
Primary metal products (17 to 22)	(27 to 30)	(11, 12, 14, 15)
Fabricated metal products (23 to 25)	(31)	(13a, 13b, 27b, 28b, 29)@
Non-electrical machinery (26, 27)	(32)	(17)$
Transportation equipment (28 to 32)	(33 to 35)	(17)$
Electrical machinery and apparatus (33, 34)	(36, 50)	(18)
Professional goods and precision instruments (35, 36)	(37)	(19)
Jewelry, musical instruments, toys and sporting goods, misc. (37 to 39)	(38, 39)	(13a, 13b, 27b, 28b, 29)@
Wood products and furniture (40 to 42)	(53, 54)	(26, 27a, 28a, 28c, 39c2)
Paper and paper products (43)	(55, 56)	(22)
Printing (44)	(57)	(23a)
Leather and leather products (45, 46)	(61, 62)	(24, 37)
Textiles (47 to 51)	(63)	(21)
Apparel (52, 53)	(64)	(36, 38a)
Food, beverages and tobacco (54 to 58)	(68, 69)	(30 to 35)

Notes

Industry 50 (for 1962–72 categories) begins in 1970; Industry 42 (for 1962–72 categories) begins in 1966; @ and $ indicate industries that were combined for 1952–61. AS indicates: Bundesministerium für Arbeit und Sozialordnung: *Arbeits- und Sozialstatistik. Hauptergebnisse*; SJ indicates: Statistisches Bundesamt: *Statistisches Jahrbuch für die Bundesrepublik Deutschland*.

include Berlin. The continuous series for female percentage in manufacture, shown in Figure 2.3, is derived from *SJ* for years prior to 1958, with data for 1952 to 1954 from the 1955 *SJ*; data for 1955 and 1956 from the 1957 *SJ*; and data for 1957 from the 1958 *SJ*. The *SJ* data are based on the average of two monthly surveys six months apart, whereas the post-1957 data, from *AS*, are annual averages. The years 1958 to 1996 are drawn from the same survey used for sectoral-level regressions.

Data for cross-sectional manufacturing regressions

Independent variables used were female union propensity (percent female unionized divided by percent female employed); the ratio of hours worked by males to hours worked by females; female percentages; and the ratio of male-to-female hourly earnings, including bonuses and premiums. These independent variables are made up of within-period averages for all evenly-numbered years, with the exception of female percentages, which are made up of within-period averages for all years.

Union membership data are not available at as disaggregated a level as other data. As a consequence, there are only ten categories of female union propensity for Japan and only seven for Germany. German data is based on membership at the end of September up to 1960 and the end of December thereafter. Japanese data is based on membership at the end of June. While Japanese data is by industry, German data is by industrial union and is thus an estimate (within the DGB for manufacture (*"Deutscher Gewerkshaftsbund"* or Federation of German Trade Unions). For Germany, the manufacturing unions include the seven unions associated with manufacturing production, as much as the data allows. The food industry union includes restaurant workers in addition to workers in food manufacture. In 1989, the Art (*Kunst*) and Printing and Paper (*Druck und Papier*) unions were combined to form the Medien unions. Data for 1989 and 1990 are adjusted by subtracting 20,000 for males and 10,000 for females, consistent with numbers on the Art union for earlier years. With or without this adjustment, the ranking by female percentage is unchanged.

Japan   Data are for production and non-production employees in firms with thirty or more employees and hourly earnings are derived from the ratio of average monthly earnings over the year to average monthly hours worked over the year.

Germany   Data on hours, wages, and unionization are from *SJ*. Data on hours and wages are for wage employees only (*"arbeiter"*), and thus differ from employment data, which also include salaried employees (*"angestellte"*). Hourly earnings are derived from the ratio of average weekly earnings over the year to average weekly hours worked over the year.

Chapter 4

This chapter makes use of the most recent versions of the OECD's *STAN Structural Analysis* databases, the *Input–Output Database* (1995) for input–output data, the *Bilateral Trade Database* (1998) for trade data, and the *STAN Database for Industrial Analysis* (1998) for output, total employment, and price deflator data (the last derived from data on value added in real and nominal terms). These datasets have the advantage of being largely standardized by industry classification, following what the OECD calls an "Adjusted ISIC Revision 2 Classification," for which there are twenty-two distinct manufacturing industries.

Input–output data for Germany do not conform perfectly to the "Adjusted ISIC Revision 2 Classification." Thus data from the *STAN Database for Industrial Analysis* and *Bilateral Trade Database* are modified to match the input–output data whenever feasible. ISIC 351+352 also includes ISIC 3522 and ISIC 383-3832 also includes ISIC 3832. ISIC 3842+44+49 is omitted, as input–output data for it is spread among industries in such a way that a correction is not feasible. In addition, employment data in Japan for ISIC 3842+44+49 and ISIC 3825 begin in only 1984. Thus other data for these industries is also truncated to match the shorter period. Trade data for Germany include regions of the former East Germany after 1990, and thus the analysis runs only to 1990.

For industry-level data on the female percentage of manufacturing employment, data for Germany are from the UNIDO *Industrial Statistics Database* (1999), for which data are classified by ISIC code. Data for Japan are from the Japanese Ministry of Labour's *Yearbook of Labour Statistics* and are for firms with five or more employees. Japanese employment data are made consistent with the "Adjusted ISIC Revision 2 Classification" by industry mapping codes shown in Table A2. UNIDO data for Germany on female percentage of manufacturing employment and Japanese Ministry of Labour's *Yearbook of Labour Statistics* data for firms with five or more employees and do not go back to the 1978–80 period. Thus data from the *ILO Yearbook of Labour Statistics* are used to obtain the female percentage of employment for the manufacturing sector as a whole for the 1978–80 period, necessary for the estimates of gender bias in relation to average employment in 1978–80. There are small differences in the female percentage of manufacturing employment between the ILO and other data (from UNIDO and country sources). Thus adjustments are made to the average female percentage of employment for the 1978–80 period from the ILO data. The assumption is made that the difference between the ILO and other data in the 1978–80 period is proportionate to the difference in the year of the industry-level data on men and women's manufacturing employment. (That is, the average female percentage of employment for 1978–80 for the manufacturing sector as a whole is divided by f^{ilo}/f^{unido}, where the numerator stands for female percentage of employment from the *ILO Yearbook of Labour Statistics* and the denominator stands for the female

Table A2 Industry mapping codes for Japanese manufacturing industries

OECD Adjusted ISIC Revision 2	Japan Yearbook of Labour Statistics industry classification
31	12,13
32	14, 15, 24
33	16, 17
34	18, 19
351+352 minus 3522	20
3522	20
353+354	21
355+356	22, 23
36	25
371	26
372	27
381	28
382 minus 3825	29
3825	30
383 minus 3832	30
3832	30
3841	31
3842+44+49	31
3843	31
3845	31
385	32
39	33, 34

percentage of manufacturing employment from the UNIDO dataset or country sources, with both terms for the manufacturing sector as a whole in the year of industry-level data on men and women's employment.) This enables one to make best use of the continuity over time provided by the ILO data and the industry detail provided by data from UNIDO and country sources. In any case, the analysis is quite robust in this regard, as demonstrated by the small differences between results in parts I and II of Table 4.2.

Notes

1 Unemployment, labor market flexibility, and women as a buffer workforce

1 Derived from the difference between average annual growth of employment in respective sectors and average annual growth of the working-age population.
2 The average annual percent growth of the working-age population from 1973 to 1990 was 1.22 in the US, 0.88 in Japan, and 0.64 in Germany (*OECD Historical Statistics*, 1960–1995).
3 As an important example, by counting incarcerated males as part of the unemployed labor force, rates of long-term unemployment for males would be essentially the same in the US and Germany (2.8 percent for the US and 2.7 percent in Germany in 1993, compared with official rates of 1.0 percent for the US and 2.4 percent for Germany) (Buchele and Christiansen 1996: Table 6).
4 Gordon only provides data for Europe as a whole, though. Looking at Germany alone and making a similar correction to account for self-employment income, Heinz König argues that the increase in the real wage gap is still observed (König 1987: 738).
5 It is also important to address the extent to which apparent differences in wage flexibility among countries actually reflect differences in seniority-rules for layoffs, or other factors causing low-wage workers to be more or less vulnerable to layoffs (Brunello 1988, Hashimoto and Raisian 1992: 94).
6 In contrast with Bruno and Sachs's arguments, Calmfors and Driffil find generally insignificant correlations between straight rankings by centralization of wage-setting and the noted measures of macroeconomic performance (Calmfors and Driffil 1988: 22).
7 In the US, growing inequality and the collapse in wages for less-skilled workers is often held to result from greater labor market flexibility in the face of similar demand shifts across the advanced economies away from less-skilled workers. This view is suggested by theories of unemployment based on marginalist principles, which underlie the unified theory. But wages are not the kind of phenomenon that can meaningfully be understood by such abstract means, via the marginalist system of simultaneous determination of distribution, output, and relative prices. Wages are inherently more historical in nature, reflecting both economic and broader social factors, including the relative power of capital and labor. Wage patterns in the US may be a reflection of the declining influence of labor, as evidenced by declining unionization rates. If this is so, growing inequality in the US does not reflect the unfettered adjustment of wages towards hypothesized market-clearing levels, the usual understanding of labor market flexibility. In this sense, one's theory of wages is of vital importance in establishing a method and evaluating the evidence regarding the relationship between unemployment and inequality.
8 The authors used 225 age-education groups in the US, 29 in Canada, and 70 in France.

9 Within the 18 to 29 age group, with employment rates of 0.55 for women in the low education group, 0.66 for women in the middle education group, and 0.78 for women in the high education group, as of 1984. This compares with employment rates for the US of 0.35 for women in the low education group, 0.68 for women in the middle education group, and 0.87 for women in the high education group, as of 1991 (Blau and Kahn 1997: figs 1a–1c).

10 Low pay is defined as the percentage of full-time workers earning less than two-thirds of median earnings for all full-time workers, which is strongly and positively correlated with earnings inequality.

11 The Beveridge curve for Japan, incidently, closely resembles those for Germany and France (Sakurai and Tachibanaki 1992: 325).

12 The evidence that lifetime employment is associated with larger firms is not unambiguous, though. A study by Abraham and Houseman indicates "only a weak relationship" between firm size and employment adjustment for the manufacturing sector in Japan, where employment adjustment is measured as an elasticity with respect to output changes (Abraham and Houseman 1989: 5).

13 Based on the Japan Bureau of Statistics Employment Status Survey, for which part-timers are classified by the employment status given by firms rather than the actual number of hours worked.

14 In a similar manner, Kurosaka writes that

> the unemployment rate [in Japan in the mid-1970s] increased only a little, principally because the female labor force participation rate fell from 48.2 percent in 1973 to 46.5 percent in 1974 and, further, to 45.7 percent in 1975, as jobless female workers did not stay in the labor market but withdrew from the labor force.
>
> (Kurosaka 1989: 32)

15 Counting discouraged workers in both the numerator and denominator.

16 For Japanese women, the average annual growth rate of labor force participation was 2.21 percent from 1987 to 1991, and 0.57 percent from 1991 to 1993; for Japanese men, the average annual growth rate of labor force participation was 1.33 percent from 1987 to 1991 and 1.05 percent from 1991 to 1993. That is, Japanese men's labor force participation was much more stable over these up- and downswings than was Japanese women's (OECD *Quarterly Labour Force Statistics* 1990a, 1992, 1994e).

2 Women's integration into the workforce

1 The number of discouraged men workers declined by an average annual rate of 9.4 percent from 1987 to 1991 and increased by an average annual rate of 10.9 percent from 1991 to 1993 (OECD 1995: 88).

2 Regarding the oil crisis years of the early 1970s, Mairesse describes the anomalous levels of discouraged workers in Japan as follows:

> Between 1973 and 1975, the number of men and women unemployed increased by 220,000 and 100,000 respectively, while the number which were discouraged and went out of the "labor force" increased by 350,000 and 840,000, respectively (!). . . . Based on a very casual look at the statistics for the U.S. and the other members of the European Community for GNP growth and unemployment, the Japanese case seems very particular indeed.
>
> (Mairesse 1984: 103)

Cf. also Hamada and Kurosaka 1984: 82 for a description of these years, noted in the previous chapter. Patrick and Rohlen describe the importance of discouraged workers in Japan, particularly women, as follows:

> Women constitute a vast reservoir of low-cost labor. Although more than half of

married women work, more than 8 million women (and 2 million men) not employed desire to work (mainly part time), although most are not actively seeking a job and do not show up in unemployment statistics.

(Patrick and Rohlen 1987: 361–2)

3 Other "characteristics" of Japanese employment practices noted by the Bank are as follows. The Bank, in a section titled "Changes in the Japanese labor market after the oil crisis," writes that

In experiencing these business downturns, Japanese companies tried to balance corporate profits against employment while improving the flexibility of employment in response to fluctuations in sales and production by taking the following measures: (1) Minimizing the increase in total employment through streamlining and labor-saving investment, and increasing part-time workers who require lower wages and are more flexible in terms of hourly wages, working hours, and volume.

(Bank of Japan 1994: 70)

Among the other measures noted were "Increasing transfers" and "reducing the upswing of seniority-based wages."

4 The Berlin Wall fell in November of 1989, the currency union occurred in July 1990, and formal political unification occurred in October 1990.

5 See Baxter and King (1995: 15–16) for a detailed explanation.

6 For the 1958 to 1996 period, for instance, the standard deviation of the logarithmic growth rate of the number of unemployed is 15.7 for men and 10.0 for women in Japan, and 34.2 for men and 31.3 for women in Germany. A similar result is obtained from Equation (1) using the number of unemployed. For the 1958 to 1996 period, the estimate of β is considerably less than 1 in Japan, at 0.71, and only somewhat less than 1 in Germany, at 0.94.

7 For example, β estimates for Germany based on logarithmic growth rates at the labor-force level are 1.19 for data to 1996 and 1.11 for data to 1991; β estimates for Germany based on the Hodrick-Prescott filter at the labor-force level are 1.26 for data to 1996 and 1.14 for data to 1991.

8 Regarding the consolidation of the lifetime employment system, Hashimoto and Raisian write that "Japanese labor turnover appears to have been quite substantial in the early 1900s and through the early 1950s" (Hashimoto and Raisian 1992: 79).

9 These results should be qualified in one respect, however. Even though women's relative labor-force and employment volatility is significantly higher in Japan, this is often relative to substantially lower labor-force or employment volatility. For example, the standard deviation of the Hodrick-Prescott filtered data for all employees, total, ($\log T_t - \log T_{t(\mathrm{HP})}$) from 1952 to 1991 was 0.018 for Germany and 0.013 for Japan, and the same measure for all employees, female ($\log F_t - \log F_{t(\mathrm{HP})}$), was 0.023 in Germany and 0.019 in Japan. The standard deviation of the Hodrick-Prescott filtered data for total labor-force participants from 1952 to 1991 was 0.010 for Germany and 0.008 for Japan, and the same measure for female labor-force participants was basically identical in Germany and Japan, at 0.015. It is only relative to men within their respective countries, then, that Japanese women are argued to serve more as a buffer workforce than German women.

10 Based on this specification, estimates are significantly greater for Japan than Germany only for all employees and non-agricultural employees, in part because of the large standard errors associated with estimates for labor-force participants and all workers for Japan.

11 The issue of change over time in women's relative employment volatility is usefully considered in the context of a study by Houseman and Abraham (1993). Houseman and Abraham test women's relative employment volatility in Japan and the US for the

manufacturing sector as a whole. Comparing the 1980s with the 1970s, their empirical work for Japan suggests that women's employment volatility declined relative to men's in the more recent period. Using monthly data, the authors construct a finite distributed lag model, regressing the logarithmic differences of, separately, women's and men's employment on the logarithmic differences of current and lagged manufacturing output. Houseman and Abraham's model also includes a constant and a linear time trend. For 1970 to 1979 period, the twelve-month elasticity (the sum of coefficient estimates on current output and output lagged through twelve months) is 0.456 and 0.160 for women and men's employment respectively; for the 1980 to 1989 period, the twelve-month elasticity is 0.316 and 0.195 for women and men's employment respectively. For both periods, women's employment elasticity is significantly greater than men's at the 5 percent level. Yet female-to-male ratios based on these elasticities declined substantially, from 2.85 in the 1970s to 1.62 in the 1980s, providing evidence that Japanese women served less strongly as a buffer workforce in the 1980s (Houseman and Abraham 1993: 47). In order to address this issue, regressions are run on modified versions of equation (2), using dummy variables to test for structural change:

$$\log F_t - \log F_{t(HP)} = \alpha + dummy_1 + dummy_2 + \beta_0(\log T_t - \log T_{t(HP)})$$
$$+ \beta_1((\log T_t - \log T_{t(HP)})*(dummy_1)) + \beta_2((\log T_t - \log T_{t(HP)})$$
$$*(dummy_2)) + \varepsilon \qquad (9)$$

where $dummy_1$ is defined as 0 for years prior to the early 1970s and 1 thereafter, and $dummy_2$ is defined as 0 for years prior to the 1980s and 1 thereafter and other variables are defined as above. The estimate of β_1 provides a test of whether the role of women as a buffer workforce changed after the early 1970s, while the estimate of β_2 provides a test of whether the role of women as a buffer workforce changed during the 1980s and after, as suggested by Houseman and Abraham's results. The Hodrick-Prescott filter is used rather than logarithmic growth rates, as the former better isolates cyclic movement in the data. The span of years from 1958 to 1996 is considered to focus on the period in Japan for which women served most strongly as a buffer workforce, the period after the consolidation of the lifetime employment system. Using 1973 and 1980 as turning points for the manufacturing sector as a whole, the estimate of β_1 is 0.609 and the estimate of β_2 is –0.373, the former significant at the 5 percent level and the latter insignificant. The estimate of β_0 is 1.232. The negative estimate on β_2 is consistent with the results of Houseman and Abraham's study that Japanese women served less as a buffer workforce in the 1980s than the 1970s. However, these results suggest that the 1980s largely marked a return to the pattern of the years before the early 1970s, and that the 1973 to 1980 period was exceptional. One finds a similar result at the aggregate level. At the labor-force level for Japan from 1958 to 1996, and again using 1973 and 1980 as turning points, the estimate of β_1 is 0.914 and the estimate of β_2 is –1.306, both significant at the 5 percent level, while the estimate of β_0 is 1.900. For all employees, the estimate of β_1 is 0.026 and the estimate of β_2 is –0.111, neither significant, while the estimate of β_0 is 1.533. These results are at odds with those in Kucera 1997b, which argued that there was a significant increase in the role of women as a buffer workforce in Japan after 1973. In this earlier study, only the span of years from 1952 on was considered, rather than 1958 on as is done here. It is this difference in the span of years considered that accounts for the difference in results, for Japanese women did not serve strongly as a buffer workforce (relative to Japanese men) in the years prior to 1958.

12 The measure considers women's share of earned income, and men and women's life expectancy, adult literacy rates, and combined primary, secondary, and tertiary education enrollment rates.

13 It may be relevant, in this regard, that Japan and Italy are the only two OECD countries (of the nineteen for which data are available) for which women's share of
part-time employment increased strongly from 1979 to 1990 (OECD 1991: 46).

14 For example, Rubery and Tarling's study of the UK and Humphries' study of the US
find much smaller estimates of women's relative employment volatility for total
employment (they do not consider labor-force participation). For the UK, Rubery and
Tarling find a β estimate of 1.064 for total employment in industry and services for the
span of years from 1959 to 1983 (Rubery and Tarling 1988: 102); for the US,
Humphries finds a β estimate of 0.930 for total non-agricultural employment for the
span of years from 1960 to 1982 (Humphries 1988: 24). Humphries's results for the US
are consistent with those of Goodman, Antczak, and Freeman 1993 and Houseman and
Abraham 1993, who also do not find evidence that women serve strongly as a buffer
workforce in the US. Goodman *et al.* examined the absolute numbers of jobs gained
and lost by men and women in five recessions from 1969 to 1991. The report states:

> In each of the last five recessions, men lost at least 9 times as many jobs as
> women did. This fact is primarily attributable to the distribution of male and
> female employees in the various industries and the degree of cyclical job loss in
> each industry during recessions. The goods-producing industries, which employ
> large numbers of men, sustain the greatest job losses during downturns. Certain
> service-producing industries that employ primarily women actually continue to
> grow in recessions.
>
> (Goodman *et al.* 1993: 26)

Houseman and Abraham's study tests women's relative employment volatility in
Japan and the US for the manufacturing sector as a whole. The authors use monthly
data to construct a finite distributed lag model, regressing the logarithmic differences of, separately, women's and men's employment on the logarithmic differences
of current and lagged manufacturing output. Elasticities are constructed for the current month, three months, and twelve months (the latter two being the sum of
coefficient estimates on current output and output lagged through three and twelve
months, respectively). These elasticities are constructed for the 1970 to 1979 and
1980 to 1989 periods. For the US, the most striking result from this study is that
while elasticities were significantly higher for women than men in the 1970s, elasticities were lower for women than men in the 1980s, though not significantly so. In
other words, while in the 1970s women in US manufacturing played a larger role
than men in employment adjustment, the pattern was reversed in the 1980s
(Houseman and Abraham 1993). Cf. also Bettio on Italy, who does not look at total
employment, but who finds an β estimate of 1.413 (significantly greater than 1 at
the 5 percent level) for employment in industry for the span of years from 1959 to
1983 (Bettio 1988: 77).

15 It should be perhaps mentioned that Houseman and Abraham's method of using
monthly data to construct a finite distributed lag model regressing output on – separately – men and women's employment is preferable to the methods used herein
regarding the role of women as a buffer workforce. However, their study looks only
at the manufacturing sector as a whole. This study's concern is not only with the
buffer hypothesis but with the job segregation and substitution hypotheses, requiring
matching data between Germany and Japan at the sectoral and manufacturing
industry levels. Given the considerable difficulty in obtaining even the annual data
used in this data (for which Germany was particularly problematic), the methods
used in this study seemed a reasonable compromise.

16 The unemployment rates for Germany shown in Table 3.1 are derived by taking the
number of unemployed as a percentage of the number of labor-force participants.
Therefore these rates include the self-employed, which are, as Nickell states,
excluded from the unemployment rates provided in the Bundesministerium für Arbeit

und Sozialordnung's *Arbeits- und Sozialstatistik. Hauptergebnisse.* See for instance the notes on page 65 of the 1997 edition.

17 Sorrentino writes that those working part-time for economic reasons includes

> one-half of the number of unemployed persons seeking part-time work and one-half of the number of those involuntarily on part-time schedules for economic reasons. The reasoning behind this formulation is that involuntary part-time workers should be counted as at least partially unemployed; similarly, unemployed persons seeking only part-time work should be given just half the weight of unemployed persons seeking full-time jobs, because their employed counterparts work, on average, only about half of a full workweek.

(Sorrentino 1995: 32)

18 In 1991, for instance, the conventional rate was 3.1 percent in Sweden and 1.9 percent in Japan. Including those working part-time for economic reasons, the rate increases to 6.0 percent in Sweden but only 2.5 percent in Japan. Including discouraged workers in addition, the rate increases to 6.9 percent in Sweden and 6.0 percent in Japan (Sorrentino 1995: 34).

19 See the appendix "Data notes".

20 Based on equation (1), the β estimate for wholesale and retail trade for years 1958 to 1991 is 1.035 and the standard error 0.056; based on equation (2), the β estimate is 1.080 and the standard error 0.069.

21 For the entire 1952 to 1991 period, the dependent variable is made up of β's from equation (1); for the 1973 to 1991 subperiod, the dependent variable is derived from a modified version of equations (1), using dummy variables to account for the shift in the constant and the shift in the slope of measures of women's relative employment volatility after 1973. It should be noted that there is generally less variation to account for among German manufacturing industries, especially for the post-1973 period as indicated by standard deviations of measures of women's relative employment volatility. These are, for the entire 1952 to 1991 post-1973 periods:

	Germany	*Japan*
1952–91	0.149	0.176
1973–91	0.190	0.390

22 Independent variables are made up of within-period averages for all evenly-numbered years, with the exception of female percentages, which are made up of within-period averages for all years. For Japan, data are for production and non-production employees in firms with thirty or more employees. Hourly earnings are derived from the ratio of average monthly earnings over the year to average monthly hours worked over the year. For Germany, data are for wage employees only (*arbeiter*). Hourly earnings are derived from the ratio of average weekly earnings over the year to average weekly hours worked over the year. Union membership data are not available at as disaggregated a level as other data. As a consequence, there are only ten categories of female union propensity for Japan and only seven for Germany. There is also little variability in the ratios of male-to-female hours worked for both Japan and Germany, suggesting the limited value of this variable.

23 For Germany using ordinal rankings, the estimate on the ratio of hourly earnings for the 1952 to 1991 period becomes significant at the 5 rather than 10 percent level; for Japan using ordinal rankings, the estimate on the ratio of hourly earnings for the 1952 to 1991 period becomes significant at the 1 rather than 5 percent level and the estimate of female union propensity for the 1973 to 1991 period becomes significant at the 10 rather than 5 percent level.

24 For the span of years from 1952 to 1991 for Japan, the correlation between β estimates derived from equation (1) and female-to-male standard deviation ratios of logarithmic growth rates of employment is 0.90.

25   At the sectoral level for years 1958 to 1991, the correlation coefficient between female percentage of employment and total employment volatility is –0.12 for Germany and –0.19 for Japan; the correlation coefficient between female percentage of employment and women's relative employment volatility is 0.24 for Germany and –0.24 for Japan.

26   At the manufacturing industry level for years 1952 to 1991, the correlation coefficient between female percentage of employment and total employment volatility is –0.24 for Germany and 0.31 for Japan; for years 1973 to 1991, the correlation coefficient between these same measures is –0.38 for Germany and 0.51 for Japan, with the latter significant at the 5 percent level.

27   At the manufacturing industry level for years 1952 to 1991, the correlation coefficient between female percentage of employment and women's relative employment volatility is –0.11 for Germany and 0.65 for Japan, with the latter significant at the 1 percent level; for years 1973 to 1991, the correlation coefficient between these same measures is 0.06 for Germany and –0.31 for Japan, with both insignificant.

28   The analysis does not consider job segregation for the seven non-agricultural sectors, as there are too few sectors for the analysis to be of much value.

29   Anker does not multiply his dissimilarity index by 100 and so "proportion" in his definition translates to "percentages" for the current chapter.

30   For a given period, that is, one sums the year-to-year values of *SEX* and evaluates this as a percentage of the sum of year-to-year differences in *DI*. For Germany, changes from 1961 to 1962 and 1972 to 1975 are left aside, to abstract from changes in data sources.

31   In her study of the US, Humphries examines the point-to-point movemnet in *DI*, from peak to trough to peak and so on, which does not appear to reveal any obvious pattern (Humphries 1988: 36). A similar analysis is considered here, taking the logarithmic growth rate of total manufacturing employment as an indicator of cyclicality and correlating this measure with, first, the logarithmic growth rate of *DI* and, second, the logarithmic growth of changes in *DI* resulting from *SEX* (that is, taking the value of *DI* in the starting point of 1952 and adding *SEX* for the change 1952 to 1953, and so on). The correlations are negative for Japan and positive for Germany. For years 1952 to 1991, the correlation coefficient for *DI* for Japan is –0.52 (significant at the 1 percent level) and for the change in *DI* resulting from *SEX* is –0.27 (significant at the 10 percent level); for Germany, the correlation coefficient for *DI* is 0.37 (significant at the 5 percent level) and for the change in *DI* resulting from *SEX* is 0.42 (significant at the 5 percent level). For the span of years from 1952 to 1996, the correlation coefficients are somewhat smaller and less significant for both Germany and Japan. Yet the cyclical movement of changes in *DI* and changes in *DI* resulting from *SEX* appears to offer few clearcut insights into the buffer, segregation, and substitution hypotheses, or into the relation among these hypotheses. These correlation are of course determined by the patterns of women's relative employment volatility among manufacturing industries, as shown in Table 2.8. But evidence for these hypotheses and the relationships among them is more clearly revealed by the analysis noted in the main body of this chapter.

32   The source for Japan noted in Table 2.11 is the same source as used elsewhere in this study, but uses data for firms with five or more employees whereas most of the data in the study is for firms with thirty or more employees. However, the former data is only available for the span of years from 1990 on. The twenty-two industry classification is based on what the OECD calls the "Adjusted ISIC Revision 2 Classification" from its *STAN Database for Industrial Analysis* (1998).

33   At the 75-occupation level, the dissimilarity index in 1990 was 60.6 in Finland, 58.6 in France, 52.3 in Germany, 45.8 in Japan, 55.6 in the Netherlands, 56.4 in Norway, 56.9 in Spain, 57.3 in Switzerland (1980), and 56.7 in the United Kingdom, with occupational classifications somewhat different for Germany, Spain and the United

Kingdom. At the 259-occupation level, the dissimilarity index in 1990 was 67.3 in Finland, 60.7 in France, 52.9 in Japan, 58.8 in the Netherlands, 64.6 in Norway, and 65.4 in Switzerland (in 1980) (Anker 1998 112, 117).

3 Industrial relations and labor market institutions

1 By these measures, the experiences of Germany and Japan were not much different from the other advanced economies. For the G7, the female percentage of the labor force increased from 37 to 43 percent over these years; for the fifteen European Union countries, the measure increased from 34 to 41 percent; for the OECD as a whole, the measure increased from 36 to 41 percent (OECD *Historical Statistics* 1997). Women's integration into the labor force is often measured by their labor-force participation rates, and by this measure Germany ranks relatively low as of 1987, with a rate of 42.0, ranking after Sweden (81.1 percent), Norway (63.7), Denmark (57.5), Canada (56.2), the US (54.2), Japan (48.6), Australia (48.3), the United Kingdom (48.2), and France (45.8) (Brinton 1993: 3). However, men's labor-force participation is also somewhat lower in Germany. A related point, cross-country comparisons of labor-force participation rates are sensitive to the age range considered. For ages 15 to 64, for instance, women's labor-force participation rates in Germany are about 60 percent (Table 6.2). In order to abstract from such country-specific factors, the comparison of the female percentage of the labor force seems a preferable measure.

2 Regarding Japan and the US, Taira provides a similar view. He writes that "the deficient proletarianization and homogenization of Japanese labor before World War I resulted in a much more pronounced labor market segmentation in later years in Japan than in the United States" (Taira 1989: 182).

3 In light of this, Rowthorn's distinction between types of corporatist economies may be instructive. Rowthorn distinguishes between corporatist economies such as Germany and Sweden and others such as Japan and Austria, the latter which he associates with "consensus." The former countries, Rowthorn writes "have an inherent dynamic toward equality" whereas the latter "are more conservative and tend to preserve the power relationships and inequalities in existence at the time these orders were established" (Rowthorn 1992: 125, quoted in Milberg 1998: 12).

4 There are considerable cultural differences between Japan and the west in the way that women and women's employment are viewed. It seems reasonable to wonder whether such cultural differences might account for differences in women's employment conditions, but this is a difficult issue not lending itself to ready resolution. If cultural differences are important, it seems they ought to manifest themselves concretely. Perhaps they do, in the institutions this chapter considers. At the same time, the consideration of culture seems of questionable value in explaining why Japanese women's employment conditions diverged from Japanese men's since the mid-1970s, as indicated by widening male–female wage differences and declining female union propensity. For during this time there appears to have been a heightened awareness of the problems of working women, partly the result of the United Nations Decade for Women beginning in 1975 and of the Japan Year of the Woman Conference the following year. It was this context that contributed to the passage in Japan of the Part-Time Labor Law in 1983, the Equal Opportunity Act in 1985, and the Law Concerning Childcare Leave of 1991 (Buckley 1994: 162–5). That Japanese women's employment conditions diverged from Japanese men's over these years suggests, though, that such cultural changes (if they may be fairly called that) were overwhelmed by the constraints of Japan's institutional legacy, as the core of the Japanese employment system came under increased pressure since the mid-1970s. Of course, the institutional legacy itself may well be a manifestation of cultural views, complicating the matter. See Dore (1973), Yasuba (1976), and Jacoby

(1979) for an introduction to the debate on the role of culture as a determinant of Japanese labor institutions, particularly regarding the historical development of the lifetime employment and seniority-based earnings systems. See Brinton (1988, 1992) for an introduction to the gender aspects of the debate.

5 The system also creates strong incentives for firms to apply what Brunello calls "reverse seniority rules" in making layoff decisions (Brunello 1988. Cf. Nakamura and Nitta 1995: 327–8 for a similar account).

6 For male workers in manufacturing in 1970, job turnover rates dropped sharply between the 20 to 24 and 25 to 29 age groups, leveling off thereafter, indicating that it often took workers several years to settle into a position following graduation (Koike 1983a: 41).

7 Nakamura takes this as evidence of the continued prevalence of seniority-based earnings, in direct contradiction with Clark and Ogawa (1992). Nakamura writes that "the seniority wage slope hardly changed after the 1970s and even steepened at the end of the 1980s. It appears the seniority wage system is still alive and well" (Nakamura 1995: 156). Yet age is only a proxy for seniority, and the widening differences may result to some extent from increased interfirm mobility of employees older than entry level age. Tachibanaki compares the 1958–70 and 1975–78 periods and, in a manner similar to Nakamura, states that

> it can be concluded that the basic nenko-wage system survived the extremely bad period in the Japanese economy. For example, experience, which measures the duration of service in a company, did not decline significantly as an important factor in explaining wage differentials.
>
> (Tachibanaki 1982: 449)

8 Jones 1976–7: 592; Kawashima 1987: 611; Tachibanaki 1987: 669; Edwards 1988: 249; Carney and O'Kelly 1990: 127; Ono 1990: 87–8; Peterson and Sullivan 1990: 172–3; Hashimoto 1993: 141; Lam 1993: 198, 218; Kumazawa 1996: 13.

9 The connection between dual labor markets and the seniority-based earnings system was emphasized by Jacoby, who argued that the "crucial enabling factors" for the development of the seniority-based earnings system were "(1) the shift from pre-industrial forms of skilled labor organization and supervision to more bureaucratic styles of management, and (2) the formation of a dual economy and labor market, with *nenko* systems concentrated in the primary or oligopoly sector" (Jacoby 1979: 190).

10 Consistent with this, it is at the second peak of the *M*-shaped curve of Japanese women's labor force participation that the male–female earnings gap is widest in Japan, at ages 45 to 49. As of 1983, Japanese women aged 16 to 19 earned about 90 percent of what Japanese men of the same age earned. This percentage declined to less than 50 percent for the 45 to 49 age group and increased thereafter, to about 60 percent for the 55 to 59 age group (Lam 1992: 48). This picture is confirmed by Koike, who looks at male–female wage differences by age groups in the early and mid-1970s for Germany and Japan as well as France, Italy, and the United Kingdom. Especially for blue-collar workers, male–female wage differences were quite stable by age group for Germany, France, Italy, and the United Kingdom, whereas they widened strongly in Japan, particularly between the 20 to 24 and 35 to 39 age groups. For white-collar workers, male–female wage differences widened for all five countries up to the 40 to 44 age group, but much more strongly so in Japan (Koike 1983b: 114). Consistent with their general exclusion from seniority-based promotion, women in Japan held only 8.8 percent of administrative and managerial positions in recent years, compared with 18.4 percent in Germany and 39.8 percent in the U.S. (Lam 1992: 15). It is something of a misnomer to refer to promotion in Japan as seniority-based, though. It is more accurate to say that Japanese firms rely exceptionally heavily on promotion from within the firm, meaning from within the pool of regular full-time employees (Brinton 1993: 123–34).

11 For instance, the share of women employees who were married increased from 38.6 to 57.8 percent from 1965 to 1993, and the average age of women employees increased from 28.1 to 36.0 over these same years (Kumazawa 1996: 160).

12 Regarding female white-collar workers in Japan, Carney and O'Kelly describe the pressure to retire early as follows:

> Unmarried women who continue to work past the "proper age for marriage" (*tekireiki*) are often subjected to strong pressures from employers and coworkers to quit. Whether unmarried or married, however, women who work beyond the "appropriate years" on a continuous basis often face a sharp diminution of status as their role of office flower is eclipsed and they must be dealt with as truly functional (and possibly threatening) administrative personnel.
>
> (Carney and O'Kelly 1987: 199)

13 Recent books by Kumazawa (1996), Price (1997), and Gordon (1998) suggest though that the characterization of Japan as a high road economy is too blithe, for it neglects the heavy price paid by Japanese workers in the core of the system in terms of stress, overwork, and a lack of independent voice. The intensification of work and the loss of worker voice in the face of a rapidly growing and increasingly competitive economy are, Price notes, reflected in a popular saying of the 1980s: "*keizai taikoku, seikatsu shokoku,*" meaning "powerful economy, impoverished life" (Price 1997: 270). These works provides a useful context for a 1992 survey by the Japanese Ministry of Labour asking Japanese women whether they would want to have the type of jobs that men had. Sixty-five percent of the women interviewed replied that they "wouldn't want them" and only 7 percent replied "definitely yes" (Gordon 1998: 192). Gordon interprets this result as follows: "They [survey respondents] seemed to be saying, 'If the only way to advance is by turning into a total company person, who needs a promotion?'" (ibid.)

14 In most OECD countries the proportion of temporary employment grew little if at all from the mid-1980s to the mid-1990s. The exceptions are Australia, France, the Netherlands, and Spain, where temporary employment grew strongly, and Belgium, Greece, Luxembourg, and Portugal, where temporary employment declined somewhat (OECD 1996: 6).

15 In Japan as of 1991, 38.6 percent of all wage and salary earners were women, compared with 41.3 percent in Germany (OECD 1993a: 24). As of 1994, 9.8 percent of German men worked as temporaries compared with 11.0 percent of German women (including eastern and western Germany). In contrast, only 5.4 percent of Japanese men worked as temporaries compared with 18.3 percent of Japanese women (OECD 1996: 8). Germany and Japan are alike in one respect, though, as regards changes in the proportions of men and women temporary employees. The study notes:

> While there are differences in levels as between men and women, the evolution in the incidence of temporary employment has tended to be similar. That is, where it has increased for men, it has also increased among women [from 1983 to 1994]. The only exceptions are Japan and Germany, where temporary employment increased slightly among men and declined slightly among women, and Denmark, which shows the opposite pattern.
>
> (OECD 1996: 6)

16 A recent ruling by the Japanese Supreme Court might improve the job security of temporary workers. This ruling holds that temporary workers whose contracts are repeatedly renewed by the same firm may not be dismissed arbitrarily, but only for "just cause" (Schregle 1993: 514). The extent to which the ruling will be enforced remains to be seen.

17 The definition has presumably been changed with the establishment of the thirty-five-hour work week for members of the German metalworkers' union, IG Metall.

18 A 1990 survey by the Ministry estimated that 21 percent of part-timers were working full-time hours (Houseman and Osawa 1995: 10).
19 Data on part-time employment are not shown for Italy, Sweden or the US for 1973 to 1989 and 1991 to 1993, as the large discontinuities with other years suggest that a different definition of part-time employment was used.
20 Based on data for the early 1990s, the distribution of part-timers among sectors was fairly similar in Germany, Japan, and the US. In Germany, the following percentages of employment was part-time by sector: in agriculture, 21 percent, in industry, 7 percent, in services, 21 percent; in Japan, the measures were: in agriculture, 25 percent, in industry, 10 percent, in services, 18 percent; in the US, the measures were: in agriculture, 26 percent, in industry, 9 percent, in services, 24 percent (Houseman 1995: 253). Given the high proportion of part-timers who were women (87.0 percent for the US in 1989 (OECD 1991: 46), these can be taken as rough measures of the distribution of women part-timers among sectors.
21 Of the characteristics of female part-timers in Japan, Carney and O'Kelly write, "Most of these women are married, their average age in 1983 was 41.7 years, and more than two-thirds of them were over the age of thirty-five" (Carney and O'Kelly 1990: 133). In contrast, the average age of female permanent regular workers during this time was only 33.5, eight years less than for female part-timers (Kawashima 1987: 604). Of German women returning to work after maternity leave, nearly one-third took up work on a part-time basis (OECD 1995: 188). Using micro datasets, Blau and Kahn note that as of the mid-1980s, 50.8 percent of married women workers in Germany worked part-time (fewer that thirty-five hours per week) compared with only 16.6 percent of single women workers, The significant difference between married and single women in this regard held for all countries Blau and Kahn studied with the exception of the US, for which the difference was much less. Japan was not inluded in the study (Blau and Kahn 1995: 122–3).
22 A similar conclusion is reached by Drobnic, Blossfeld, and Rohwer in their recent study of women's employment patterns in Germany and the US. They write,

> Compared with the U.S., a large number of part-time jobs in Germany are relatively "good" jobs that do not marginalize the workers. . . . In Germany, part-time work seems to be used systematically as a strategy to combine employment and childrearing. However, this form of employment successfully reconciles market work and family for women who primarily depend on their partners for support.
> (Drobnic, Blossfeld, and Rowher 1999: 144)

23 Japan was the only one of seventeen OECD countries for which the former exceeded the latter, though it is not indicated in the source how this is possible or whether the discrepancy results from the use of two different surveys or estimates.
24 Referring to the work of Koike (1983a) and Dore (1973), Lincoln and McBride write of

> how Japanese companies strive to reduce the gap in status and working conditions between blue- and white-collar workers. All employees are on salary; there are no segregated parking lots and cafeterias for production workers; the company union includes lower supervisors and other white-collar workers; and the management/worker wage gap is considerably lower than in the United States.
> (Lincoln and McBride 1987: 292)

25 Union representation in Germany increased from 33.0 percent in 1970 to 35.6 in 1980 (OECD 1994b: 184).
26 The number of women works councilors in the DGB increased little from 1959 to 1969, from 15,281 to 16,246. By 1982, however the number was 38,356 and by 1987 it had increased to 39,032. The female percentage for all work councilors in Germany increased from 11.4 to 19.3 percent from 1968 to 1981 and reached 22.2 percent in 1987 (Cook 1984: 75, Cook *et al.* 1992: 89).

27 Sakuma, for example, attributes much of the declining unionization rate of the economy as a whole to the inclusion of part-timers into the workforce (Sakuma 1988: 3). Yet even Japanese women belonging to unions are likely to be disproportionately affected by layoffs. The problem is described by Hanami, who writes as follows:

> In negotiating or consulting on such matters, companies and unions generally adopt one of two standards for selecting those who must be laid off. One is to select employees whose performance is poor, a standard that might apply more to men than to women; the other is to search out those workers whose personal financial circumstances will presumably be least affected by dismissal. This means, first, young, unmarried employees of both sexes, and, next, married women whose husbands are wage earners, on the assumption that such women are secondary breadwinners and hence that their income is dispensable.
>
> (Hanami 1984: 223–4)

28 It is worth noting that the persistence of Japan's core employment system and the diverging patterns of women's relative employment conditions in Germany and Japan are at odds with the hypothesis predicting the convergence of labor-management relations among countries. A similar conclusion is reached by Locke and Kochan, regarding studies of changing employment relations in ten countries, including Germany and Japan. The authors write as follows:

> The variations in employment practices and outcomes in the country chapters demonstrate that there is not a single natural response to increased market competition. Nor are the variations observed simply random deviations from a single market-determined result. Instead, employment relations are shaped in systematic and predictable ways by institutions that filter these external pressures and by the strategies of key actors. . . . [W]e hope this volume puts to rest the old debate over convergence or lack of convergence of employment systems around the world. In its place should be an active search for both common patterns that reflect the growing interdependence of national economies, the ease of transfer of technologies, information, and organizational innovations, and systematic variations that can be explained by differences in local history the strength of institutions, and the values and strategic choices of key actors.
>
> (Locke and Kochan 1995: 382–4)

29 Women working in the public sector also had the option of taking several years' unpaid leave following the birth of every child, with full job guarantees (Allen 1988: 250).
30 An OECD study on childcare indicates that less than 1 percent of German mothers work part-time while on maternity leave (OECD 1995: 187).
31 Also suggestive is a study by Joshi and Davies of estimated foregone earnings as a result of having children. Compared with women with no children, these authors estimate that German women with one child earn 30 percent less, those with two children nearly 50 percent less, and those with three children 60 percent less over a lifetime. These measures are somewhat higher in Great Britain and very much lower in Sweden and France, and the authors note that "These patterns . . . show a close correlation with the availability of child care facilities" (Joshi and Davies 1992: 576). These sources of earnings loss can be decomposed into the effects of lost years, lost hours, and lower pay. In Germany for women with two children, 60 percent of the estimated loss in lifetime earnings results from lost years, 18 percent from lost hours and 22 percent from lower pay (ibid.: 572). In addition, the seniority-based work rules of many German firms work in disfavor of women who leave employment for extended periods of time. This problem is described by Cook *et al.* as follows:

> [T]he seniority principle as it is used in Germany . . . discriminates against women. Because it assumes continuous employment as the norm, a condition

few women have been able to achieve during the childbearing years, women are handicapped. Further, since years of employment in a single firm are often taken as equivalent to enriched experience and even advancing skill, these qualities are rewarded with wage improvement.

(Cook *et al.* 1992: 95)

More recent studies by Trappe and Rosenfeld (1999) and Stier, Lewin-Epstein, and Braun (1998) reach different conclusions, though, regarding the effect of children and continuous employment on women's earnings in Germany. The result of Trappe and Rosenfeld's study are summarized in Chapter 5. Trappe and Rosenfeld summarize the findings of Stier, Lewin-Epstein, and Braun's comparative study as follows:

Stier, Lewin-Epstien and Braun show that in 1994, mothers "paid" less of their earnings for past reduced and intermittent employment in Germany than in Sweden, the UK, Australia, Canada, Norway, and the US. They suggest that women who conform to the German "male breadwinner" model and stay home with young children or take reduced hours are not penalized later for doing so.

(Trappe and Rosenfeld 1999: 25)

32 Before 1958, two-thirds of women taking career breaks had no children. This declined to 26 percent in the years from 1973 to 1977. Increasingly, then, career breaks in Germany came to be associated less with marriage and more with child-bearing (Kolinsky 1989: 158. Cf. Langkau and Langkau-Herrman 1980: 36).
33 The employment rate of German mothers in 1988 was 31 percent for those with youngest child up to age 2, 41 percent for youngest child between ages 3 and 6, and 50 percent for youngest child between ages 7 and 15, the employment rate of Swedish mothers was 73, 82 and 88 percent and the employment rate of French mothers 50, 59 and 67 percent for each of the respective age groups of youngest children, with mothers' age ranging from 16 to 59 for all three countries (Joshi and Davies 1992: 563).
34 According to Ogawa and Ermisch, the proportion of those aged 60 and over living in extended, three-generation family households was 32 percent in Japan in 1990, compared with 3 percent in Germany and less than 1 percent in the U.S. and Great Britain (Ogawa and Ermisch 1996: 679).

4 Foreign trade, employment, and earnings

1 The focus is on the period up to 1990, as trade data include the former East Germany thereafter.
2 The sixteen-industry classification is used whenever average female percentages over time are considered, as these data are not consistently available over time by the twenty-two industry "Adjusted ISIC Revision 2 Classification." For Japan, the sixteen-industry-level data include firms with thirty or more employees, compared with five or more employees for the twenty-two-industry level data.
3 For a recent summary of economic theories of gender segregation, see Anker's chapter titled "Theories and explanations for occupational segregation by sex" (1998).
4 Based on the period from 1978 to 1995 (1990 for Germany) and using three-year endpoint averages for twenty-two manufacturing industries (noted in Table 2.12), the correlation coefficient between the percentage point difference in net exports relative to domestic consumption and 1990 labor coefficients are as follows: for Germany, 0.68 for OECD trade and 0.14 for non-OECD trade, a difference of 0.54; for Japan, −0.14 for OECD trade and −0.50 for non-OECD trade, a difference of 0.36. These positive differences, what one might call a Heckscher-Ohlin gap, provide evidence that labor-intensive industries are less competitive as regards non-OECD than OECD trade, based on the assumption that Germany and Japan's relative labor endowments are smaller than those of their non-OECD than OECD trading partners.

5 Based on the sixteen-manufacturing-industry classification noted in Table 2.8 using annual averages from 1970 to 1991, correlation coefficients between the female percentage of employment and labor intensity are 0.43 for Germany and 0.46 for Japan, with both significant at the 10 percent level. Based on the twenty-two-manufacturing-industry classification noted in Table 2.12 using data for 1990, correlation coefficients between these measures are 0.44 for Germany and 0.55 for Japan, with the former significant at the 10 percent level and the latter significant at the 1 percent level.

6 That is, trade demand vectors T contain zeros for non-manufacturing industries, and indirect effects from manufacturing trade on non-manufacturing industries (in L) are deleted.

7 For instance, employment and production data are missing for ISIC 383-3825 and 3825 for years prior to 1976.

8 This is revealed by considering average annual growth rates of export and import propensities for Japan for the 1970 to 1995 and 1978 to 1995 periods. For world trade, the annual average growth of import propensities was 3.27 for the period beginning in 1970, and 4.31 for the period beginning in 1978, not a dramatic difference. However, the annual average growth of export propensities for the period beginning in 1970 was 1.96, nearly five times higher than the average for the period beginning in 1978, 0.42. In short, the gap between the average annual growth of export and import propensities was much greater in the 1978 to 1995 than in the 1970 to 1995 period, with the difference accounted for largely by exports.

9 In order to match the averages for export and import propensities and export and import levels in 1993–95, three-year averages are also used for employment levels in the beginning of the period (1978–80) and the female percentage of employment for the manufacturing sector as a whole in the beginning of the period (1978–80).

10 For the construction of average technical coefficients for the 1978 to 1995 period, technical coefficients derived from input–output data for 1990 are averaged with technical coefficients derived from input–output data for 1975 for Japan and 1978 for Germany. Industry-level price deflators are used in the construction of average labor coefficients. Price data are missing for Japan for ISIC 3825, office and computing equipment. Thus labor coefficients for the year of the input–output data are used for this industry for both Germany and Japan. Given the rapid pace of technical change in this industry, this almost certainly results in a more conservative estimate of employment change from trade expansion.

11 For instance, the gender bias for Germany from world trade was –0.43 excluding these industries, compared with –0.49 including them; for Japan, the gender bias from world trade was –3.98 excluding these industries, compared with –3.88 including them.

12 Overall earnings inequality is measured for instance by Gini coefficients or ratios of earnings for workers in higher to lower earnings deciles.

13 From 1974 to 1990, for instance, the female-to-male hourly earnings ratio increased in Germany and decreased in Japan in fourteen of sixteen manufacturing industries. The unweighted average for these sixteen industries increased in Germany from 0.75 to 0.77 and decreased in Japan from 0.55 to 0.51 over these years.

14 With GDP data from the OECD *Economic Outlook* for June 1999.

15 Looking at manufacturing employment as a percentage of non-agricultural employment, the patterns are very similar (based on data noted in Figure 3.2 and 3.3). Specifically, in no year after 1960 was the measure of manufacturing employment as a percentage of all employment one percentage point less than the measure of manufacturing employment as a percentage of non-agricultural employment, for either Germany or Japan.

16 Data for all firms is based on labor-force surveys compiled in the *ILO Yearbook of Labour Statistics* while data on firms for thirty or more employees is based on establishment surveys from the Japan Ministry of Labour's *Yearbook of Labour Statistics*.

17 The industry-level data from which the correlation coefficients are derived indicate that the strong negative correlation in Germany is driven in large part by employment losses in three industries: textiles; apparel; and leather and leather products. These industries rank in the top three by female percentage of employment and the bottom three by employment growth. The average annual decline of relative employment growth from 1970 to 1991 was –3.26 percent for textiles, –4.18 percent for wearing apparel, and –4.49 percent for leather products and footwear (relative to the manufacturing sector as a whole). These industries experienced three to four times more employment loss than non-metallic mineral products, which had the next greatest employment loss.

18 Wood (1994: 407–4, 1995: 67) argues for the importance of defensive labor displacing technical change while Burtless (1995: 811–13) expresses skepticism.

19 A similar result regarding the increased importance of job tenure and age was found by Hill, who evaluates the span of years from 1965 to 1988. After controlling for age, job tenure, and firm size, Hill finds that the female-to-male hourly wage ratio narrowed strongly from 1969 to 1976, from about 0.74 to 0.83. This adjusted ratio remained flat thereafter, averaging about 0.83 (Hill 1996: 153–4). Hill's and Tachibanaki's work appears to make use of the same micro dataset, referred to as the "Basic Survey on Wage Structure" by Hill (1996: 161) and the "Wage Structure Survey" by Tachibanaki (1996: 25). The evidence from both Hill and Tachibanaki regarding job tenure also suggests the persistence and even increased importance since the mid-1970s of seniority-based earnings in Japan.

20 In a sense, the finding that in Japan gender is in and of itself the most important determinant of overall wage differences creates an opening for institutional explanations. But even if, say, the gender wage gap in Japan completely disappeared when controlling for job tenure, the opening would still exist, as is suggested by the discussion here. This holds for other "slice in time" analyses of wage determinants, which too often beg the question of what truly underlies wage differences. That is, it is not a sufficient explanation to show that lower-paid workers are less educated, are in lower-paying occupations, and have less job tenure. For the questions remains as to why lower-paid workers have these characteristics and the extent to which they are true measures of productivity.

21 Regarding Japan, Freeman cites two studies (Nakamura, Sato, and Kamiya 1988; Osawa 1989) finding that union membership is associated with 10 percent higher wages for Japanese women but no higher wages for Japanese men (Freeman 1994: 288). In their study of earnings inequality in the US and Japan, Kalleberg and Lincoln find a negative union membership effect on earnings for both male and female workers in Japan. But, as the authors write:

> [T]here is little evidence from past research on Japanese collective bargaining to suggest that they [unions] actually depress earnings. Since the zero-order correlation between the presence of a union contract and earnings is positive in both countries (though this correlation is smaller in Japan), it could be that the negative effect of unionization in Japan . . . reflects its collinearity with the many other variables associated with the incidence of unionism that are included in our model.
> (Kalleberg and Lincoln 1994: S146–S147)

Though they consider men and women separately, the results of Kalleberg and Lincoln's study are generally consistent with those of Tachibanaki (1982, 1996). They write for instance of the greater importance for earnings in the US of "job characteristics, positions in the authority hierarchy, and (for workers) unions representation" whereas in Japan they write that earnings "are conditioned more by 'life-cycle' variables such as age and by the organizational structures and processes associated with firm internal labor markets – seniority, promotions, internal training" (Kalleberg and Lincoln 1994: S121).

22 From 1990 to 1996, for instance, the female-to-male hourly earnings ratio increased

in Japan in sixteen of sixteen manufacturing industries. The unweighted average for these sixteen industries increased in Japan from 0.51 to 0.55 over these years.

23 To summarize briefly, the number of part-time workers, men and women alike, increased in both Germany and Japan since the mid-1970s (Table 4.4). As of the late 1980s, about 30 percent of female employees in both Germany and Japan worked as part-timers (OECD 1991: 46). But there were substantial differences in the nature of women's part-time employment in Germany and Japan, differences that appear relevant to the diverging pattern of male–female wage differences. About 40 percent of German part-timers (those working more than 21 hours per week) are considered "regular part-time workers," with similar wages, benefits, and job security to regular full-time employees (Kolinsky 1989: 178, 180–1; OECD 1991: 44, 48). In Japan, part-timers are classified not by data collection agencies but by employers (Hashimoto 1993: 141). As of the mid-1980s, an estimated one-quarter of Japanese part-timers actually work full-time (Saso 1990: 145). Japanese employers have a strong monetary incentive to classify workers as part-timers, since they then are not part of the regular system of benefits and seniority-based earnings. Japanese part-time female employees over age twenty received only 60 to 70 percent of a regular female employee's wages, as well as far fewer benefits (Kawashima 1987: 604; Houseman 1995: 257).

Temporary employees are typically paid a good deal less than regular employees. In Germany and Japan in recent years, one out ten employees worked on a temporary basis, with the proportion somewhat smaller for manufacturing employees. For Germany, 45.1 percent of temporaries were women in 1991, somewhat higher than the female percentage of employees. For Japan, 72.3 percent of temporaries were women, highest among the sixteen OECD countries for which such data are available (OECD 1993a: 24). Also significant is the age distribution of temporary employees. In Germany, the majority of temporaries (58.3 percent) were in the 15 to 24 age group, whereas the majority of temporaries in Japan (58.0 percent) were in the 25 to 54 age group. Given the context of the seniority-based earnings system in Japan, the high proportion of mostly women temporary workers in the older age group likely plays a role in the pattern of male–female wage differences in Japan.

5 German reunification

1 Some provide a higher figure for the percentage of East German women employed on a part-time basis, at about 25 percent, but without offering a clear definition of part-time work (e.g. Brander 1990: 42). That the percentage of women working part-time is higher in East than West Germany is also indicated by Gillian Preece, who writes that "part time work is not as prevalent in the former German Democratic Republic (GDR) where one in 20 mothers worked less than 25 hours per week in contrast to one in five in the FRG" (Preece 1992).

2 One of the causes of the labor shortage was the large-scale emigration from East to West that continued from 1949 until 1961, when the Berlin Wall went up. During these years, 2.7 million persons moved from East to West Germany, 14 percent of the East's 1949 population (Sorensen and Trappe 1995: 399).

3 As of 1988, the average age at first marriage was 25.0 for men and 22.9 for women in the East, compared with average ages of 28.0 for men and 25.5 for women in the West; as of 1989, the average age of women at the birth of the first child was 22.9 in the East and 26.7 in the West; and 90 percent of East German women had at least one child, compared with 85 percent of West German women (Quack and Maier 1994: 1260; Walper 1995: 5; Adler 1997: 41; Trappe and Rosenfeld 1999: 10).

4 On an hourly basis, women in West Germany made between 70 and 75 percent as much as men in the manufacturing and non-agricultural sectors in the 1980s (Figures 3.1 and 3.2).

5 Occupations are measured in two ways. First, by the female percentage of workers in forty-seven occupations, grouped in five quintiles. Second, using a set of twenty-four occupational dummy variables. Either measure provides "virtually the same results" (Sorensen and Trappe 1995: 401, 403).

6 Trappe and Rosenfeld use the *West German Life History Study* and the *East German Life History Study* datasets to estimate the effect on earnings of having children for men and women workers (Trappe and Rosenfeld 1999). The authors find that the gender earnings gap in East Germany persisted even after accounting for the influence of having children and a range of other plausible determinants of earnings. The authors examine monthly earnings for all full-time and part-time workers, in the West for birth cohorts 1954 to 1956 and 1959 to 1961 in 1991, in the East for birth cohorts 1951 to 1953 and 1959 to 1961 in 1989. In the West, having children is estimated to have a sizeable positive effect on men's earnings and a sizeable negative effect on women's earnings. The "child penalty" influenced West German women's earnings not through labor-force experience or job tenure, but through part-time employment status (Trappe and Rosenfeld 1999: 25). For East Germany, the most striking finding is that having children had essentially no effect on men or women's earnings (ibid.: Table 1). In some model specifications, having children had an estimated positive effect on men's earnings in East Germany, but this finding is not robust with respect to alternative model specifications (ibid.: 25).

7 In West Germany, for a 1988 sample of 45,000 firms with more than twenty employees or more than 2 million marks in annual revenues (Antal and Krebsbach-Gnath 1993: 50).

8 The convergence of social policies was far-ranging, as Rosenberg points out. She writes,

> Upon unification on October 3, 1990, the West Germany legal code took effect (with certain exceptions) in GDR territory. The Bonn coalition had announced August 23, 1990, that all superior rights or benefits provided in the GDR would be reduced to FRG levels.
>
> (Rosenberg 1991: 134)

9 There was also from 1989 to 1991 a sharp increase in mortality rates for a wide age range of men and women in the East (Eberstadt 1994: 146).

10 Since the number of women labor-force participants actually declined from 1991 to 1996 by 163,000 greater than the decline of the population of women in this age group, the equalization of women's labor-force participation in East and West means that 901,000 women (163,000 plus 738,000) would have had to leave the labor force from 1991 to 1996 (that is, after adjusting for the decline in the population of women aged 15 to 64 in the East from 5,392,000 in 1991 to 5,204,000 in 1996) (*Arbeits- und Sozialstatistik*).

Bibliography

Abraham, Katherine and Susan Houseman. 1989. "Job Security and Work Force Adjustment: How Different are U.S. and Japanese Practices?" *NBER Working Paper Series*, Working Paper no. 3155.

Adler, Marina. 1997. "Social Change and Declines in Marriage and Fertility in Eastern Germany." *Journal of Marriage and the Family* 59 (Feb.): 37–49.

Adler, Marina and April Brayfield. 1997. "Women's Work Values in Unified Germany: Regional Differences as Remnants of the Past." *Work and Occupations* 24(2): 245–66.

Allen, Joseph. 1988. "European Infant Care Leaves: Foreign Perspectives on the Integration of Work and Family Roles," in Edward Zigler and Meryl Frank (eds), *The Parental Leave Crisis: Toward a National Policy*. New Haven, Conn. and London: Yale University Press.

Andrews, Edmund. 1997. "Bonn's Blank Check Buys Hollow Economy." *New York Times* (April 17).

Anker, Richard. 1998. *Gender and Jobs: Sex Segregation of Occupations in the World*. Geneva: International Labour Organization.

Antal, Ariane Berthoin and Camilla Krebsbach-Gnath. 1993. "Women in Management in Germany: East, West, and Reunited." *International Studies of Management and Organization* 23(2): 49–69.

Atkins, Ralph. 1999. "German Jobs Figures Take Shine off Euro." *Financial Times* (Jan. 9–10): 3.

Bank of Japan. 1994. "The Japanese Employment System." *Bank of Japan Quarterly Bulletin* (May): 52–85.

Bastelaer, Alois van, Georges Lemaitre, and Pascal Marianna. 1997. "The Definition of Part-Time Work for the Purpose of International Comparisons." *OECD Labour Market and Social Policy Occasional Papers*, no. 22.

Baxter, Marianne and Robert King. 1995. "Measuring Business Cycles: Approximate Band-Pass Filters for Economic Time Series." *NBER Working Paper Series*, Working Paper no. 5022.

Bean, Charles. 1994. "European Unemployment: A Survey." *Journal of Economic Literature* 32 (June): 573–619.

Beck, Barbara. 1998. "Where East Meets West." *Economist* (July 18): S5.

Bednarzik, Robert and Clinton Shiells. 1989. "Labor Market Changes and Adjustments: How do the US and Japan Compare?" *Monthly Labor Review* 112(2): 31–42.

Beissinger, Thomas and Joachim Moeller. 1998. "Wage Flexibility and Employment Performance: A Microdata Analysis of Different Age-Education Groups for Germany." *Regensburger Diskussionsbeitraege*, nr. 307 (May).

Belman, Dale and Thea Lee. 1996. "International Trade and the Performance of US Labor Markets," in Robert Blecker (ed.), *U.S. Trade Policy and Global Growth: New Directions in the International Economy*. Armonk, NY: M. E. Sharpe.

Bettio, Francesca. 1988. "Sex-Typing of Occupations, the Cycle, and Restructuring in Italy," in Jill Rubery (ed.), *Women and Recession*. London and New York: Routledge and Kegan Paul.

Bhagwati, Jagdish and Marvin Kosters (eds). 1994. *Trade and Wages: Leveling Wages Down?* Washington, D.C.: AEI Press.

Blanchflower, David and Andrew Oswald. 1995. "An Introduction to the Wage Curve." *Journal of Economic Perspectives* 9(3): 153–67.

Blank, Rebecca. 1994. *Social Protection versus Economic Flexibility: Is There a Trade-off?* Chicago: University of Chicago Press.

—— 1997. "Is There a Trade-Off Between Unemployment and Inequality?" *Jerome Levy Economics Institute of Bard College Public Policy Brief*, 33.

Blau, Francine and Lawrence Kahn. 1994. "International Differences in Male Wage Inequality: Institutions Versus Market Forces." *NBER Working Paper Series*, Working Paper no. 4678 (March).

—— 1995. "The Gender Earnings Gap: Some International Evidence," in Richard Freeman and Lawrence Katz (eds), *Differences and Changes in Wage Structures*. Chicago: The University of Chicago Press.

—— 1997. "Gender and Youth Employment Outcomes: The US and West Germany, 1984–1991." *NBER Working Paper Series*, Working Paper no. 6078.

Bleakley, Hoyt and Jeffrey Fuhrer. 1997. "Shifts in the Beveridge Curve, Job Matching, and Labor Market Dynamics." *New England Economic Review* (Sept.–Oct.): 3–19.

Blöndal, Sveinbjörn and Mark Pearson. 1995. "Unemployment and Other Non-Employment Benefits." *Oxford Review of Economic Policy* 11(1): 136–69.

Brander, Sylvia. 1990. "The Employment of Women in the Former GDR." *Info Digest* 43(4): 42–7.

Braun, Michael, Jacqueline Scott, and Duane Alwin. 1994. "Economic Necessity or Self-Actualization? Attitudes Toward Women's Labour-Force Participation in East and West Germany." *European Sociological Review* 10(1): 29–47.

Brinton, Mary. 1988. "The Social-Institutional Bases of Gender Stratification: Japan as an Illustrative Case." *American Journal of Sociology* 94(2): 300–34.

—— 1992. "Christmas Cakes and Wedding Cakes: The Social Organization of Japanese Women's Life Course," in Takie Sugyama Lebra (ed.), *Japanese Social Organization*. Honolulu: University of Hawaii Press.

—— 1993. *Women and the Economic Miracle: Gender and Work in Postwar Japan*. Berkeley: University of California Press.

Brodsky, Melvin. 1994. "Labor Market Flexibility: A Changing International Perspective." *Monthly Labor Review* 117(11): 53–60.

Brown, Clair, Yoshifumi Nakata, Michael Reich, and Lloyd Ulman. 1997. *Work and Pay in the United States and Japan*. Oxford: Oxford University Press.

Brunello, Giorgio. 1985. "Labour Adjustment in Japanese Incorporated Enterprises: An Empirical Analysis for the Period 1965–1983." *Hitotsubashi Journal of Economics* 26(2): 165–80.

—— 1988. "Organizational Adjustment and Institutional Factors in Japanese Labour Market Adjustment: An Empirical Evaluation." *European Economic Review* 32(4): 841–60.

—— 1990. "Hysteresis and 'The Japanese Unemployment Problem': A Preliminary Investigation." *Oxford Economic Papers* 42 (June): 483–500.

Bruno, Michael and Jeffrey Sachs. 1985. *The Economics of Worldwide Stagflation*. Oxford: Blackwell.

Buchele, Robert and Jens Christiansen. 1996. "Does Employment and Income Security Cause Unemployment? A Comparative Study of the U.S. and the E-4." Paper presented at the Conference on European Employment Systems and the Welfare State.

Buckley, Sandra. 1994. "A Short History of the Feminist Movement in Japan," in Joyce Gelb and Marian Lief Palley (eds), *Women of Japan and Korea: Continuity and Change*. Philadelphia: Temple University Press.

Burtless, Gary. 1995. "International Trade and the Rise in Earnings Inequality." *Journal of Economic Literature* 33 (June): 800–16.

Calmfors, Lars and John Driffil. 1988. "Centralization of Wage Bargaining." *Economic Policy* (April): 13–61.

Card, David, Francis Kramarz, and Thomas Lemieux. 1995. "Changes in the Relative Structure of Wages and Employment: A Comparison of the United States, Canada, and France." Industrial Relations Section, Princeton University, Working Paper no. 355 (December).

Card, David and Alan Krueger. 1995. *Myth and Measurement: The New Economics of the Minimum Wage*. Princeton, NJ: Princeton University Press.

Carney, Larry and Charlotte O'Kelly. 1987. "Barriers and Constraints to the Recruitment and Mobility of Female Managers in the Japanese Labor Force." *Human Resource Management* 26 (Summer): 193–216.

—— 1990. "Women's Work and Women's Place in the Japanese Economic Miracle," in Kathryn Ward (ed.), *Women Workers and Global Restructuring*. Ithaca, NY: ILR Press.

Casey, Bernard, Rüdiger Dragendorf, Walter Heering, and Gunnar John. 1989. "Temporary Employment in Great Britain and the Federal Republic of Germany: An Overview." *International Labour Review* 128(4): 449–66.

Clark, Robert and Naohiro Ogawa. 1992. "Employment Tenure and Earnings Profiles in Japan and the United States: Comment." *American Economic Review* 82(1): 336–54.

Cole, Robert. 1971. *Japanese Blue Collar: The Changing Tradition*. Berkeley, Calif.: University of California Press.

Cook, Alice. 1984. "Federal Republic of Germany," in Alice Cook, Val Lorwin, and Arlene Kaplan Daniels (eds), *Women and Trade Unions in Eleven Industrialized Countries*. Philadelphia: Temple University Press.

Cook, Alice, Val Lorwin, and Arlene Kaplan Daniels. 1992. *The Most Difficult Revolution: Women and Trade Unions*. Ithaca, NY and London: Cornell University Press.

Curry, James. 1993. "The Flexibility Fetish: A Review Essay on Flexible Specialisation." *Capital and Class* 50 (Summer): 99–126.

de Neubourg, Chris. 1985. "Part-time Work: An International Quantitative Comparison." *International Labour Review* 124 (Sept.–Oct.): 559–76.

Deven, Fred, Sheila Inglis, Peter Moss, and Pat Petrie. 1998. "State of the Art Review on the Reconciliation of Work and Family Life for Men and Women and the Quality of Care Sevices." European Commission Department for Education and Employment Research Report no. 44.

Doeringer, Peter and Michael Piore. 1971. *Internal Labor Markets and Manpower Analysis*. Lexington, Mass.: D. C. Heath.

Dölling, Irene. 1991. "Between Hope and Helplessness: Women in the GDR after the 'Turning Point'." *Feminist Review* 39 (Winter): 3–15.

Dombois, Rainer. 1989. "Flexibility by Law? The West German Employment Promotion Act and Temporary Employment." *Cambridge Journal of Economics* 13 (June): 359–71.

Dore, Ronald. 1973. *British Factory, Japanese Factory: The Origins of Diversity in Industrial Relations*. Berkeley, Calif.: University of California Press.

Drobnic, Sonja, Hans-Peter Blossfeld, and Götz Rohwer. 1999. "Dynamics of Women's Employment Patterns over the Family Life Course: A Comparison of the United States and Germany." *Journal of Marriage and the Family* 61 (Feb.): 133-46.

Eatwell, John and Lance Taylor. 2000. *Global Finance at Risk: The Case for International Regulation*. New York: New Press.

Eberstadt, Nicholas. 1994. "Demographic Shocks After Communism: Eastern Germany, 1989–93." *Population and Development Review* 20(1): 137–52.

Edwards, Linda. 1988. "Equal Employment Opportunity in Japan: A View from the West." *Industrial and Labor Relations Review* 41 (Jan.): 240–50.

Engelbrech, Gerhard. 1991. "The Labor Market for Women in the Old and New Länder of the Federal Republic of Germany." *Labour* 5 (Winter): 105–21.

Ferree, Myra Marx. 1993. "The Rise and Fall of 'Mommy Politics': Feminism and Unification in (East) Germany." *Feminist Studies* 19(1): 89–115.

Fortin, Nicole and Thomas Lemieux. 1997. "Institutional Changes and Rising Wage Inequality: Is There a Linkage?" *Journal of Economic Perspectives* 11(2): 75–96.

Freeman, Richard. 1994. "American Exceptionalism in the Labor Market: Union–Nonunion Differentials in the United States and Other Countries," in Clark Kerr and Paul Staudohar (eds), *Labor Economics and Industrial Relations*, Cambridge, Mass.: Harvard University Press.

—— 1995. "Are Your Wages Set in Beijing?" *Journal of Economic Perspectives* 9(3): 15–32.

Freeman, Richard and Lawrence Katz. 1994: "Rising Wage Inequality: The United States vs. Other Advanced Countries," in Richard Freeman (ed.), *Working Under Different Rules*. New York: Russell Sage Foundation.

Fukui, Haruhiro, Peter Merkl, Hubertus Müller-Groeling, and Akio Watanabe. 1993. *The Politics of Economic Change in Postwar Japan and West Germany, Volume 1: Macroeconomic Conditions and Policy Responses*. New York: St Martin's Press.

Fuji Economic Review. 1990. "The Current Labor Shortage and Its Prospects." (March–April): 5–13.

Galbraith, James, William Darity, Jr. and Jiaqing Lu. 1998. "Measuring the Evolution of Inequality in the Global Economy." *Center for Economic Policy Analysis Working Papers on International Capital Markets and the Future of Economic Policy*, Working Paper no. 4 (May).

Glyn, Andrew. 1995. "The Assessment: Unemployment and Inequality." *Oxford Review of Economic Policy* 11(1): 1–25.

Godley, Wynne. 1998. "Motor Starts to Sputter." *Financial Times* (July 10): 12.

Goodman, William, Stephen Antczak, and Laura Freeman. 1993. "Women and Jobs in Recessions: 1969–1992." *Monthly Labor Review* 116(7): 26–35.

Gordon, Andrew. 1998. *The Wages of Affluence: Labor and Management in Postwar Japan*. Cambridge, Mass.: Harvard University Press.

Gordon, David. 1996. *Fat and Mean: The Corporate Squeeze of Working Americans and the Myth of Managerial "Downsizing."* New York: Free Press.

Gordon, Robert. 1987. "Productivity, Wages, and Prices Inside and Outside of Manufacturing in the U.S., Japan, and Europe." *European Economic Review* 31 (Apr.): 685–739.

Gornick, Janet, Marcia Meyers, and Katherin Ross. 1997. "Supporting the Employment of Mothers: Policy Variation Across Fourteen Welfare States." *Journal of European*

Social Policy 7(1): 45–70.

Green, Francis and Thomas Weisskopf. 1990. "The Worker Discipline Effect: A Disaggregative Analysis." *Review of Economics and Statistics* (May): 241–9.

Gustafsson, Siv. 1992. "Separate Taxation and Married Women's Labor Supply." *Journal of Population Economics* 5: 61–85.

Gustafsson, Siv, Cecile Wetzels, Jan Dirk Vlasblom, and Shirley Dex. 1996. "Women's Labor Force Transitions in Connection with Childbirth: A Panel Data Comparison between Germany, Sweden and Great Britain." *Journal of Population Economics* 9: 223–46.

Hamada, Koichi and Yoshio Kurosaka. 1984. "The Relationship Between Production and Unemployment in Japan: Okun's Law in Comparative Perspective." *European Economic Review* 25(1): 71–94.

—— 1986. "Trends in Unemployment, Wages and Productivity: The Case of Japan." *Economica* 53(210(S)): 272–96.

Hanami, Tadashi. 1984. "Japan," in Alice Cook, Val Lorwin, and Arlene Kaplan Daniels (eds), *Women and Trade Unions in Eleven Industrialized Countries*. Philadelphia: Temple University Press.

Hashimoto, Masanori. 1993. "Aspects of Labor Market Adjustments in Japan." *Journal of Labor Economics* 11 (Jan.): 136–61.

Hashimoto, Masanori and John Raisian. 1985. "Employment Tenure and Earnings Profiles in Japan and the United States." *American Economic Review* 75(4): 721–35.

—— 1992. "Aspects of Labor Market Flexibility in Japan and the United States," in Kazutoshi Koshiro (ed.), *Employment Security and Labor Market Flexibility: An International Perspective*. Detroit: Wayne State University Press.

Hesse, Beate. 1984. "Women at Work in the Federal Republic of Germany," in Marilyn Davidson and Cary Cooper (eds), *Working Women: An International Survey*. Chichester, UK: Wiley.

Hill, M. Anne. 1996. "Women in the Japanese Economy," in Susan Horton (ed.), *Women and Industrialization in Asia*. London: Routledge.

Houseman, Susan. 1995. "Part-Time Employment in Europe and Japan." *Journal of Labor Research* 16(3): 249–62.

Houseman, Susan and Katharine Abraham. 1993. "Female Workers as a Buffer in the Japanese Economy." *AEA Papers and Proceedings* 83 (May): 45–51.

Houseman, Susan and Machiko Osawa. 1995. "Part-Time and Temporary Employment in Japan." *Monthly Labor Review* (Oct.): 10–18.

Humphries, Jane. 1988. "Women's Employment in Restructuring America: The Changing Experience of Women in Three Recessions," in Jill Rubery (ed.), *Women and Recession*. London and New York: Routledge and Kegan Paul.

Hunt, Jennifer. 1997. "The Transition in East Germany: When is a Ten Point Fall in the Gender Wage Gap Bad News?" *NBER Working Paper Series*, Working Paper no. 6167 (September).

—— 1999. "Determinants of Non-Employment and Unemployment Durations in East Germany." *NBER Working Paper Series*, Working Paper no. 7128 (May).

Ifo Institute for Economic Research and Sakura Institute of Research. 1997. *A Comparative Analysis of Japanese and German Economic Success*. Tokyo: Springer.

International Herald Tribune (anonymous) 1999. "In Germany, West Gains as More Lose Jobs in East" (November 10): 17.

Ishibashi, Asako. 1995. "Career Women Finally Get a Break – To Have Babies." *Nikkei Weekly* (Sept. 25): 1, 4.

Jackman, R. and R. Layard and S. Nickell. 1996. "Combatting Unemployment: Is Flexibility Enough?" *Centre for Economic Performance Discussion Paper* no. 293 (March).

Jacoby, Sanford. 1979. "The Origins of Internal Labor Markets in Japan." *Industrial Relations* 18(2): 184–96.

Japan Statistics Bureau. 1995, 1997. *Japan Statistical Yearbook.* Tokyo: Nihon Tokei Kyokai.

Jones, H. J. 1976–7. "Japanese Women and the Dual-Track Employment System." *Pacific Affairs* 49 (Winter): 589–606.

Joshi, Heather and Hugh Davies. 1992. "Day Care in Europe and Mothers' Forgone Earnings." *International Labour Review* 132(6): 561–79.

Kalleberg, Arne and James Lincoln. 1994. "The Structure of Earnings Inequality in the United States and Japan." *American Journal of Sociology* 94 (Supplement): S121–S153.

Katz, Lawrence, Gary Loveman, and David Blanchflower. 1995. "A Comparison of Changes in the Structure of Wages in Four OECD Countries," in Richard Freeman and Lawrence Katz (eds), *Differences and Changes in Wage Structures.* Chicago: University of Chicago Press.

Kawamura, Hiroshi. 1994. "Lifetime Employment in Japan: Economic Rationale and Future Prospects." *United Nations Department for Economic and Social Information and Policy Analysis Working Paper Series*, no. 5.

Kawashima, Yoko. 1987. "The Place and Role of Female Workers in the Japanese Labor Market." *Women's Studies International Forum* 10(6): 599–611.

Koike, Kazuo. 1983a. "Internal Labor Markets: Workers in Large Firms," in Taishiro Shirai (ed.), *Contemporary Industrial Relations in Japan.* Madison, Wisc.: University of Wisconsin Press.

—— 1983b. "Workers in Small Firms and Women in Industry," in Taishiro Shirai (ed.), *Contemporary Industrial Relations in Japan.* Madison, Wisc.: University of Wisconsin Press.

Kolinsky, Eva. 1989. *Women in West Germany: Life, Work, and Politics.* Providence and Oxford: Berg.

König, Heinz. 1987. "Comments: 'Productivity, Wages, and Prices Inside and Outside of Manufacturing in the U.S., Japan, and Europe,' by Robert J. Gordon." *European Economic Review* 31 (April): 736–9.

Krueger, Alan and Jörn-Steffan Pischke. 1995. "A Comparative Analysis of East and West German Labor Markets: Before and After Unification," in Richard Freeman and Lawrence Katz (eds), *Differences and Changes in Wage Structures.* Chicago: University of Chicago Press.

—— 1997. "Observations and Conjectures on the U.S. Employment Miracle." *NBER Working Paper Series*, Working Paper no. 6146 (August).

Kucera, David. 1997a. *Labor Adjustment in Japan and the Former West Germany: The Role of Women as a Buffer Workforce.* Unpublished dissertation, New School for Social Research.

—— 1997b. "Women and Labor Market Flexibility: The Cases of Japan and the Former West Germany in the Postwar Years," in Ellen Mutari, Heather Boushey, and William Fraher IV (eds), *Gender and Political Economy: Incorporating Diversity into Theory and Policy.* Armonk, NY: M. E. Sharpe.

—— 1998. "Foreign Trade and Men and Women's Employment and Earnings in Germany and Japan." *CEPA Working Papers on Globalization, Labor Markets, and Social Policy: A Project Funded by the John D. and Catherine T. MacArthur*

Foundation, Working Paper no. 9, April 1998 (revised August 1998).

Kucera, David and William Milberg. 2000. "Gender Segregation and Gender Bias in Manufacturing Trade Expansion: Revisiting the 'Wood Asymmetry'." *World Development* 28(7): 1191–1210.

Kumazawa, Makoto. 1996. *Portraits of the Japanese Workplace: Labor Movements, Workers, and Managers*. Boulder, Colo.: Westview.

Kume, Ikuo. 1998. *Disparaged Success: Labor Politics in Postwar Japan*. Ithaca, NY: Cornell University Press.

Kurosaka, Yoshi. 1989. "The Japanese Economy and the Labor Market." *Japanese Economic Studies* 17(4): 3–40.

Kuznets, Stanley. 1968. "Notes on Japan's Economic Growth," in Lawrence Klein and Kazushi Ohkawa (eds), *Economic Growth: The Japanese Experience since the Meiji Era*. Homewood, Ill.: R. D. Irwin.

Lam, Alice. 1992. *Women and Japanese Management: Discrimination and Reform*. London and New York: Routledge.

—— 1993. "Equal Employment Opportunities for Japanese Women: Changing Company Practice," in Janet Hunter (ed.), *Japanese Women Working*. London: Routledge.

Langkau, Jochem and Monika Langkau-Herrmann. 1980. "Federal Republic of Germany," in Alice Yohalem (ed.), *Women Returning to Work: Policies and Progress in Five Countries*. Montclair, NJ: Allanheld, Osmun.

Leamer, Edward. 1994 "Trade, Wages and Revolving-Door Ideas." *NBER Working Paper Series*, Working Paper no. 4716.

Lee, Thea and John Schmitt. 1996. "Trade and Income Distribution: Theory, New Evidence, and Policy Alternatives," unpublished paper prepared for the Center for Economic Policy Analysis Workshop Series.

Lincoln, James and Kerry McBride. 1987. "Japanese Industrial Organization in Comparative Perspective." *Annual Review of Sociology* 13: 289–312.

Locke, Richard and Thomas Kochan. 1995. "Conclusion: The Transformation of Industrial Relations? A Cross-National Review of the Evidence," in Richard Locke, Thomas Kochan, and Michael Piore (eds), *Employment Relations in a Changing World Economy*. Cambridge, Mass.: MIT Press.

Locke, Richard, Thomas Kochan, and Michael Piore. 1995. "Introduction: Employment Relations in a Changing World Economy," in Richard Locke, Thomas Kochan, and Michael Piore (eds), *Employment Relations in a Changing World Economy*. Cambridge, Mass.: MIT Press.

McKinsey Global Institute. 1997. "Executive Summary," in *Removing Barriers to Growth and Employment in France and Germany*. Frankfurt, Paris, Washington: McKinsey Global Institute.

Macpherson, W. J. 1987. *The Economic Development of Japan, 1868–1941*. Basingstoke: Macmillan.

Mahnkopf, Birgit. 1992. "The 'Skill-Oriented' Strategies of German Trade Unions: Their Impact on Efficiency and Equality Objectives." *British Journal of Industrial Relations* 30(1): 61–81.

Maier, Friederike. 1993. "The Labour Market for Women and Employment Perspectives in the Aftermath of German Unification." *Cambridge Journal of Economics* 17(2): 267–80.

Mairesse, Jacques. 1984. "Comments on 'The Relationship Between Production and Unemployment in Japan: Okun's Law in Comparative Perspective.' by K. Hamada and Y. Kurosaka." *European Economic Review* 25(1): 99–105.

Metcalf, David. 1987. "Labour Market Flexibility and Jobs: A Survey of Evidence from OECD Countries with Special Reference to Europe," in Richard Layard and Lars Calmfors (eds), *The Fight Against Unemployment: Macroeconomic Papers from the Centre for European Studies*. Cambridge, Mass.: MIT Press.

Meulders, Daniele, Robert Plasman, and Valerie Vander Stricht. 1993. *Position of Women on the Labour Market in the European Community*. Aldershot, UK: Dartmouth.

Milberg, William. 1997. "Globalization and International Competitiveness," in Paul Davidson and Jan Kregel (eds), *Improving the Global Economy: Keynesianism and the Growth in Output and Employment*. Cheltenham, UK: Elgar.

—— 1998. "Technological Change, Social Policy and International Competitiveness." *Center for Economic Policy Analysis Working Papers on Globalization, Labor Markets, and Social Policy*, Working Paper no. 7.

Mincer, Jacob and Yoshio Higuchi. 1988. "Wage Structures and Labor Turnover in the United States and Japan." *Journal of the Japanese and International Economies* 2(2): 97–133.

Nakamoto, Michiyo. 1999. "Japan Struggling to Adjust to the End of Jobs for Life." *Financial Times* (June 2): 4.

Nakamura, Keisuke and Michio Nitta. 1995. "Developments in Industrial Relations and Human Resource Practices in Japan," in Richard Locke, Thomas Kochan, and Michael Piore (eds), *Employment Relations in Changing World Economy*. Cambridge, Mass.: MIT Press.

Nakamura, K., H. Sato, and T. Kamiya. 1988. *Do Labor Unions Really Have a Useful Role?* Tokyo: Sogo Rodo Kenkyujo (in Japanese).

Nakamura, Takafusa. *1995. The Postwar Japanese Economy: Its Development and Structure, 1937–1994* (2nd edn). Tokyo: University of Tokyo Press.

Nakanishi, Tamako. 1983. "Equality or Protection? Protective Legislation for Women in Japan." *International Labour Review* 122 (Sept.–Oct.): 609–21.

Nickell, Stephen. 1997. "Unemployment and Labor Market Rigidities: Europe versus North America." *Journal of Economic Perspectives* 11(3): 55–74.

Nishikawa, Shunsaku and Yoshio Higuchi. 1980–1. "Determinants of Female Labor-Force Participation." *Japanese Economic Studies* 9 (Winter): 62–87.

OECD. 1986. *Flexibility in the Labour Market: The Current Debate*. Paris: Organisation for Economic Cooperation and Development.

—— 1987, 1988, 1990b, 1991, 1993a, 1994b, 1995, 1996, 1997, 1998, 1999. *Employment Outlook*. Paris: Organisation for Economic Cooperation and Development.

—— 1990a, 1992, 1994e. *Quarterly Labour Force Statistics*. Paris: Organisation for Economic Cooperation and Development.

—— 1993b. Labour Force Statistics. Paris: Organisation for Economic Cooperation and Development.

—— 1994a. *The OECD Jobs Study, Evidence and Explanations, Part I: Labour Market Trends and Underlying Forces of Change*. Paris: Organisation for Economic Cooperation and Development.

—— 1994c. *The OECD Jobs Study, Facts, Analysis, Strategies*. Paris: Organisation for Economic Cooperation and Development.

—— 1994d. *New Orientations for Social Policy*. Paris: Organisation for Economic Cooperation and Development.

Ogawa, Naohiro and John Ermisch. 1996. "Family Structure, Home Time Demands, and the Employment Patterns of Japanese Married Women." *Journal of Labor Economics* 14(4): 677–702.

Ohno, Taiichi. 1988. *Toyota Production System: Beyond Large-Scale Production*. Cambridge, Mass.: Productivity.

Ono, Tsuneo. 1990. "The Maturing of the Labor-Management Relationship and a Macroeconomic Analysis of Wage Change." *Japanese Economic Studies* 18(4): 65–91.

Osawa, M. 1989. "The Service Economy and Industrial Relations in Small- and Medium-Size Firms in Japan." *Japan Labor Bulletin* (July).

Osawa, Machiko. 1995. "The Changing Women's Employment and the Role of Social Policies in Japan," in Briitta Koskiaho (ed.), *Women, the Elderly and Social Policy in Finland and Japan: The Muse or the Worker Bee?* Hants, UK and Vermont: Ashgate.

Patrick, Hugh and Thomas Rohlen. 1987. "Small-Scale Family Enterprises," in Kozo Yamamura and Yasukichi Yasuba (eds), *The Political Economy of Japan: Volume 1: The Domestic Transformation*. Stanford, Calif.: Stanford University Press.

Peterson, Richard and Jeremiah Sullivan. 1990. "The Japanese Lifetime Employment System: Whither it Goest?" in S. Benjamin Prasad (ed.), *Advances in International Comparative Management: A Research Annual*. Greenwich, Conn. and London: JAI Press.

Pfau-Effinger, B. 1994. "The Gender Contract and Part-Time Paid Work by Women – Finland and Germany Compared." *Environment and Planning* 26(9): 1355–76.

Piore, Michael and Charles Sabel. 1984. *The Second Industrial Divide: Possibilities for Prosperity*. New York: Basic Books.

Preece, Gillian. 1992. "German Reunification: How Demographic Changes Have Affected the Employment of Women in the German Banking Sector." *Management Services* 36(1): 22–5.

Price, John. 1997. *Japan Works: Power and Paradox in Postwar Industrial Relations*. Ithaca, NY: ILR Press.

Quack, Sigrid and Friederike Maier. 1994. "From State Socialism to Market Economy – Women's Employment in East Germany." *Environment and Planning* 26(7): 1257–6.

Raschke, Freddy. 1993. "Labour Markets in Japan and Germany," in Haruhiro Fukui, Peter Merkl, Hubertus Müller-Groeling, and Akio Watanabe (eds), *The Politics of Economic Change in Postwar Japan and Germany: Volume 1: Macroeconomic Conditions and Policy Responses*. New York: St Martin's Press.

Rekko, Ange, Hans Doodeman, Peter de Gijsel, Joop Schippers, and Jacques Siegers. 1993. "The Effects of Temporary Withdrawals on Women's Gross Wage Rates: A Comparison between the Federal Republic of Germany and the Netherlands." *Jahrbuch für Nationalökonomie und Statistik* 212(1–2): 105–19.

Rosenberg, Dorothy. 1991. "Shock Therapy: GDR Women in Transition from a Socialist Welfare State to a Social Market Economy." *Signs* 17(1): 129–51.

Rowthorn, Robert. 1992. "Corporatism and Labour Market Performance," in Jukka Pekkarinen, Matti Pohjola, and Robert Rowthorn (eds), *Social Corporatism: A Superior Economic System?* Oxford: Clarendon.

Rubery, Jill (ed.). 1988. *Women and Recession*. London and New York: Routledge.

Rubery, Jill and Roger Tarling. 1988. "Women's Employment in Declining Britain," in Jill Rubery (ed.), *Women and Recession*. London and New York: Routledge and Kegan Paul.

Rudolph, Hedwig, Eileen Appelbaum and Friederike Maier. 1990. "After German Unity: A Cloudier Outlook for Women." *Challenge* (Nov.–Dec.): 33–40.

Rueschemeyer, Marilyn. 1993. "Women in East Germany: From State Socialism to

Capitalist Welfare State," in Valentine Moghadam (ed.), *Democratic Reform and the Position of Women in Transitional Economies*. Oxford: Clarendon Press.

Sachs, Jeffrey and Howard Shatz. 1994. "Trade and Jobs in US Manufacturing." *Brookings Papers on Economic Activity* (1): 1–84.

Sakuma, Ken. 1988. "Changes in Japanese-Style Labor-Management Relations." *Japanese Economic Studies* 16(4): 3–48.

Sakurai, Kojiro and Toshiaki Tachibanaki. 1992. "Estimation of Mis-Match and U-V Analysis in Japan." *Japan and the World Economy* 4(3): 319–32.

Saso, Mary. 1990. *Women in the Japanese Workplace*. London: Hilary Shipman.

Sassen, Saskia. 1988. *The Mobility of Labor and Capital: A Study in International Investment and Labor Flow*. Cambridge: Cambridge University Press.

Schiersmann, Christiane. 1991. "Germany: Recognizing the Value of Child Rearing," in Sheila Kamerman and Alfred Kahn (eds), *Child Care, Parental Leave, and the Under 3s: Policy Innovation in Europe*. New York: Auburn House.

Scharpf, Fritz. 1997. "Employment and the Welfare State: A Continental Dilemma," *Max Planck Institute for the Study of Societies Working Paper* no. 97/7 (July).

Scherer, Peter. 1994. "Trends in Social Protection Programs and Expenditures in the 1980s," in Rebecca Blank (ed.), *Social Protection versus Economic Flexibility: Is There a Trade-off?* Chicago: University of Chicago Press.

Schoer, Karl. 1987. "Part-Time Employment: Britain and West Germany." *Cambridge Journal of Economics* 11 (March): 83–94.

Schregle, Johannes. 1993. "Dismissal Protection in Japan." *International Labour Review* 132(4): 507–20.

Schumacher, Dieter. 1984. "North-South Trade Shifts in Employment: A Comparative Analysis of Six European Community Countries." *International Labour Review* 123(3) (May–June): 333–48.

Seki, Hideo. 1980. "Employment Problems and Policies in an Ageing Society: The Japanese Experience." *International Labour Review* 119 (May–June): 351–65.

Shimada, Haruo. 1993. "Recession and Change in Labour Practices in Japan." *International Labour Review* 132(2): 159–60.

Shingo, Shigeo. 1989. *A Study of the Toyota Production System From an Industrial Engineering Viewpoint*. Cambridge, Mass.: Productivity Press.

Simpson, Diane. 1985. "Women in Japan's Struggle for Labor Reform," in Norbert Soldon (ed.), *The World of Women's Trade Unionism: Comparative Historical Essays*. Westport, Conn.: Greenwood.

Singh, Ajit. 1998. "'Asian Capitalism' and the Financial Crisis." *Center for Economic Policy Analysis Working Papers on International Capital Markets and the Future of Economic Policy* no. 10.

Solow, Robert. 1997. "What is Labor-Market Flexibility? What is it Good For?" British Academy Keynes Lecture.

Sorensen, Annemette and Heike Trappe. 1995. "The Persistence of Gender Inequality in Earnings in the German Democratic Republic." *American Sociological Review* 60 (June): 398–406.

Sorrentino, Constance. 1993. "International Comparisons of Unemployment Indicators." *Monthly Labor Review* (March): 3–24.

—— 1995. "International Employment Indicators, 1983–93." *Monthly Labor Review*, 118(8): 31–50.

Soskice, David. 1990. "Wage Determination: The Changing Role of Institutions in Advanced Industrialized Countries." *Oxford Review of Economic Policy* 6(4): 36–61.

Standing, Guy. 1989. "Global Feminization through Flexible Labor." *World Development* 17(7): 1077–95.

Stier, Haya and Noah Lewin-Epstein, and Michael Braun. 1998. "The Institutional Context of Women's Employment Consequences: Evidence from Eight Industrialized Countries." Paper presented at the conference in Tel Aviv on "The Welfare State at Century's End."

Stiglitz, Joseph. 2000. "Democratic Development as the Fruits of Labor." Keynote Address to the Industrial Relations Research Association.

Taira, Koji. 1989. "Labor Market Segmentation, Human Resource Utilization, and Economic Development: The Case of Japan in Historical Perspective," in Ryuzo Sato and Takashi Negishi (eds), *Developments in Japanese Economics*. Tokyo: Academic Press.

Tachibanaki, Toshiaki. 1982. "Further Results on Japanese Wage Differentials: Nenko Wages, Hierarchical Position, Bonuses and Working Hours." *International Economic Review* 23 (June): 447–61.

—— 1987. "Labour Market Flexibility in Japan in Comparison with Europe and the US." *European Economic Review* 31 (April): 647–84.

—— 1996: *Wage Determination and Distribution in Japan*. New York: Oxford University Press.

Trappe, Heike. 1996. "Work and Family in Women's Lives in the German Democratic Republic." *Work and Occupations* 23(4): 354–77.

Trappe, Heike and Rachel Rosenfeld. 1999. "How Do Children Matter? A Comparison of Gender Earnings Inequality for Young Adults in the Former East Germany and the Former West Germany." Paper prepared for Tanja Van Der Lippe and Liset Van Dijk (eds), *Women's Employment in a Comparative Perspective: Integrating Micro and Macro Approaches*. New York: Aldine de Gruyter.

United Nations Development Programme. 1995. *Human Development Report 1995*. New York: Oxford University Press.

Vogelheim, Elisabeth. 1988. "Women in a Changing Workplace: The Case of the Federal Republic of Germany," in Jane Jenson, Elisabeth Hagen, and Ceallaigh Reddy (eds), *Feminization of the Labor Force: Paradoxes and Promises*. New York: Oxford University Press.

Walper, Sabine. 1995. "Youth in a Changing Context: The Role of the Family in East and West Germany," in James Youniss (ed.), *After the Wall: Family Adaptations in East and West Germany*. San Francisco: Jossey-Bass.

Witte, James and Gert Wagner. 1995. "Declining Fertility in East Germany after Unification: A Demographic Response to Socioeconomic Change." *Population and Development Review* 21(2): 387–97.

Wood, Adrian. 1991a. "How Much Does Trade with the South Affect Workers in the North?" *World Bank Research Observer* 6(1) (Jan.): 19–36.

—— 1991b. "North–South Trade and Female Labour in Manufacturing: An Asymmetry." *Journal of Development Studies* 27(2) (Jan.): 168–89.

—— 1994. *North–South Trade, Employment and Inequality: Changing Fortunes in a Skill-Driven World*. Oxford: Clarendon Press.

—— 1995: "How Trade Hurt Unskilled Workers." *Journal of Economic Perspectives* 9(3): 57–80.

Yasuba, Yasukichi. 1976. "The Evolution of the Dualistic Wage Structure," in Hugh Patrick (ed.), *Japanese Industrialization and its Social Consequences*. Berkeley, Calif.: University of California Press.

Index

116–21, 191n31, 192n33 (*see also* child care, maternity); as part-time workers 31, 36, 62, 83, 88–90, 95, 101–7, 113, 115, 153, 157; as percentage of workforce 44–6, 74, 189n15; substitution for men 34, 39, 58, 66–7, 72–3, 89; as temporary workers 36, 79, 83, 90, 95, 97–100, 113, 115, 153; unemployment levels 46, 159, 162, 166–70; unionization of 38, 62, 67, 74, 78, 83–4, 89, 107–14, 123, 147, 150–2, 177, 191n27; wage levels of 16–17, 67–8, 74–7, 83, 85, 87, 90, 95, 117, 122, 140–1, 146, 163–4, 167; withdrawal from work-force during twenties and thirties 82–3, 90–5, 118; working in Germany

38, 44–6, 56–9, 62, 66, 71, 78–84, 90, 92, 97–9, 112–21, 146, 155–8, 164, 166–70; working in Japan 28, 31, 44–6, 66, 71, 78–97, 110, 146, 152–4; working in smaller firms 110, 152
Women and Recession 33–5, 40
wood products, trade in 124, 136, 138
Wood, A. 13, 122, 124, 127, 130, 134, 140, 141, 146, 194n18
"Worker Discipline Effect, The" 58
works councils 35, 82, 112, 116, 190n26
World Bank 22

Yasuba, Y. 187n4
year of statistical analysis *see* time span
Year of the Woman Conference 187n4
Year of the Working Woman 112